D1001182

Liang Ch'i-ch'ao
and Intellectual Transition
in China, 1890–1907

HARVARD EAST ASIAN SERIES 64

The East Asian Research Center at Harvard University
administers research projects designed to further
scholarly understanding of China, Japan, Korea,
Vietnam, and adjacent areas.

Liang Ch'i-ch'ao

and Intellectual Transition in China,
1890–1907

HAO CHANG

HARVARD UNIVERSITY PRESS

Cambridge, Massachusetts

1971

Distributed in Great Britain
by Oxford University Press, London

Preparation of this volume has been aided by
a grant from the Ford Foundation.

Library of Congress Catalog Card Number 75–162635
SBN 674–53009–8

Printed in the United States of America

To the memory of my mother

Acknowledgments

This book is an outgrowth of the Ph.D. dissertation I wrote at Harvard in the mid-1960's. In the process of transforming the dissertation into a book I have become indebted to a number of my teachers and friends. Among them I must first of all express my profound gratitude to Professor Benjamin I. Schwartz who has given me guidance, encouragement, and support at every step of writing and revising the manuscript for publication. I must also indicate my deep thankfulness to Professor John K. Fairbank for the firm and sustained support he gave to publishing this book. I would like to acknowledge the generosity of Professor John L. Loos, Louisiana State University, and the East Asian Research Center at Harvard University in providing the research funds which enabled me to expand and revise my dissertation for publication during the summer and fall of 1967.

Among those who have indirectly helped me in writing this book, I must pay tribute to Professor Thomas A. Metzger, whose warm friendship, devotion to scholarship, and imaginative approach to history have been an unfailing source of intellectual stimulation. I am grateful to Professor Robert N. Bellah for his criticism of the manuscript at its early stage and also for the intellectual influence of his writing and lectures.

Finally, to my wife, Jung-Jung, I owe much gratitude for helping me in many ways to make this manuscript publishable.

Contents

Liang Ch'i-ch'ao and Intellectual Transition
in China, 1890–1907

Abbreviations

Prologue

This book explores a crucial period of intellectual transition in modern China, the years from mid-1890's to mid-1900's, by tracing the metamorphoses of the mind of Liang Ch'i-ch'ao, a central figure during this time. Liang was chosen because his formative years coincided with the period under study; he reached mental adulthood in the early 1890's and throughout the remainder of this period was active at the center of China's intellectual scene. Through his powerful pen and voluminous writings Liang exerted a shaping influence on the intellectual climate of the period. A study of Liang's mind thus provides an ideal vantage point for exploring the changing consciousness of his time.

"Western impact" was a primary factor in the formation of Liang's mind, but, like other broad concepts, this one must be used with care. Benjamin Schwartz has warned against a too complacent assumption that the West is a completely known quantity.[1] Even more insidious is the implication that traditional Chinese culture in confrontation with the West was inert, capable of response only when stimulated from without. Thus the concept of "impact" may lead to underestimating the complex and dynamic qualities of the traditional culture. To focus on

1. Benjamin Schwartz, *In Search of Wealth and Power: Yen Fu and the West* (Cambridge, 1964), pp. 1–4.

1

an external influence carries the danger of overlooking the inner dimensions of Chinese tradition.

To be sure, the late Ch'ing period was not an age of intellectual vigor like the Southern Sung or the late Ming. Yet it would be quite wrong to overlook intellectual development within the traditional world of the late Ch'ing. Close examination indicates that Confucian scholars continued to be engaged in such lively intellectual debates as those between the schools of Han Learning and Sung Learning, those between the New Text School and the Ancient Text School, or even those between the Ch'eng-Chu School and the Lu-Wang School of Neo-Confucianism. Thus for scholars in the late nineteenth century, Confucianism, not to say the whole Chinese cultural tradition, was by no means a monolithic whole but a vast and complex intellectual world divided into competing schools of thought.[2]

For the modern student it is, however, still much easier to see the variety within a religio-cultural tradition than to grasp its inner dynamics. Here, I think, much hinges upon the distinction between outside observation and inside participation. For the modern student of Chinese history, who more often than not stands outside the Chinese cultural tradition, Confucianism may seem to be no more than a set of ideological beliefs imposed by the state on the minds of the Chinese people or a philosophy which has intellectual interest primarily for Confucian scholars. But Confucianism was also a practicable faith for those who lived within tradition as did most Chinese intellectuals in the nineteenth century.[3] If one admits that there is some difference between a non-Christian scholar who studies the

2. *CCHS*, II, 596–622, 622–632.

3. For a clarification of the concept of faith, see Wilfred C. Smith, *The Meaning and End of Religion* (New York, 1964), pp. 109–138; see also his *The Faith of Other Men* (Cleveland, 1963), pp. 8–101.

Bible with a scholar's interest and a Christian believer who reads the Bible for spiritual direction, one must also admit that there is some difference between a modern scholar who studies the *Analects* for purely intellectual purposes, and a nineteenth-century Confucian scholar reading the *Analects* for spiritual meaning. To the former a religio-cultural tradition is a subject of disinterested study, but to the latter, it was a faith which needed to be practiced. In this perspective, it is very important for students of late Ch'ing thought to try to keep in mind this inner dimension of Confucian tradition and to explore its meanings. In attempting such an exploration there may be no better procedure than to follow Max Weber's concept of "imaginative participation," that is, to try to imagine oneself in the position of the Confucian literati and to see those problems which the practice of Confucianism as a living personal faith would pose for them.[4] It is important not only to see the problems but to view their development in a historical perspective, for this is the best way to grasp the inner dynamics of Confucianism in the late Ch'ing.

An awareness of the inner variety and dynamics of tradition is necessary in order to understand China's response to the West. For it is mainly in terms of a particular set of concerns and problems inherited from Confucian tradition that Chinese intellectuals responded to the Western impact in the late Ch'ing. We cannot appreciate these considerations unless we begin with the inner dimension of Confucian tradition.

While such an approach is valuable for the study of the intellectual history of modern China in general, it is particularly relevant to the study of the years immediately before and after 1900, a period during which Liang Ch'i-

4. Max Weber, *The Theory of Social and Economic Organization* (New York, 1964), p. 91; *Sociology of Religion* (Boston, 1963), pp. 1–2.

ch'ao was a central intellectual figure. In general it can be maintained that for most of the nineteenth century, after the beginning of contact with the West in 1840, the intellectual impact of the West on China remained superficial. Except for a small number of scholar-officials in positions of official responsibility and a few figures of marginal status in the treaty ports, Western influence had hardly penetrated into the scholarly world of China. An examination of the thought of such important intellectual figures in late nineteenth-century China as Ch'en Li, Chu T'zu-ch'i, Chu I-hsin, and Wang K'ai-yün reveals surprisingly few traces of the West.[5] For these figures as for the majority of the scholar-gentry in the fifty years after 1840, the central concerns remained those classical problems of Confucian tradition.

Thus unlike nineteenth-century Japan, where Western impact quickly became the dominant concern of most Japanese intellectuals, Western learning aroused little intellectual response in China. Even among the growing yet still small number of Chinese who were more or less affected by Western learning, there was not as much vigorous response as might have been expected. Some of these people had perhaps too superficial an understanding of Western learning to allow them to relate it significantly to the concerns and problems of traditional thought. Others like Wang T'ao or Cheng Kuan-ying, who might have had a better understanding, however, did not belong to the elite group of gentry-literati and hence were "marginal men" lacking the traditional respectability in the Chinese intellectual world, and perhaps as a result their voices were not often heard. Thus for almost half a century after the 1840's, conscious intellectual interaction between Chinese tradition and Western learning remained

5. *CCHS*, II, 596–622, 622–632, 639–641.

isolated and superficial. One may even be tempted to maintain that just as the economy of nineteenth-century China was divided into modern and traditional sectors with little significant interaction between them, two separate intellectual worlds had existed side by side in China without any intercourse of transformative consequence.

The tempo of intellectual change was drastically stepped up in the last decade of the nineteenth century, mainly because of the emergence of a reform movement. This movement has usually been studied as a political event, to the neglect of its intellectual aspect, which, in the long-term historical perspective, is much more significant. For the present purpose, two points need to be made. This reform movement was launched by a group of young Chinese who came to their intellectual adulthood in the 1890's. They were thoroughly grounded in the Chinese cultural tradition and deeply involved with the central problems and concerns of traditional thought. Moreover, some of them had sustained contact with a wide range of Western learning that was hardly possible before. Through their efforts a cultural interaction on a significant scale was established between Western and traditional culture. This interaction touched off a series of vigorous debates which eventually engulfed a sizable segment of Chinese gentry-scholars. The reform movement of the 1890's was therefore a genuinely intellectual movement.

The significance of this movement would have been much reduced if its effects had been confined to those articulate gentry-scholars. But it produced a cultural fermentation which had a nationwide effect made possible chiefly by the emergence of a new kind of newspaper. True, China had had newspapers long before this period, but they were either operated by foreigners or by those Chinese of little respectability in the treaty ports. Moreover, these publications were in the main commercially oriented and consequently had little intellectual influence.[6] The reform movement in the 1890's, however, brought a tremendous change in this respect. For the purpose of propagating their ideas, young intellectuals started to experiment with the publication of newspapers. Their success inspired directly or indirectly many similar efforts and led to a mushrooming of newspapers more politically oriented and more ideological in content.[7] The fact that many of these newspapers were operated by gentry-scholars themselves aided their circulation in the country. Through this new medium the young reformers had a much broader audience than was previously possible. The cultural gap which had separated the world of Western learning from the world of traditional thought in the greater part of the nineteenth century was thus gradually bridged. Although people might still be divided by many problems posed by the encounter between these two worlds, Chinese intellectuals were faced by a more or less common set of new problems and concerns. A new set of problems, concerns, and ideals were forged out of the intellectual interaction between two cultures, and these ideals and concerns became part of the national cultural transformation which continued well into the 1900's.

6. Ko Kung-chen, *Chung-kuo pao-hsüeh shih* (Taipei, 1964), pp. 87–144
7. T'ang Chih-chün, *Wu-hsü pien-fa shih lun-ts'ung* (Hankow, 1957), pp. 222–270.

1

The Intellectual Setting

The intellectual change that resulted from the reemergence of the Confucian ideal of practical statesmanship and the revolt against Han Learning in the late Ch'ing period were to have a profound influence on Liang. Both phenomena must be understood as developments of the inner dynamics of Neo-Confucianism. Hence a preliminary characterization of these developments within the framework of Neo-Confucianism is essential to an understanding of Liang's intellectual background.

Neo-Confucianism as a late revival of Confucianism was essentially a faith at the root of which lay the ideal of *jen* (humanity). Certainly *jen* was a vital ideal in classical Confucianism, but it did not attain its indisputable central place until the Neo-Confucian stage. By then *jen* had become universally recognized in the Confucian scheme of things as the *telos*, the intrinsic aim of existence.[1] Although the meaning of *jen* has undergone considerable development in the long course of the evolution of Confucianism, its basic meaning has remained more or less fixed and can best be ascertained by an examination of two other Confucian ideals which were taught in the

1. See Wing-tsit Chan, "The Evolution of the Confucian Concept of Jen," *Philosophy East and West*, 4.4:295–319 (1955); see also Liang Ch'i-ch'ao, *Ju-chia che-hsüeh* (Confucian philosophy) in *YPSHC-CC*, ts'e 24, 103:19.

7

Analects as the dual way to attain the ideal of *jen,* namely, *chung* and *shu.* As Chu Hsi said, *chung* meant an imperative to the utmost realization of self, while *shu* meant the commitment to extend one's self-realization, so to speak, in order to help others attain self-realization.[2] In other words, *jen* signified a life-ideal with a dual reference. In the first place, it denoted a commitment to an unending moral cultivation of personality, or in Confucian terms, self-cultivation (*hsiu-shen*). But this self-cultivation was not conceived as a self-sufficient value in itself. It was imperative that in cultivating one's moral character, one should also "extend" one's moral cultivation, so to speak, to help others to achieve moral cultivation. Hence, inseparably linked to the self-regarding commitment to *chung* was an other-regarding commitment to *shu.* But what was characteristic of Confucianism was the often implicit assumption that the other-regarding commitment could be only fulfilled through political engagement by way of public service. In Confucian terms, the other-regarding commitment for a gentleman (*chün-tzu*) was almost necessarily a commitment to "practical statesmanship." [3]

Both commitments, the commitment to self-cultivation and that to practical statesmanship, then, were indispensable to the realization of *jen;* and the relationship between the two commitments may be characterized as correlative. According to the Confucian personality ideal, a man could not be called a sage no matter how morally cultivated he was, unless he fulfilled his commitment

2. For Chu Hsi's commentaries on the two concepts, *chung* and *shu,* in *Analects* and *Doctrine of the Mean* see *Lun-yü hsin-chieh,* vol. 1, in *Ssu-shu tu-pen* (Taipei, 1952), pp. 55–56; *Chung-yung hsin-chieh, Ssu-shu tu-pen,* p. 14; see also Fan Shou-k'ang, *Chu-tzu chi ch'i che-hsüeh* (Taipei, 1964), pp. 162–164.

3. *Ju-chia che-hsüeh,* pp. 2–3; see also Benjamin Schwartz, "Some Polarities in Confucian Thought," in Davis S. Nivison and Arthur F. Wright, eds., *Confucianism in Action* (Stanford, 1959), pp. 52–54.

to public service; by the same token, he could not claim statesmanship no matter how spectacular his public achievement as long as he was not morally cultivated. This dual commitment of *jen* is crystallized in the all-important Confucian ideal of sage-statesmanship, or "inner sagehood and outer kingship" *(nei-sheng wai-wang)*.[4] It must be noted, however, that in the framework of Confucianism the ideal of sage-statesmanship applied primarily to *chün-tzu*, the moral elite, rather than to men in general. True, *chün-tzu* as understood in Confucianism referred to a spiritual stature attainable by merit. Furthermore, it was assumed in Confucianism that any man had the potential for achieving moral perfection and hence could become a *chün-tzu* by moral effort and striving. But it was also assumed, and increasingly so, in Confucianism that although *chün-tzu* was a stature attainable by anyone, only a minority could be expected to go through the hard process of cultivation and discipline to achieve it; and it was the morally cultivated few who were qualified to assume the responsibility of ruling and administering the land. In this sense the sage-statesmanship ideal was meaningful only for the cultural elite.

The above characterization of Confucianism as a faith and the delineation of its *telos* have the important implication that the central motive of Confucianism was a pragmatic one, namely, to implement its moral ideals in individual life and in society. This pragmatic motive should be kept in mind when we try to comprehend the place of learning in Confucianism. To be sure, for Confucianism, which stressed textual authority, learning *(hsüeh)*, in the sense of a knowledge of the Confucian

---

4. *Ju-chia che-hsüeh,* pp. 2–3, 21; Benjamin Schwartz, "Some Polarities in Confucian Thought," pp. 52–54; see also Hsü Fu-kuan, *Hsüeh-shu yü cheng-chih chih chien* (Taichung, 1963), pp. 44–62.

classics in particular and cultural heritage in general, was always an important value. But learning was important only as an instrumental value, not as an intrinsic one. Given the ultimacy of *jen* in Confucianism, it is obvious that learning could have value only insofar as it helped realize that ultimate ideal.[5]

Confucianism, then, seen in the eyes of its practitioners, was never simply a philosophical system or a kind of intellectual pursuit. Although scholasticism inevitably played an important part in it, the tendency to identify Confucianism as a philosophical system or a scholastic pursuit is dangerous because it overshadows its central pragmatic motive and obscures its identity as a living faith. From this standpoint, scholasticism posed just as much of a threat to Confucianism's identity from within as Buddhism and Taoism did from without.

The emergence of Neo-Confucianism in the Sung dynasty meant that it had withstood the challenges of Buddhism and Taoism and reestablished its activistic ideal of sage-statesmanship. As Lu Hsiang-shan so aptly put it, Confucianism advocated "managing the world" (*ching-shih*), while Buddhism taught "withdrawal from the world" (*ch'u-shih*).[6] Yet success in repudiating Buddhism and Taoism did not mean that the reaffirmation of the activistic ideal of sage-statesmanship in the mainstream of Confucianism was an untroubled one. As Neo-Confucianism developed in the last several centuries, its commitment to that activistic life-ideal had been fraught with tensions.

One important source of controversy resulted from the place of learning in the scheme of Confucianism. The problem revolved around how much or to what extent

5. *Ju-chia che-hsüeh*, pp. 1–4.
6. Feng Yu-lan, *History of Chinese Philosophy*, tr. Derk Bodde (Princeton, 1953), II, 578.

Confucianism as an inner faith could be served by scholarly investigation. Herein lies a conflict familiar to almost all religious and cultural traditions: to fulfill a moral faith, one needs to know the teachings of the founder. Scholarship is necessary, at least for the purpose of clarifying the meaning of the sage's words, but scholarship has its temptations for many; and who could guarantee against the possibility of submitting to its temptations and thereby losing sight of the end it is supposed to serve? The task of keeping the balance between scholasticism and faith in a religio-cultural tradition is always a delicate one.

The problem of the usefulness of learning to faith lay at the heart of the dispute between the two major schools within Neo-Confucianism. In the view of the orthodox Ch'eng-Chu School, learning, at least in the Confucian scholastic sense, was essential for the realization of the Confucian life-ideal. Underlying this view was the belief that knowledge of the organizing principles of outer reality would make possible a true comprehension of the inner reality of human nature, and would thus lead ultimately to the intellectual enlightenment required for self-cultivation.[7] Opposed to this school of Neo-Confucianism was the Lu-Wang School which upheld the primacy of moral intuition and hence the self-sufficiency of the human mind. It thus tended to consider learning as of only peripheral relevance for the concern of self-cultivation.[8]

This so-called "Idealistic School" had a great upsurge in the late Ming and for a time even dominated the intellectual world. But in the seventeenth century an intellectual reaction set in against this "idealistic tendency." In the eyes of many Confucian scholars the approach of the Lu-Wang School had the dangerous tendency of be-

7. Ibid., II, 551–571.
8. Ibid., pp. 572–592; see also Hsü Fu-kuan, "Hsiang-shan hsüeh-shu," in *Chung-kuo ssu-hsiang-shih lun-chi* (Taichung, 1959), pp. 12–71.

11

coming excessively concerned with abstract metaphysical speculation on the nature of the innate knowledge of the mind, which could become very remote from the concrete problems of human life.[9] Furthermore, its tendency to view "inner light" as a sufficient source of moral direction might also have the dangerous consequence of overstepping the moral prescriptions of Confucianism. Hence the intellectual reaction started with a clamor for the repudiation of the "idealistic approach" and with a plea for "prudent conduct" (shih-hsing). Since "prudent conduct" in the Confucian sense can be practiced only by following the prescriptions of Confucian canons, a call was also sounded for "substantial learning" (shih-hsüeh) in the sense of "empirical" study of Confucian literature. Meanwhile this call for substantial learning was also reinforced by considerable revulsion against the careerism of the examination system. Thus shih-hsing and shih-hsüeh became the commonly felt needs among Chinese scholars who lived in that age of cultural crisis in late Ming and early Ch'ing.[10] Yet in the course of the next two centuries, the call for substantial learning became the dominant trend and the relationship between learning and conduct was increasingly neglected. The tendency eventually culminated in the eighteenth century in a national vogue of textual and philological scholarship among Confucian scholars under the loose name of the School of Empirical Research.

It must be emphasized that at first the School of Empirical Research was by no means a consciously planned intellectual movement guided by the clear purpose of valuing scholarship for its own sake. In the beginning, its scholasticism was justified as no more than an essential

9. CCHS, I, 7–21; see also Feng Yu-lan, History of Chinese Philosophy, II, pp. 596–629.
10. CCHS, I, 18–20.

means to explore the moral implications of Confucianism and thereby to serve the broad concerns of human life and society. This is nowhere more clearly shown than in the thought of Ku Yen-wu who was generally regarded as the founder of the School of Empirical Research in the Ch'ing. According to Ku Yen-wu, textual criticism and philological investigation are indispensable for the canonical study of Confucianism; but the ultimate purpose of study is still what he called the "understanding of the Confucian *tao*" (*ming-tao*) and the "salvation of the world" (*chiu-shih*).[11] Even at the height of the School of Empirical Research in the eighteenth century, its central figure, Tai Chen, still justified his textual and philological studies by the rationale that only by minute word-by-word and sentence-by-sentence study of Confucian canons was a realization of the Confucian *tao* possible.[12]

Whatever the original justification, the important fact remains that in the course of the eighteenth century Confucian scholarship had become so divorced from its alleged socio-moral concern that the relationship between learning and conduct could hardly be perceived. Modern Chinese scholars are generally inclined to ascribe this cult of "empirical research" to the political pressure exerted by the Manchu government which presumably in the interest of political stability preferred to see Chinese intellectuals all engrossed in a study devoid of moral and political meaning. While political pressure was perhaps a contributing factor, any explanation of an intellectual movement of such magnitude as the School of Empirical Research must not overlook factors inherent in the development of Confucianism. It is entirely conceivable that in trying to get at the original vision and true meaning of Confucianism,

11. *CCHS*, I, 144–146.
12. *CCHS*, I, 306–379.

scholars in the seventeenth and eighteenth centuries found that the annotative scholarship of, at first, Confucianism, and then, by extension, of ancient historical and philosophical literature was an intellectual world in itself and was attractive enough to hold their scholarly interest. Here, then, is the universal phenomenon of the means being unwittingly transformed into the end. Once the new "end" was created, it took on a momentum of its own and a power to move men's minds.

Of course, the intellectual world of the mid-Ch'ing, dominated as it was by the School of Empirical Research, was never entirely monopolized by it. At least Ch'eng-Chu Neo-Confucianism, now popularly known as Sung Learning, was still the orthodox creed of the Ch'ing court; it thus not only had a place among scholarly circles, but also retained considerable influence through the requirements of the civil examination. But its ability to serve as the vehicle of Confucian inner faith was not much better than the School of Empirical Research. To begin with, it was much impaired by the careerism prevalent among many who read Chu Hsi's commentaries on the Confucian classics exclusively as a means to self-advancement in officialdom. On the other hand, the limited number of scholars who retained a genuine interest in Sung Learning were usually engaged in hairsplitting debate over the metaphysical meaning of Confucian self-cultivation to the neglect of the social meaning of Confucianism.[13] Thus the combined effects of the School of Empirical Research and the School of Sung Learning in the mid-Ch'ing intellectual world resulted in the decline of Confucianism as a faith, especially insofar as its socio-political meaning was concerned.

13. *CCHS*, II, 453–522; see also Chang Shun-hui, *Ch'ing-tai Yang-chou hsüeh-chi* (Shanghai, 1962), pp. 1–39, 83–99, 106–136, 142–158.

Given the central pragmatic motive of Confucianism, the dominance of the School of Empirical Research could at best be a precarious one. Confucian scholars might rest content with the vogue of scholasticism as long as they lived in an untroubled age of peace and prosperity like the seventeenth and eighteenth centuries. But in an age of trouble and crisis, which inevitably drove Confucian scholars to reflect upon the purpose and meaning of their studies, scholasticism was bound to come under criticism as a failure of ideals and a distraction from faith.

Such were the roots of the sense of cultural malaise which started to spread gradually among Confucian scholars toward the end of the eighteenth century.[14] Beset by this deepening sense of unease, Confucian scholars felt the need to reassert the now obscured Confucian ideal of sage-statesmanship and thereby to rekindle socio-political consciousness in the country. As the symptoms of dynastic decline accumulated in the course of the early nineteenth century, their efforts gradually crystallized into a new alignment of intellectual attitudes which shaped the cultural transformation of the following decades.

The motivating force behind the general reaction to the dominance of scholasticism in the late Ch'ing was doubtless the Confucian ideal of practical statesmanship. A clear indication is the fact that while a widely accepted scholarly syllabus of the eighteenth century comprised three major categories — k'ao-cheng (textual criticism), tz'u-chang (poetical literature), and i-li (moral philosophy of self-cultivation), syllabi made by scholars of the nineteenth century usually added the significant category of ching-shih (practical statesmanship). [15] Because the ideal of

14. *CCHS*, II, 523–595; see also Liang Ch'i-ch'ao, *Intellectual Trends in the Ch'ing Period*, tr. Immanuel C. Y. Hsü (Cambridge, 1959), pp. 83–85.
15. *CCHS*, I, 317; II, 628.

practical statesmanship was susceptible to different emphases, the reaction naturally took different forms and resulted in divergent intellectual trends during the century.
One principal reaction resulted in a reinforcement of
the socio-political consciousness of scholars of Sung Learning. The scholars of this school had earlier tended to focus
their attention on the moral philosophy of self-cultivation (*i-li*) to the neglect of the socio-political commitment
of Confucianism. Now in the course of the early nineteenth century a group of scholars of Sung Learning tried
to redress the balance and revive the socio-political concern as an indispensable part of Confucian faith. This
development can be seen most clearly in the thought of
T'ang Chien, a central figure in the School of Sung Learning in the early nineteenth century. While one part of his
teachings was still centered around the distinctive traditional concern of Sung Learning, *hsiu-shen* (self-cultivation), the other part focused on the socio-political concern
of *shou-tao chiu-shih* (maintain the Way in order to save
the world). Thus, for T'ang Chien, Sung Learning was
valuable as a source of the principles of Confucian self-
cultivation and above all as a source of the principles of
Confucian statesmanship.[16]

Although this new development of Sung Learning meant
a reassertion of the Confucian ideal of practical statesmanship, it involved nothing new because its approach was
still strongly marked by traditional moral idealism. According to this view, Confucian statesmanship consisted
primarily in the setting of moral examples by the cultural
elite. For by cultivating character, the elite could achieve
a sort of moral charisma which qualified them for the

16. Hellmut Wilhelm, "Chinese Confucianism on the Eve of the Great
Encounter," in Marius B. Jansen, ed., *Changing Japanese Attitudes toward
Modernization* (Princeton, 1965), pp. 299–303.

all-important task of "moral education and transformation" (*chiao-hua*) of the people and would in effect inspire the people automatically to follow their model. In this way, a moral custom would then be gradually created. Once a moral custom was created, the state and society would be easily put in order. Thus in this view of Confucian statesmanship, the coercive and managerial functions of the state were considered as only peripheral; the primary concern was the moral transformation of society by exemplary leadership.[17]

No wonder, then, in T'ang Chien's mind as in those of other scholars in this school, that self-cultivation retained its central importance. In line with the tradition of the School of Sung Learning, T'ang Chien's thought was centered around two concepts, namely, *shou-ching* (abiding in reverence) and *ch'iung-li* (exhausting the principle). In the framework of Ch'eng-Ch'u moral philosophy, *ch'iung-li* meant essentially an intellectual approach to the problem of self-cultivation at the heart of which was the belief that an indispensable part of self-cultivation consisted in the comprehensive study of cultural heritage, or more briefly, in book-learning (*tu-shu*). *Shou-ching* aimed to cultivate a kind of single-minded seriousness bordering on religious reverence as an essential condition for the realization of the moral self. For many scholars of Sung Learning, this reverence involved imposing strict discipline on one's outer behavior in accordance with Confucian rules of propriety (*li*).[18] An emphasis on the combination of *shou-ching* and *ch'iung-li* thus had the definite implication that directions for the cultivation of personality stem chiefly from external sources, either in the sense of book learning

17. For a typical Confucian view of statesmanship see Tseng Kuo-fan, "Yüan ts'ai," in *Tseng Wen-cheng-kung ch'üan-chi* (Shanghai, 1935), *Wen-chi*, pp. 4–5.
18. Hellmut Wilhelm, pp. 299–303.

or in the sense of conforming with traditional rules of propriety.

Two other currents of thought were closely related to the School of Sung Learning. The first was the T'ung-ch'eng School which, although primarily a literary school, was also mainly concerned with the socio-moral meaning of Confucianism; true to its Neo-Confucian lineage, it regarded literature essentially as the vehicle of Confucian faith. In this sense the T'ung-ch'eng School may be regarded as a popularized variant of the School of Sung Learning. With such an intellectual kinship, it naturally sided with the School of Sung Learning in bewailing the hollowness of the scholasticism of the mid-Ch'ing. It is thus no surprise that the most searing attack on the School of Empirical Research in the early nineteenth century came from Fang Tung-shu, a central figure in this school.[19]

More important, the attack on the School of Empirical Research from the camp of Sung Learning and its allied school resulted in an eclectic movement among Ch'ing scholars to combine both approaches in their scholarly works. Many scholars of Han Learning tended to admit the inadequacy of their exclusive concern with "empirical research" and to emphasize the importance of going beyond "empirical" Confucian scholarship to search for its moral meaning. This eclectic approach was already discernible in the scholarly works of Juan Yüan, a high-ranking official and well-known scholar of Han Learning in the late eighteenth and early nineteenth centuries. He was greatly interested in the various disciplines involved in Han Learning, but only as a means to understanding the Sage's *tao*.[20] In Canton, Juan Yüan, who had long served as the governor-general there, founded the famous academy,

19. *T'ung-ch'eng pai yen-chiu lun-wen chi* (Anhui, 1963), pp. 1–223.
20. *CCHS*, II, 478–490.

Hsüeh-hai t'ang, which later became a center of Confucian scholarship in South China. Perhaps owing to Juan Yüan's influence, this eclecticism seems to have taken hold particularly among scholars in the Canton area in the nineteenth century.[21] Two of these scholars were central figures in the movement. Ch'en Li, himself an outstanding scholar in the field of Han Learning, strongly deplored the academic fashion of writing commentaries without studying the moral meaning of Confucian canons. The remedy, as he saw it, was not to forsake empirical research, but to superimpose on it a search for moral meaning on the model of Chu Hsi's approach. He often urged scholars to use the methods of empirical research for a thorough mastery of one canon for the purpose of cultivating character.[22]

This revolt against exclusive addiction to "empirical" scholarship was shared in an even stronger way by Ch'en Li's associate at Hsüeh-hai t'ang, Chu Tz'u-ch'i, who later became K'ang Yu-wei's teacher. In Chu's view, the distinction between Han Learning and Sung Learning must be transcended and an effort must be made to return to the broader view of Ku Yen-wu or Chu Hsi, namely, that "empirical scholarship" was worthwhile but must be applied with an eye to its social and moral significance. "Confucius' teaching makes no distinction between Han Learning and Sung Learning. Its substance consists in no more than self-cultivation and study." [23] This emphasis on the moral orientation of learning can also be seen in the curriculum he drew up for his students, which was divided

21. Ibid.; Liang Ch'i-ch'ao considered this eclectic approach to combine Han Learning and Sung Learning in Confucian scholarship as the distinguishing characteristic of what he called *Yüeh-hsüeh* (Kwangtung learning), which centered around Hsüeh-hai t'ang in the nineteenth century. See *YPSHC-CC*, ts'e 24, 103:67.

22. *CCHS*, II, 602, 609–616.

23. Chien Ch'ao-liang, *Chu Chiu-chiang hsien-sheng nien-p'u*, in Chien Ch'ao-liang, ed., *Chu Chiu-chiang hsien-sheng chi*, p. 25.

into two parts: moral cultivation, and the study of Confucian scholarship. In this curriculum moral cultivation was introduced before scholastic study and was given greater importance in the whole program.[24] The arrangement of this curriculum later served as a model in part for K'ang Yu-wei when he set up his own private school at Canton.[25] For Ch'en Li the emphasis was laid almost exclusively on the moral import of Confucian scholarship and the broader concern of state and society was largely left implicit. Chu went further. He related moral cultivation to the larger socio-political purpose: "Why should we study? Study is undertaken for the purpose of intellectual enlightenment. Intellectual enlightenment is sought for the purpose of managing affairs; one should first put the body and mind in order so as to be ready to serve the world and the state." [26]

We have seen that the intellectual reaction against the dominance of Han Learning had brought about a significant reorientation of thought in the late Ch'ing, as reflected in the development of three intellectual currents: Sung Learning, the T'ung-ch'eng School, and the eclectic movement to synthesize Han Learning and Sung Learning. While these trends were marked by a commitment to practical statesmanship in Confucian scholarship, what they achieved practically was often no more than a resurgence of interest in Ch'eng-Chu's Neo-Confucian moral philosophy on the premise that Confucian statesmanship can best be attained by self-cultivation. However intellectual reaction in the late Ch'ing also took forms which called for outer renovations of institutions as the major means of realizing the ideals of Confucian statesmanship. One trend

24. *CCHS*, II, 639–640.
25. *CCHS*, II, 639–641.
26. Chien Ch'ao-liang, p. 29.

in this direction was the resurgence of the New Text School.

The New Text School in the late Ch'ing had its origin in the inner logic of the philosophical rationale of the School of Empirical Research. The latter started as a revolt against the metaphysical proclivity of Sung-Ming Neo-Confucianism, which, according to the scholars of "empirical research," had obscured and adulterated the pristine wisdom of Confucius. In order to reverse this trend, they argued, one had to return to antiquity (*fu-ku*) in order to recover original Confucian teachings.[27] This tendency of the School of Empirical Research to revive ancient Confucian teachings developed by stages. The first stage looked back in time, past Wang Yang-ming's school, to Chu Hsi's version of Sung Neo-Confucianism, which was regarded as more solid and balanced in its interpretation of the Sage's message. From there they went even further back in order to seek authentic Confucian scholarship in commentaries written during the Sui-T'ang period and the Six Dynasties. Finally they reached the Later Han, where Ch'ing scholars found a mine of exegetical scholarship in the works of such masters of the Ancient Text School as Cheng Hsüan, Hsü Shen, Ma Jung, and Chia K'uei. Thus at the apogee of the development of the School of Empirical Research in the eighteenth century there was such a cult of the annotative scholarship of the Later Han that the School of Empirical Research was simply identified as the School of Han Learning.[28]

The logic of searching for the ancient sources of Confucian scholarship had created a compelling tendency for certain scholars to probe even further back. Thus when

27. Immanuel C. Y. Hsü, pp. 21–25.
28. Ibid.; see also Chou Yü-t'ung, *Ching chin-ku-wen-hsüeh* (Commercial Press, 1926), pp. 27–36.

the annotative scholarship of the Ancient Text School had been well explored, it was only natural for certain Ch'ing scholars to turn their attention to the exegetical scholarship of the Former Han dynasty, which was dominated by the New Text School. In their view, since the New Text versions of Confucian classics were obviously closer in time to the age of Confucius, these versions were a more likely channel for getting at his true teachings. In this way the commentaries of New Text School which had long been obscured were brought back to the attention of Ch'ing scholars and the old intellectual controversy between the New Text School and the Ancient Text School was thus revived.[29]

On the surface the disputes between the New Text School and the Ancient Text School were largely textual and philological. These differences, however, were not without what we may call "ideological" implications. To begin with, the different images of Confucius were involved in the dispute. The Ancient Text School held that Confucius was a great teacher who inherited the cultural legacy of the past and then edited it and faithfully transmitted it to posterity. The New Text School projected an image of Confucius as a sort of messianic prophet who could foretell the future of mankind and who had a message to deliver to posterity.[30] Related to this prophetic image of Confucius was the belief that Confucius wrote the *Six Classics* mainly for the purpose of applying his sociomoral ideals to the world. Thus, in studying the *Six Classics*, particularly the *Spring and Autumn Annals (Ch'un-ch'iu)*, which was regarded by the New Text scholars as the primary repository of Confucius' moral and political

29. Immanuel C. Y. Hsü, pp. 25, 87; Chiang Po-ch'ien and Chiang Tsu-i, *Ching yü ching-hsüeh* (Shanghai, 1948), pp. 229–232.

30. Hsiao Kung-ch'üan, "K'ang Yu–wei and Confucianism," *Monumenta Serica*, 18:175–196.

ideals, the goal was an imaginative grasp of the subtle religious and moral implications rather than a historically accurate understanding. According to the New Text tradition, in writing the *Spring and Autumn Annals* Confucius was interested not so much in recording events but in enunciating social and moral principles. The New Text School also believed that the teachings of Confucius were not all contained in the Canons because much of his teaching was transmitted orally. All these characteristics point to a central belief of the New Text tradition: that the core of Confucianism is its socio-moral pragmatism and that, true to this pragmatic spirit, a free "ideological" interpretation of Confucianism is preferable to a literal and prosaic understanding.[31]

Another salient feature of the New Text School was its distinctive views of history. Though somewhat ambivalent about regarding history as cyclical change or progressive development, the scholars believed that history developed by stages and that each historical period required distinctive "institutions" for cosmological reasons. This belief gave rise to the idea that institutions should change with different periods and that institutional reform (*kai-chih*) was sanctioned by Confucianism.[32] To be sure, in the New Text interpretation of Confucianism all these ideals were mixed up with many elements of magic or "extravagant and strange views."[33] But it is nonetheless undeniable that inherent in the New Text interpretation was a pronounced socio-political orientation and ambiguous attitudes toward institutional reformism.

The revival of the New Text School in the late Ch'ing was mainly a result of the inherent tendency of the School of Empirical Research to "return to antiquity"; in the

31. Ibid., pp. 136–143.
32. Ibid., pp. 166–175.
33. Feng Yu-lan, *History of Chinese Philosophy*, II, 7–132.

beginning the New Text School was not marked by social consciousness or political purpose, as is evident from the writings of such pioneering scholars as Chuang Ts'un-yü and Liu Feng-lu in the eighteenth century.[34] But given its emphasis on the socio-political orientation of Confucianism and its image of Confucius as an institutional reformer, it was by no means accidental that two prominent nineteenth-century scholars of the New Text School, Wei Yüan and Kung Tzu-chen, became active advocates of the Confucian ideal of practical statesmanship. Wei Yüan must be regarded as the pivotal figure, for he was among the first scholars in the late Ch'ing who consciously rebelled against the scholasticism of the School of Empirical Research and reaffirmed the centrality of social orientation in Confucianism. In his view, "true Han Learning" was to be sought in the New Text School of the Former Han dynasty rather than in the Ancient Text School of the Later Han dynasty.[35]

Although in the cases of Wei Yüan and Kung Tzu-chen the revived New Text School became a channel for political reformism, the development of the New Text School during the rest of the nineteenth century was not necessarily linked with any reformist movement. In fact, we find among its members such scholars as Shao I-ch'en, Tai Wang, Wang K'ai-yün, and P'i Lu-men, who were generally very removed from politics and seem to have had an almost purely academic interest in New Text commentaries on Confucian classics.[36] But through the labor of these scholars and others, the Confucian scholarship of the New Text School, which, in the hands of such pioneering figures as Chuang Ts'un-yü and Liu Feng-lu in the

34. *CCHS*, II, 523–528; see also Immanuel C. Y. Hsü, pp. 88–91.
35. *CCHS*, II, 524, 523–568.
36. Ibid.; see also Immanuel C. Y. Hsü, pp. 88–91.

eighteenth century, had been almost completely concentrated on the *Kung-yang Commentary on the Ch'un-ch'iu,* had now extended to other Confucian classics. By the time such outstanding late Ch'ing scholars as Wang K'ai-yün and P'i Lu-men became active this school constituted a serious challenge to the authority of the Han Learning among Chinese scholars.[37] In the late 1880's, Liao P'ing, a disciple of Wang K'ai-yün, wrote a book entitled *Chin-ku-hsüeh k'ao* (On the new text and ancient text learning.) Drawing on the works of his predecessors in the New Text School he put forth the provocative thesis that all Ancient Text scholarship was spurious because all the Ancient Text classics were the forgeries of an unscrupulous Han scholar, Liu Hsin. The true repository of Confucius' teachings, Liao P'ing argued, should be found in the New Text scholarship, which held that Confucius composed the *Six Classics* with the purpose of setting forth his ideas on institutional reform for posterity.[38] Liao P'ing did not seem to have enunciated this thesis with any noticeable political purpose. However, after K'ang Yu-wei learned it from him, it was to become the central part of K'ang's reformist ideology.[39]

While some scholars in the New Text School evinced a significant tendency to reassert the vital value of practical statesmanship in Confucianism, they left open the all-important question of how to implement this value. As we have seen, the School of Sung Learning and its allied schools shared this reaffirmation of socio-political purposes.

---

37. Chiang Po-ch'ien and Chiang Tsu-i, pp. 230–231; Immanuel C. Y. Hsü, pp. 91–92.

38. *CCHS,* I, 643–653; Joseph R. Levenson, "Liao P'ing and the Confucian Departure from History," in Arthur F. Wright and Denis Twitchett eds., *Confucian Personalities* (Stanford, 1962), pp. 317–325.

39. *CCHS,* II, 642–652; see also Hsiao Kung-ch'üan, "K'ang Yu-wei," pp. 126–132.

Yet they remained committed to the traditional notion that Confucian statesmanship can be best realized by way of self-cultivation and moral leadership. In the New Text literature there is some tendency toward "institutional reformism," but "institutional reform" is not an exact rendering of the term *kai-chih.* The word *chih,* as understood in the New Text literature of the Former Han, referred to rituals at least as much as it did to institutions. In other words, *kai-chih* might mean more of a ritual change than any kind of institutional reform as understood in the present sense. Thus the cultural sanction given to institutional reform in the New Text literature was at best an ambiguous and problematical one.[40]

Akin to and overlapping to a certain extent with the New Text School was another group which, as a reaction against the socio-moral indifference of Han Learning, upheld the ideal of practical statesmanship on the level of intrinsic value and emphasized professional statecraft as a principal approach to implementing that ideal. This type of thinking is often loosely identified as the School of Statecraft. Few scholars in this school went so far as to reject moral cultivation as a necessary condition for the realization of their broader socio-political goals. But their stress on professional statecraft and the institutional approach as legitimate and important concerns of Confucian scholars implied that moral cultivation in itself was not adequate to attain practical statesmanship; it had to be supplemented by institutional arrangements.[41] It should be em-

40. Ku Chieh-kang, *Han-tai hsüeh-shu shih-lüeh* (Shanghai, 1948), pp. 1–24.

41. This emphasis on professional statecraft is evident in the design and content of *Huang-ch'ao ching-shih wen-pien* (Peking, 1826), ed. Ho Ch'ang-ling and Wei Yüan. In its first section the moral orientation of Confucian learning is stressed and the rest of the compilation deals with the professional statecraft required for the different branches of bureaucracy.

phasized, however, that by institutional arrangements they meant *administrative* rather than *political* renovation.

This differentiation can be understood in the light of the comparative rigidity of the Chinese tradition of political thought. While there had doubtless been considerable development in the realm of administrative thought ever since China became a centralized bureaucratic empire two millennia previously, there had been little change in the realm of political principles. This comparative rigidity of Confucian political tradition can be seen most clearly in three critical areas. In the first place, the principle of kingship remained an unchanging fixture of Chinese political tradition down to the nineteenth century. Admittedly, among some Neo-Confucian scholars, there had been many arguments centered around the problem of centralized bureaucracy (*chün-hsien*) versus feudalism (*feng-chien*).[42] But the real focus of dispute was the problem of centralized or decentralized political power, rather than a questioning of the ideal of kingship as the basic organizing principle of political system. Underlying this basic acceptance of the institution of the monarchy was the fact that the grounds for political legitimation had also remained unchanged throughout the traditional period of China. Down to the eve of modern times, heaven had always been upheld as the ultimate source of legitimation, and kingship as the only institutional device to keep the human world in harmony with heaven by articulating the mandate of heaven. Thus kingship had a particularly secure place in Chinese political tradition because it was thought to have the all-important function of mediating between Heaven and the human order in the Chinese religious world view.

42. T'ao Hsi-sheng, *Chung-kuo cheng-chih-ssu-hsiang shih* (Chungking, 1942), IV, 133–156.

In addition, the Confucian political tradition envisaged universal empire as the only desirable form of political community. Alternative forms such as the city-state and the nation-state, which figure so prominently in the Western tradition, do not exist in Confucian culture.

In the orthodox Neo-Confucian view the prime goal of the Confucian state was the maintenance of Confucian moral teachings rather than collective achievement either in terms of political expansion or of economic development. This view is clearly manifested in the Neo-Confucian stress on the ideal of the "kingly way" (*wang-tao*) and the "way of hegemony" (*pa-tao*). Another indication is the Neo-Confucian attack on the Legalist ideal of wealth and power (*fu-ch'iang*) as the legitimate goal of the state and its repudiation of the Han and T'ang, the two glorious dynasties in Chinese history from the standpoint of collective achievement, as models for later dynasties.[43]

In regard to the organizing principles of the political system as well as the form of the political community, the School of Statecraft still operated within the parameters of traditional political thought. The thought of such central figures in this school in the early nineteenth century as Wei Yüan, Pao Shih-ch'en, and Chou Chi was characterized by an almost exclusive concern with the organizational and managerial issues predicated on an unquestioned acceptance of the political premises of the traditional Confucian state.[44]

However, with respect to the moral goal of the Confucian state, the School of Statecraft is bound to be sig-

43. S. N. Eisenstadt, *The Political Systems of Empires* (New York, 1963), pp. 225–238; Hsiao Kung-ch'üan, *Chung-kuo cheng-chih-ssu-hsiang shih* (Taipei, 1954), IV, 461–469; see also T'ao Hsi-sheng, IV, 133–156; Mou Tsung-san, *Cheng-tao yü chih-tao* (Taipei, 1960), pp. 203–269.

44. Ch'i Ssu-ho, "Wei Yüan yü wan-Ch'ing hsüeh-feng," *Yen-ching hsüeh-pao*, 39:185 (1950); see also Ho Ch'ang-ling, ed., *Huang-ch'ao ching-shih wen-pien* (Peking, 1826), "Hsü-li" 1:1–1b, "table of contents," 1:1–38.

nificantly ambivalent. This attitude is manifested in the *Huang-ch'ao ching-shih wen-pien* (Compilation of essays on statecraft), which was published under the editorship of Wei Yüan and Ho Ch'ang-ling in 1826. This compilation represented an almost unprecedented effort to mobilize all available thought in order to attack the various managerial and organizational problems of the bureaucratic state — the administration of the Six Boards and such related problems as taxation, the salt gabelle, grain transport, the military system, and the Inner Asian frontier defense.[45] A quick glance at its contents shows no deviation from the traditional orientation of the Confucian state, for the whole corpus of technical administrative thought was prefaced with an assertion of the Confucian ideals of learning and government. But the very fact that such a large-scale collection of technical ideas about the organization and management of bureaucracy was undertaken by Confucian scholar-officials implies a recognition that a specialized knowledge of statecraft in addition to a general knowledge of Confucian classics was useful.

This position was a significant departure from the orthodox image of the Confucian scholar-official, whose grasp of Confucian moral teaching was presumed to be adequate for setting the state and society in order. What is more interesting, though, is the emergence of certain tendencies in the writings of Wei Yüan, the chief editor of this compilation, which accommodated certain Legalist goals of statehood within the framework of Confucianism. By paying tribute to the princes of *Realpolitik* in the late Chou and to the Legalist emperor, Ch'in Shih-huang-ti, Wei tried to blur the distinction between hero and sage and to close the gap between the ideals of *wang-tao* and *pa-tao*. Not only did such ideals as practical achievement and

45. Ibid.

29

profit making receive a positive evaluation in his work, but the Legalist goals of wealth and power also found a legitimate place in his view of Confucian statesmanship: "In this world there is wealth and power without the kingly way. But there is no kingly way without wealth and power." [46] With such a view, it is little wonder that Wei Yüan did not find it unbecoming for a Confucian scholar to write an enthusiastic account of the outward expansion of the early Ch'ing empire and sing praises for the military accomplishments of the K'ang-hsi Emperor. [47] Although such ideas of Wei Yüan's cannot be taken as representative of the whole School of Statecraft, the ideal of collective power and achievement was already present in late Ch'ing thought before China's encounter with the West.

The T'ung-chih Restoration in the 1860's is generally characterized as a reassertion of the orthodox political goals of the Confucian state. [48] This characterization is true of the court, whose official patronage of Sung Neo-Confucianism naturally committed it to the orthodox Confucian goals of statehood. But for that galaxy of Confucian statesmen who shared power in the provinces, the picture is a more complicated one. The central figure in the group, Tseng Kuo-fan, clung by and large to the political views of Sung Neo-Confucianism, but the positions of some other figures in the group were more ambiguous. [49] Feng Kuei-fen, for instance, was a direct descendant of the School of Statecraft in the early nineteenth century and an important intellectual spokesman at this time. To him the ideal of wealth and power was an accepted value. [50] Tso

46. Ch'i Ssu-ho, p. 191.
47. Ibid., pp. 188–201.
48. Mary C. Wright, *The Last Stand of Chinese Conservatism: The T'ung-chih Restoration, 1862–1874* (Stanford, 1957), pp. 43–67.
49. Ibid.; see also *CCHS*, II, 569–595.
50. Feng Kuei-fen, *Chiao-pin-lu k'ang-i* (Personal proposal from the Studio of Chiao-pin), exerpted in *Wu-hsü pien-fa*, I, 15, 28.

Tsung-t'ang, quite unlike Tseng Kuo-fan, whose models were always ancient Confucian sages, sometimes cited ancient Legalist statesmen. Indeed, in view of Tso's dynamic political style, it is difficult to think that his goal could have been other than that of wealth and power.[51] Therefore in the political outlook of the T'ung-chih Restoration we find the Legalist ideal of wealth and power, peripheral as it was, offering counterbalance to the dominant cultural goals of the Confucian state.

In spite of all the conflicting elements in the tradition of statecraft, it was not until the 1870's and 1880's when the Self-strengthening Movement got under way in China under the pressure of the Western challenge that the ideal of wealth and power gradually gained widespread acceptance as a legitimate goal of state policies. A prevalent view was found in Ma Chien-chung's words: "The basis for governing a country is wealth and power; the attainment of wealth must precede the achievement of power." [52] What had started as a sidestream in the School of Statecraft had gradually been transformed under the stimulus of Western impact into a dominant political ideal in the late nineteenth century.

The political goal of collective achievement, once it was widely accepted, was bound to transform the Confucian view of practical statesmanship which, as it emerged in the early nineteenth century, confined its attention mainly to problems of moral leadership and administrative management. In the first place, the goal of wealth and power provided a sanction and motivation for the acceptance of

51. For Tso's intellectual background and political achievements, see Ch'in Han-ts'ai, *Tso Wen-hsiang-kung tsai hsi-pei* (Chungking, 1945), pp. 11–16.

52. Benjamin Schwartz, *Yen Fu*, pp. 16–17; Ma Chien-chung, *Shih-k'o-chai chi-yen chi-hsing* (Notes from the Shih-k'o studio) excerpted in *Wu-hsü pien-fa* I, 163.

31

Western industrialism and profit-making activities. Even more significant was the fact that it eventually led to the transformation of some basic political principles of Confucianism, which underlay late Ch'ing thought on practical statesmanship. Again contact with the West provided the indispensable stimulant.

Soon after the 1870's and certainly by the early 1890's there was a general feeling among some reform-minded Chinese intellectuals that behind the wealth and power of the Western nations there was not only technological and wealth-producing ingenuity but also a remarkable capacity for united will and collective action. In contrast to the West where the government and the people were closely welded together, China suffered from a political gap between the ruler and the ruled. To bridge this gap and to strengthen political support for the government, political communication between the ruling and the ruled must be established.[53] The idea of establishing communication and seeking popular support, to be sure, was also present in Confucian political thought, but in very different form. While communication with the ruled was traditionally thought to be best channeled through bureaucracy and political support was usually tacit and passive acquiescence, what was sought by late Ch'ing reformists Wang T'ao, T'ang Chien, Ch'en Chih, Ch'en Ch'iu, and Cheng Kuanying in the 1880's and the 1890's was active political support expressed through some sort of participation.[54]

More important, they even accepted the Western in-

53. Onogawa Hidemi, "The Reform Movement of 1898 and Hunan Province," in *Shimmatsu seiji shisō kenkyū* (Kyoto, 1960), pp. 276–342.
54. In Neo-Confucianism the organic relationship between different parts of the human body has often been upheld as the model for human relationships in society. See Feng Yu-lan, *History of Chinese Philosophy*, II, 407–629; Onogawa Hidemi, pp. 276–342; Chou Fu-ch'eng, "Cheng Kuanying ti ssu-hsiang," in *Chung-kuo chin-tai ssu-hsiang-shih lun-wen chi* (Shanghai, 1958), pp. 95–97.

stitutional means of achieving such aims: the institution of a parliament. As Ch'en Chih argued, to "adopt the Western methods" one must know "the source of the military power and national wealth of the European and American countries which make them expand across the four seas." The source, he emphasized, lay in the Western parliament, because "the methods of the Western parliament combine the monarch and the people into one body, and channel the ruling and the ruled into one mind." [55] Thus a door was opened to the possibility of organizing China's political system along different lines and legitimizing it by different principles, a possibility which had never been conceived of in the Confucian view of practical statesmanship or in what may be called the *ching-shih* tradition.

Furthermore, as China had increasing contact with the world in the course of the nineteenth century, the ideal of world empire as embodied in the concept of the Middle Kingdom was being eroded. This would eventually lead to the transformation of the form of political community in the Chinese mind. To summarize, one significant upshot of the intellectual encounter between China and the West in the latter half of the nineteenth century was the gradual shift in the late Ch'ing *ching-shih* tradition from *moral-administrative* reformism to a *political* transformation of the ground rules of traditional Chinese polity.

Up to this point it has been argued that in the course of the nineteenth century the dominant scholasticism of Han Learning had been subject to intellectual reactions from various quarters, all in the name of the Confucian ideal of practical statesmanship. While all these intellectual reactions shared the *ching-shih* ideal of political engagement and social responsibility, different emphases were

55. Ch'en Chih, *Yung-shu,* exerpted in *Wu-hsü pien-fa,* I, 245; Onogawa Hidemi, pp. 276–342.

discerned in various interpretations of this protean Confucian ideal. In the case of the School of Sung Learning and its allied schools, the reaction was mainly directed against the atrophy of socio-moral concern in the School of Han Learning and took the form of emphasizing self-cultivation and moral leadership as the primary means of fulfilling the Confucian ideal of practical statesmanship.

Meanwhile some elements in a revived New Text School sought to uphold the Confucian commitment to practical statesmanship and a vaguely defined "institutional reformism" as the central concerns of "true Han Learning" and thus tried to deny the title of Han Learning to the School of Empirical Research. Finally in the School of Statecraft, which was often though wrongly identified as the sole preserve of the ideal of *ching-shih,* a particular stress was laid upon administrative renovation as an essential ingredient in the syndrome of Confucian statesmanship. These trends of thought and their interaction with Western impact were to form the points of departure for Liang Ch'i-ch'ao's intellectual development in the early 1890's through the mediation of his teacher, K'ang Yu-wei.

2

K'ang Yu-wei's Intellectual Role in the Late Nineteenth Century

In the early 1890's K'ang Yu-wei, who had already attracted some attention for his interest in reform, burst upon the intellectual scene in China with a call for radical institutional renovation, which dominated the attention of Chinese gentry-literati for the whole decade. K'ang's reformist philosophy, a product of different intellectual influences, was a syncretic one. His syncretism, in the last analysis, was an attempt to incorporate ideas from different sources in an intellectual framework which is basically Confucian. The Confucian character of his framework will become clear when we examine his intellectual development from the 1870's to the 1890's.

K'ang Yu-wei came from a strongly Neo-Confucian family background. Both his great-grandfather and grandfather were devoted students of the moral philosophy of the Ch'eng-Chu School. K'ang, who was brought up mainly under the care of his grandfather, received intensive training in Sung Neo-Confucian moral precepts during his childhood and early youth; he was said to have developed an image of himself as a Confucian sage at the early age of five, whereupon he began to act differently from other children.[1]

1. Richard C. Howard, "K'ang Yu-wei (1858–1927): His Intellectual Background and His Early Thought," in Arthur F. Wright and Denis Twitchett, eds., *Confucian Personalities* (Stanford, 1962), pp. 296–297, 298–299; see also Liang Ch'i-ch'ao, "Nan-hai K'ang-hsien-sheng chuan," (A biography of K'ang Yu-wei) in *YPSHC-WC*, ts'e 3, 6:59–60.

Apart from his Neo-Confucian family background, the second great intellectual influence to which K'ang was exposed during his early youth came from his teacher, Chu Tz'u-ch'i, who was a leading figure in the late Ch'ing eclectic movement which advocated the merger of Han and Sung Learning. Chu's central educational ideal was to gear scholastic studies to the all-important Confucian concerns of moral cultivation and practical statesmanship.[2] There is no question that this dual emphasis in Chu's intellectual outlook influenced K'ang, as he admitted later. Decisive as Chu's influence was, it is significant that after only two years of study K'ang began to rebel against some of Chu's methods of teaching and soon terminated his study with him.[3]

In the absence of sufficient evidence, one can only speculate on the reasons behind K'ang's departure. A reliable source suggests that, while studying under Chu, K'ang also gradually developed a profound interest in the straightforward and dynamic approach of Lu-Wang Neo-Confucianism.[4] Thus K'ang might have rebelled against Chu because he thought Chu's eclectic approach was overburdened with traditional textual study and hence not very effective for achieving the Confucian ideal of sage-statesmanship. K'ang's shift of interest from the Ch'eng-Chu to the Lu-Wang School was significant because the intellectual approach of the Lu-Wang School was to become an important element in his thought.

In the late 1870's K'ang also became interested in Buddhism. This development was not exceptional, since it was well known that in traditional times Confucian scholars often took a profound interest in Buddhist studies. In fact

2. Chien Ch'ao-liang, pp. 24b–32b.
3. K'ang Yu-wei, *K'ang Nan-hai tzu-pien nien-p'u* in *Wu-hsü pien-fa*, IV, 112–114.
4. Liang, "Nan-hai K'ang-hsien-sheng chuan," p. 61.

in the late Ch'ing there seems to have been a resurgence of interest in Buddhism among certain circles of Confucian literati. We are told that many scholars in the New Text School happened to have intellectual affiliations with Buddhism, but there is no evidence to suggest that K'ang's interest was in any way influenced by this general intellectual current. He seems to have developed it when he lived like a hermit in the mountain retreat Hsi-ch'iao-shan near his home.

K'ang's interest does not seem to have been mere intellectual dabbling. Aside from studying Buddhist canons, he also practiced intense meditation and experienced successive stages of mystic enlightenment. In 1879 he gave this summary of his meditations: "I reflected upon the perils and hardship in the life of the people and upon how I might save them with the powers of wisdom and ability granted to me by Heaven. Out of commiseration for all living beings, and in anguish over the state of the world, I made it my purpose to set in order all under Heaven." [5]

The tone of this statement suggests that behind the professed Confucian goal there may have existed a strong Buddhistic motivation to bring salvation to the world. Indeed, a close examination of K'ang's idea of Buddhism, in its Mahayana form, reveals that instead of negating the activistic world view of Confucianism as is often supposed, Buddhism could actually supplement and reinforce Confucianism. In his mind the image of a Confucian sage and that of Buddhist savior merged into one.

To understand the Buddhistic element in K'ang's desire to set the world in order, it is important to examine exactly how he identified Mahayana Buddhism with Confucianism. The Buddhist teaching which most interested K'ang was the Hua-yen School. The general tendency of

5. K'ang, *K'ang Nan-hai tzu-pien nien-p'u*, pp. 114–115.

Mahayana Buddhism was to replace the dualistic world view of Hinayana Buddhism with a monistic one: there was no gap between Samsara and Nirvana; Samsara was actually a manifestation of Nirvana; thus Nirvana need not be sought beyond the realm of Samsara.[6] This monistic approach was inherited by the Hua-yen School. According to its teaching, there is a close interpenetration and mutual identification between the realm of phenomenon and the realm of noumenon, the result of which is the merger of the two into an organic whole. Hence the central doctrine of the Hua-yen world view that all is one and one is all.[7]

K'ang, though aware of the original dualism of the Buddhist world view, eventually emerged from his studies of Buddhism with a monistic world view which denied the existence of a spiritual world separate from the finite world. To be sure, K'ang did not altogether deny an otherworldly spiritual realm; he continued to believe in an ultimate world of eternal bliss beyond the world of distinctions, but he was referring to the future. In the world of here and now, K'ang did not postulate a separate spiritual realm. Integral to the Buddhist world view was an injunction to renovate the finite world, to "create a spiritual world in the world of finite existence," so as to make "a spiritual world *of* the world of finite existence." In this way K'ang found in Buddhism an acceptance of the world and hence nothing which divorced it from this-worldly

6. K'ang Yu-wei never gave any specific account of his early view of Mahayana Buddhism. The following presentation of his view of Buddhism is based on Liang Ch'i-ch'ao's recollection of K'ang's view which K'ang must have held when he studied with K'ang at Ch'ang-hsing hsüeh-she in the early 1890's. Liang's account was written in 1901 and hence can be regarded as a very reliable recount of K'ang's early view of Buddhism.

7. Feng Yu-lan, *History of Chinese Philosophy*, II, 339–359; also Kenneth Ch'en, *Buddhism in China: A Historical Survey* (Princeton, 1964), pp. 313–320.

Confucianism. Confucianism, K'ang stated, is Hua-yen Buddhism.[8]

Doubtless, in K'ang's view, the embodiment of this Buddhist activistic world view was the Mahayana ideal of the compassionate bodhisattva. In Mahayana literature, the bodhisattva is portrayed as one who is not only enlightened, but also has developed such infinite compassion for the unending suffering manifested in the finite world that he chooses to delay the supreme bliss of attaining Buddhahood and remain in this world to save the souls of the unenlightened. This is the self-image which K'ang often held alongside that of a Confucian sage.[9]

While in K'ang's mind, consciously or unconsciously, the image of the bodhisattva and that of the Confucian sage often blurred into one, different degrees of commitment may actually have distinguished the two ideals. The typical image of the bodhisattva which emerged from Mahayana literature was that of an enlightened being who had made a solemn and unshakable resolve at the beginning of his career, not only to pity and help all mortal beings, but also to share their most intense sufferings.[10] Such an image was closely akin to the image of the suffering savior in Christianity or in ancient Chinese Mohism, but rather different from that of the Confucian sage, who seemed always to convey an impression of moderation and

8. Liang, "Nan-hai K'ang-hsien-sheng chuan," pp. 83–84, 1, 69.

9. As a branch of Mahayana Buddhism, the Hua-yen School naturally put strong stress on this ideal of a compassionate Buddha. Thus Buddha is seen by the Hua-yen School as possessing not only supreme wisdom but also immense compassion. After achieving supreme wisdom, they do not dwell in Samsara, nor, having achieved immense compassion, do they stay in Nirvana. See Liang, "Nan-hai K'ang-hsien-sheng chuan," pp. 61, 70; also K'ang, *K'ang Nan-hai tzu-pien nien-p'u*, p. 118.

10. See Wm. Theodore de Bary et al., eds., *Sources of Indian Tradition* (New York, 1958), pp. 161–165.

poise. In view of the fact that K'ang often vowed to save the world in the fashion of a bodhisattva, it is not too far-fetched to argue that in identifying the Confucian sage with the Mahayana bodhisattva he channeled an intense religious motivation into Confucian statesmanship.

While K'ang was gradually freeing himself of the influence of the orthodox Ch'eng-Chu School through his study of Buddhism and Lu-Wang Neo-Confucianism, he also read early Chinese studies of the West and Chinese translations of Western works. These works were accessible to him because he lived very close to the Canton area, where missionaries were active in spreading Christian teachings and Western secular knowledge. Although his knowledge of the West remained fragmentary and superficial, it could have had a profound impact upon his mind.[11] An awareness of the existence of competing civilizations and of the many dynamic nations in the West could go a long way toward shattering Chinese ethnocentrism and establishing a pluralistic world view.

Toward the end of the 1880's, through his acquaintance with Liao P'ing, an important scholar in the New Text School, K'ang became very interested in the literature of that school and soon accepted its version of Confucian scholarship.[12] With this step, the ingredients of his socio-moral philosophy were complete. When K'ang set up a private school called Ch'ang-hsing hsüeh-she, also known as Wan-mu ts'ao-t'ang, at Canton in 1890, he began to formulate a new syncretic interpretation of Confucianism from these ingredients for his students. The core of his interpretation can be found in the curriculum.

11. K'ang, *K'ang Nan-hai tzu-pien nien-p'u,* pp. 115–118; see also Richard C. Howard, "K'ang Yu-wei," p. 311.
12. *CCHS,* II, 642–652.

In contrast to the limited offerings of many other scholars in the nineteenth century, K'ang's program was exceedingly broad in scope and eclectic in content. The subjects he offered ranged from Confucian classics, histories, and Neo-Confucian moral philosophy to Buddhism, Western learning, and ancient non-Confucian classics.[13] But an examination of K'ang's educational syllabus, *An Account of Study at Ch'ang-hsing Alley* (Ch'ang-hsing hsüeh-chi), which he drew up at this time, shows that its design was still Confucian, based as it was on his new interpretation of Confucianism.

What, then, was this new interpretation? In keeping with the eclectic approach advocated by his teacher Chu Tz'u-ch'i and many other scholars in the late nineteenth century, K'ang maintained that the true Confucian scholar should transcend the disputes between Han Learning and Sung Learning and that the complete Confucian scholarship should encompass both.[14] Although this dichotomous view of Confucian scholarship sounds very like Chu Tz'u-ch'i's eclectic approach, on closer examination K'ang's view of Han and Sung Learning differed considerably from Chu's. Chu and K'ang both agreed that the central concern of Sung Learning was moral cultivation, but their interpretations of Sung Learning diverged. K'ang was closer to the Lu-Wang School, whereas Chu adhered to the Chu Hsi School. For Chu, Han Learning meant primarily the annotative studies of the School of Empirical Research,

13. Liang, "Nan-hai K'ang-hsien-sheng chuan," p. 62. Liang Ch'i-ch'ao who studied with K'ang at this time summed up the intellectual content of K'ang's teaching program at Ch'ang-hsing hsüeh-she in the following formula: "Confucianism, Buddhism, and Sung-Ming Neo-Confucianism for fundamental principles, history and Western learning for practical application."

14. K'ang Yu-wei, *Ch'ang-hsing hsüeh-chi,* in Su Yü, *I-chiao ts'ung-pien* (1898), 4:15b–16.

which generally took the exegetical scholarship of the Later Han as its model. But for K'ang, who by this time had already accepted the approach of the New Text School, Han Learning meant primarily the Kung-yang doctrines as interpreted and promoted by Tung Chung-shu during the Former Han dynasty. These Kung-yang doctrines, it must be recalled, involved a cryptical view of historical progress and a tendency to regard institutional reform, however ill-defined, as the principal approach to the Confucian ideal of practical statesmanship.[15]

Thus when K'ang said that Confucian scholarship was composed of Han Learning and Sung Learning, he meant in effect that it had essentially two aspects: cultivation of the personality and practical statesmanship.[16] In line with the eclectic approach of many scholars in the nineteenth century, for example, Tseng Kuo-fan, Ch'en Li, and Chu I-hsin, he still divided the curriculum into four categories, namely, moral philosophy (*i-li chih hsüeh*), practical statesmanship (*ching-shih chih hsüeh*), textual criticism (*k'ao-chu chih hsüeh*), and composition of poetry and prose (*tz'u-chang chih hsüeh*).[17] But since K'ang regarded textual criticism and composition of poetry and prose as supplementary to moral philosophy and practical statesmanship, the two cardinal categories of Confucian scholarship remained, in his view, the two latter subjects. Thus by reinterpreting Han Learning as the branch of Confucian scholarship concerned mainly with practical statesmanship and welding this new view to Sung Learning, K'ang reoriented Confucianism toward what he termed the two primary goals of self-cultivation and practical statesmanship, or, in

---

15. *CCHS*, II, 596–622, 639–640; K'ang, *Ch'ang-hsing hsüeh-chi*, pp. 18b–20b.

16. K'ang, *Ch'ang-hsing hsüeh-chi*, pp. 15b–16.

17. Ibid., pp. 10b–11b.

his new terms, "moral conduct" (te-hsing) and "political affairs" (cheng-shih).[18]

He emphasized that within the broad stream of Confucianism it was mainly Sung Neo-Confucianism which developed a concern for self-cultivation. The philosophy of this school centered on the *Four Books*, among which, according to K'ang, the *Analects* furnished the central precepts of Confucius' dictum: "Set your heart upon the Way, support yourself by its power, lean upon humanity, seek diversion in the arts." [19]

Although K'ang often acknowledged Chu Hsi's central place in the development of Sung-Ming Neo-Confucianism, he tended to draw closer to the idealistic teachings of Lu Hsiang-shan, Ch'en Pai-sha, and Wang Yang-ming. To begin with, K'ang's interpretation of the first precept, "set your heart upon the Way," was clearly in line with the Lu-Wang School. According to K'ang, this dictum meant taking as one's goal the Confucian Way, which, he emphasized, was centered on the ideal of *jen*. This was what Mencius and Lu Hsiang-shan meant when they said: "First establish the most important. Then, on small things, one will not be conquered by the outside world." [20] Having set one's mind on the Confucian Way, one should watch oneself constantly and discipline one's will relentlessly.

In emphasizing the importance of preserving the moral will, K'ang used the term *shen-tu* (constant self-surveillance), which was the central concept in the moral philosophy of Liu Tsung-chou, an important thinker in the Lu-Wang School in the late Ming.[21] More significant was

18. Ibid., p. 16. As K'ang said: "Moral philosophy (*i-li*) means nothing but moral conduct, practical statesmanship (*ching-shih*) means nothing but political affairs."

19. Ibid., pp. 3b–4, 3–3b, 4b–5.

20. Ibid., pp. 4b–5.

21. Ibid., pp. 5b–6b, pp. 4b–5, 6b.

K'ang's resorting to the concept of *ko-wu* (investigation of things), for his interpretation of this concept was especially indicative of his preference for the Lu-Wang School over the Ch'eng-Chu School. The interpretation of the category *ko-wu* was one of the central problems of Neo-Confucianism, as reflected in the division between the "intellectual" approach of the Ch'eng-Chu School and the "idealistic" approach of the Lu-Wang School. According to Chu Hsi *ko-wu* meant patient and extensive "investigation of things" in order to grasp the organizing principles underlying the myriad phenomena of reality and hence to achieve the intellectual enlightenment required for self-cultivation. Lu Hsiang-shan and Wang Yang-ming, however, believed that the human mind had an innate capacity for moral judgment and that self-cultivation consisted of no more than the effort to realize this moral discernment in action. In this context, *ko-wu* was interpreted as the "rectification of affairs," which meant invoking the inner light of one's mind to cope with the moral situations that confront people daily. K'ang himself defined *ko-wu* as the assertion of an inner will to resist and prevail over external distractions. Thus, in upholding the primacy and potency of the inner moral mind over the external world, he apparently allied himself with Wang Yang-ming's approach to the Confucian concern of self-cultivation.[22]

Following the emphasis on setting one's heart upon the Way was the precept "support yourself by its power," and once again K'ang drew upon Ch'en Pai-sha and Wang Yang-ming for such techniques of character discipline as the achievement of mental tranquility and emotional con-

22. Feng Yu-lan, *History of Chinese Philosophy*, II, 602–603. The criticism made of K'ang's idea of *ko-wu* in the *I-chiao ts'ung-pien* also argued that K'ang's idea is very close to those of Ch'en Pai-sha and Wang Yang-ming. See Su Yü, *I-chiao ts'ung-pien* 4:42b–43b.

trol.[23] He then went on to deal with the communal implications of self-cultivation under the precept "lean on humanity." Humanity (*jen*), was, according to K'ang, the moral ideal which distinguished human beings from beasts, for it was by virtue of *jen* that human beings associated with each other and formed communities. In other words, *jen* lay at the basis of human community (*ch'ün*). Hence the realization of *jen* was the ultimate purpose of men's learning.[24]

In discussing these first three precepts, K'ang focused on defining the moral goal of study and cultivation of character involved in pursuing that goal. Only in treating the last precept — "seek diversion in the arts" — did he set forth his ideas of intellectual study. This order of treatment is highly significant, for it was characteristic of Confucianism, especially the Lu-Wang School of Neo-Confucianism, that moral concerns must control intellectual pursuits. In his program of intellectual study K'ang followed the late Ch'ing eclectic scholars and classified his program for intellectual study into the time-honored four categories: moral philosophy, practical statesmanship, textual criticism, and poetic literature.[25] But the scope and contents of K'ang's intellectual concerns were broader and more varied than the categories suggest.

23. K'ang, *Ch'ang-hsing hsüeh-chi*, p. 7, 7–9; in *I-chiao ts'ung-pien* there was also a detailed criticism of K'ang's ideas under this category, emphasizing that K'ang derived his ideas from Ch'en Pai-sha and Wang Yang-ming. See *I-chiao ts'ung-pien*, 4:46–49.

24. K'ang, *Ch'ang-hsing hsüeh-chi*, p. 9, 9–9b.

25. Ibid., pp. 10b–11b. This fourfold classification of Confucian scholarship had been in vogue since the beginning of the nineteenth century. This classification is different from the one commonly used by the scholars of the eighteenth century in that while the former has four categories, the latter has only three categories, namely moral philosophy, textual study, and literary study, without the category of practical statesmanship. See *CCHS*, II, 637.

Although K'ang's *Ch'ang-hsing hsüeh-chi* does not go into detail about the contents of his program for intellectual training, a teaching curriculum, *Replies to Inquiries about Study at Kwangsi* (Kuei-hsüeh ta-wen), which he wrote in 1894, does provide some general idea.[26] K'ang's program was roughly divided into five parts: Confucian canons and canonical commentaries, Chinese dynastic histories, ancient Chinese non-Confucian philosophies, the moral philosophy of Neo-Confucianism, and Western learning.[27] This last category consisted for the most part of specialized subjects of a practical nature and was certainly an outgrowth of the tendency already apparent in the School of Statecraft in the early nineteenth century in that it sought to provide some specialized knowledge and professional education for the Confucian scholar. Although in K'ang's scheme this professional education was still morally directed and ideologically controlled, it nonetheless represented a further erosion of the orthodox image of the Confucian scholar as a generalist.

This then was the moral and intellectual outlook reflected in K'ang's writings around 1890. The Confucian ideals of *jen* and sage-statesmanship were still basic, and K'ang held that Confucian self-cultivation was the prin-

26. The following summary of K'ang's study program is based on his *Kuei-hsüeh ta-wen* and Liang Ch'i-ch'ao's *Tu-shu fen-yüeh k'o-ch'eng* which is modeled on the former. See Liang Ch'i-ch'ao, *Tu-shu fen-yüeh k'o-ch'eng* (The monthly study schedule), in *YPSHC-CC*, ts'e 15, 69:1–15. For K'ang's *Kuei-hsüeh ta-wen*, see Lo-sang P'eng-ts'o, "K'ang Nan-hai chiang-hsüeh Wan-mu ts'ao-t'ang chih hsüeh-yüeh," *Cheng-feng tsa-chih*, 4.5:407–413. According to Lo-sang P'eng-ts'o this article is almost an exact account of K'ang's *Kuei-hsüeh ta-wen* with only very minor differences. He claimed to have copied it from K'ang's disciple, Mai Meng-hua in 1903. According to Lo Jung-pang who is K'ang Yu-wei's grandson and has engaged in collecting K'ang's works for many years, the book of *Kuei-hsüeh ta-wen* is not available in any library in North America. This article is then perhaps the only reliable account of K'ang's *Kuei-hsüeh ta-wen* now available.

27. Lo-sang P'eng-ts'o, pp. 407–413.

cipal approach to the attainment of such ideals. In regard to self-cultivation, however, K'ang departed from the mainstream of moral thought in the nineteenth century as represented by the Ch'eng-Chu School. In Confucian terms, Ch'eng-Chu's approach to self-cultivation meant an emphasis on the outer realm rather than the inner realm of reality. K'ang, following the Lu-Wang tradition, preferred to shift the emphasis to the inner realm, implying an assertion of inner moral will and a consequent stress on the primacy of setting a goal for life. The result was an ideal of personality more committed to voluntary action than that envisaged by the Ch'eng-Chu School. It must be emphasized, however, that K'ang by no means rejected completely the Chu Hsi approach. His switch from the orthodox Ch'eng-Chu School to the Lu-Wang School was primarily a subtle shift of emphasis from the primacy of Confucian canonical studies to the primacy of asserting the inner moral will and setting the life goal for the cultivation of character.

Confucianism, according to K'ang, was not only oriented toward the ideal of self-cultivation but toward the ideal of practical statesmanship, mainly articulated in what he called the "true Han Learning" — the New Text School of Confucianism. Although K'ang had already accepted the New Text interpretation of Confucianism when he wrote *Ch'ang-hsing hsüeh-chi* in 1891, his own reinterpretation was developed in the two works which he wrote between 1891 and 1897.[28] These two works, whose intellectual repercussions were compared to a typhoon and a volcano respectively, shook the world of Chinese scholar-officials to its foundation in the last decade of the nineteenth century.[29]

28. K'ang, *Ch'ang-hsing hsüeh-chi,* pp. 15b–16, 17b–18, 18b–20b.
29. Liang Ch'i-ch'ao, *Ch'ing-tai hsüeh-shu kai-lun* (Hong Kong, 1963), p. 57.

The first work, *An Inquiry into the Classics Forged during the Hsin Period* (Hsin-hsüeh wei-ching k'ao), was written to discredit on textual grounds the authenticity of Ancient Text versions of the Confucian classics. Almost all the Ancient Text classics had been disputed individually, but there had been no effort to relate these disputations in a systematic way or to refute the Ancient Text interpretations *in toto*. This task now fell to Liao P'ing and K'ang Yu-wei, who synthesized all the previous ad hoc refutations within a systematic framework. For them it was no longer just one or several of the Ancient Text classics which needed to be refuted. Instead, the whole New Text School and the totality of the Ancient Text classics were at stake.[30]

K'ang's provocative book argued that the Ancient Text classics were all forged by an unscrupulous scholar, Liu Hsin, who lived toward the end of the Former Han dynasty and was a close friend of Wang Mang. Liu Hsin's purpose was to provide the ideological underpinnings for Wang Mang's usurpation of the Han throne, as well as for the institutional reforms advocated by Wang. But most unfortunately, K'ang emphasized, these Ancient Text versions were accepted by a number of prominent scholars in the Later Han dynasty, for example, Chia K'uei, Ma Jung, Hsü Shen, and most important of all, Cheng Hsüan. Even more disastrous, through the authority of these scholars the Ancient Text literature became the foundation of the exegetical scholarship of the School of Empirical Research in the Ch'ing dynasty. Thus many scholars in recent centuries had become the victims of Liu Hsin's fraud. K'ang charged: "All that has been regarded by posterity as Han Learning was scholarship advocated by Chia, Ma, Hsü,

30. Ibid., p. 55.

and Cheng. This was the learning of the Hsin dynasty, rather than Han Learning." [31]

The authentic Han Learning, K'ang asserted, should be sought in the New Text School which had prevailed in the Former Han dynasty. Here he defended the New Text School against the Ancient Text School on both textual and philological grounds.[32] With these arguments K'ang attempted to cut the ground from under the Ancient Text versions of classics which were the foundation of the School of Empirical Research and thereby to establish the New Text versions as the genuine repository of Confucius' teachings. K'ang's next step was to show that the central ideal of the New Text School was practical statesmanship and that in fact Confucianism was oriented toward institutional reform rather than toward the preservation of ancient doctrines and institutions.

This K'ang did in *Confucius as Reformer* (K'ung-tzu kai-chih k'ao), which he published in 1897. In this work K'ang began by arguing that prior to the late Chou period the history of China was shrouded in obscurity because "before the *Six Canons* there was no record." [33] All records of antiquity were later idealizations and rationalizations. Recorded history started in the late Chou, when many men of wisdom rose to found schools and propagate their teachings. Tending to cast a romantic glow over antiquity, they all tried to promote their ideals under the cloak of a utopian past. K'ang pointed to Lao-tzu, Mo-tzu, and many other ancient thinkers as examples; in his view, the appeal to ancient sages or legendary kings to justify an ideal was a common practice among late Chou thinkers.[34]

31. K'ang Yu-wei, *Hsin-hsüeh wei-ching k'ao* (Shanghai, 1956), p. 3.
32. Ibid., pp. 5–15; see also Ch'ien Hsüan-t'ung, "Ch'ung-lun chin-ku-wen-hsüeh wen-t'i," appended to K'ang Yu-wei's *Hsin-hsüeh wei-ching k'ao,* pp. 443–454.
33. See K'ang Yu-wei, *K'ung-tzu kai-chih k'ao* (Shanghai, 1958), p. 1.
34. Ibid., pp. 9–32, 47–100.

Confucius was one of these late Chou thinkers; his blueprint for reform was set forth in the *Six Canons*, which he wrote but claimed to have inherited from the great tradition handed down by such sage-kings as Yao and Shun, the founding kings of the Chou dynasty, and the Duke of Chou. K'ang emphatically rejected the notions, often advanced by the scholars of the Ancient Text School, that the founding sage of Confucianism was the Duke of Chou and that Confucius was merely a great teacher whose main purpose was to preserve and to transmit an ancient cultural tradition.[35]

In K'ang's view, Confucius was a "sage-king" (*sheng-wang*) or an "uncrowned king" (*su-wang*), intent on institutional reform. Drawing on certain cryptic ideals in the Kung-yang doctrines, K'ang argued that Confucius, shortly before his death, received a mandate from heaven to establish a new dynasty. This meant that Confucius had to lay down a set of new institutions for the new dynasty, for according to the Kung-yang doctrine of "three sequences" (*san-t'ung*), different historical periods require different institutional arrangements.[36] It must be noted, however, that in the Kung-yang tradition the doctrine of "three sequences" still implied a cyclical conception of history. In order to portray Confucius as a forward-looking sage-king who viewed history as linear progress through determinate stages toward an ideal future, K'ang drew upon another historical ideal of the Kung-yang tradition, the doctrine of "three ages" (*san-shih*) which contained an embryonic concept of historical progress. Human history, K'ang said, passes from the Age of Disorder (*chü-luan shih*), through the Age of Approaching Peace (*sheng-p'ing shih*), toward the final Age of Universal Peace (*t'ai-p'ing shih*), or as

35. Ibid., pp. 164–165.
36. Ibid., pp. 194–213, 214–242, 195–199, 214–225.

K'ang put it in a later scheme, through the Age of Small Peace (*hsiao-k'ang*) toward the final Age of Great Unity (*ta-t'ung*). Each of the three ages has its appropriate political system: absolute monarchy is suitable for the Age of Disorder; constitutional monarchy for the Age of Approaching Peace; and republican government for the Age of Universal Peace.[37]

Through this ingenious and provocative interpretation of Kung-yang doctrine to establish Confucius as sage-statesman and institutional innovator, K'ang argued that the ideal of practical statesmanship lay at the core of Confucianism and required institutional reform for its realization. But what did institutional reform (*kai-chih*) really mean in K'ang's scheme? In the original literature of the New Text School in the Former Han, *kai-chih* was a broad but vague concept with strong religio-mystical overtones more suggestive of ritual change than of institutional renovation in its modern sense. In this connection K'ang's concept of history as a unilinear progress which lay behind his ideal of institutional change is of particular significance. K'ang claimed that he derived the concept of historical progress from the Kung-yang doctrine of "three ages." But the latter was a long-forgotten side-stream in Confucianism. In developing a view of history which involved a distinctly modern concept of progress K'ang seems to have projected into this doctrine what he had learned from his study of the Western learning or his observation of Westerners' activities in treaty ports. Inevitably, this acceptance of a modern concept of historical progress invested K'ang's ideal of *kai-chih* with all the modern connotations of institutional reform. This was clearly reflected later in the reform programs which he submitted to the Kuang-hsü Emperor,

37. Ibid., pp. 267–300; Hsiao Kung-ch'üan, "K'ang Yu-wei and Confucianism," 18:126–143.

as well as in his recommendation to the emperor that China take as her model the Petrine reforms of Russia and the Meiji reforms of Japan.[38]

K'ang's espousal of Western concepts of historical progress and institutional reform naturally implied an acceptance of the ideal of wealth and power as the primary political goal of China at her present stage of history, and almost all of his reform proposals were centered around this ideal.[39] In this respect K'ang seemed to differ little from many of the other reform-minded Chinese scholars of the late nineteenth century. What distinguished K'ang's approach to this common goal, however, was the broad and bold reform program he designed to implement that goal. His program embraced administrative reform, promotion of industry and commerce, political participation through the establishment of a national assembly and an outright abolition of the civil service examination system, and a nationwide system of schools as the principal institutional means for educating the people.[40]

K'ang's advocacy of institutional reform and his belief in the ideal of wealth and power must not lead one to regard him as a modern nationalist. In the framework of

38. Richard C. Howard, "Japan's Role in the Reform Program of K'ang Yu-wei," in Lo Jung-pang, ed., *K'ang Yu-wei: A Biography and a Symposium* (Tucson, 1967), pp. 288–302.

39. T'ang Chih-chün, *Wu-hsü pien-fa shih lun-ts'ung*, pp. 154–177; see also Feng Yu-lan, "K'ang Yu-wei ti ssu-hsiang," in *Chung-kuo chin-tai ssu-hsiang-shih lun-wen-chi* (Shanghai, 1958), pp. 110–127; see also Onogawa Hidemi, pp. 128–238. In his first memorial presented to the Emperor Kuang-hsü he promised that if the Ch'ing court carried out reform, "wealth and power can be achieved within ten years." See K'ang Yu-wei, "Shang Ch'ing-ti ti-i-shu" (The first memorial presented to the Ch'ing emperor), in *Wu-hsü pien-fa*, II, 129; see also "Shang Ch'ing-ti ti-erh-shu" (The second memorial presented to the Ch'ing emperor), in *Wu-hsü pien-fa*, II, 140–147 and "Shang Ch'ing-ti ti-ssu-shu," (The fourth memorial presented to the Ch'ing emperor), in *Wu-hsü pien-fa*, II, 174–188, 178.

40. T'ang Chih-chün, pp. 157–158, 165–167, 169, 222–225; K'ang Yu-wei, "Shang Ch'ing-ti ti-ssu-shu," in *Wu-hsü pien-fa*, II, 176–177.

K'ang's theory of "three ages" these ideals are only meant for China at her present stage of history. Beyond the present stage K'ang looked forward to a utopian future when distinctions of whatever variety, including that of nationality, were all transcended and China as a nation joined other nations in the world to form a universal moral community which he called the world of "universal peace" or "great unity." [41] In brief, for K'ang the ultimate goal was not the nation-state but a universal moral community.

The germ for K'ang's utopianism must be sought in the Confucian ideal of *jen*. In one of his important works he regarded the Age of Great Unity as the age in which *jen* would prevail. As he said, "the Age of Great Unity is the age of perfect humanity." [42] It is no wonder that Liang Ch'i-ch'ao in his biography of K'ang said: "The philosophy of my teacher K'ang is the philosophy of the school of universal love. In his doctrine he considered *jen* as the one fundamental principle, believing that the foundation of the world, the birth of all creatures, the existence of states, and the development of moral institutions are all based on it." [43]

41. Liang, "Nan-hai K'ang-hsien-sheng chuan," pp. 73–85. Although it is true that the detailed description of this future golden age had not yet been spelled out in the 1890's, the moral *Weltanschauung* which lay at the core of K'ang's vision of a "great unity" in the future was already present in his mind in the early 1890's. As Liang later recalled, when K'ang confided to him and Ch'en T'ung-fu his ideal of the "great unity" in 1891, Liang immediately became excited about this ideal and spread it about in spite of K'ang's disapproval. See Liang, *Ch'ing-tai hsüeh-shu kai-lun*, p. 61. The following interpretation of K'ang's ideal of "great unity" is mainly based on Liang's account of it in his biography of K'ang Yu-wei which was published before K'ang's *Ta-t'ung shu* (Book of great unity) was brought out in 1902. Liang maintained that he wrote this account out of his memory of K'ang's personal explication in the early 1890's. See Liang, "Nan-hai K'ang-hsien-sheng chuan," p. 83.

42. Laurence G. Thompson, tr., *Ta T'ung Shu: The One-World Philosophy of K'ang Yu-wei* (London, 1958), p. 266.

43. Liang, "Nan-hai K'ang-hsien-sheng chuan," p. 71.

Liang Ch'i-ch'ao also suggested why the concept of *jen* constituted the core of K'ang's moral *Weltanschauung*. In Neo-Confucianism, which had a distinctive tendency to view the ground of being as both moral and cosmological, *jen* was conceived not just as a moral ideal but also as a life-giving and unifying cosmic force, through the working of which the whole world was formed and all sentient beings therein were given birth. The Neo-Confucian idea of *jen* can be best grasped by looking at the organismic analogy with which Neo-Confucian philosophers tried to understand it. To begin with, *jen* was often compared to a kernel of fruit, which in the Chinese language was literally called *jen*. Just as a whole plant may wither and die without the vital kernel, the whole cosmic order and human society would fall apart without the working of this life-giving force of *jen*. The vital function of *jen* was also clearly suggested in the expression *pu-jen* (not-*jen*) as a technical term for paralysis in Chinese medicine. In Neo-Confucian usage, the concept of *jen* thus had the definite connotations of organic unity and vitality often associated with plants and the human body. These organic analogies suggest how *jen* was conceived by K'ang as a unifying and vitalizing moral force capable of bringing this fragmented human world together into a harmonious universal brotherhood.[44]

There is no doubt that Neo-Confucianism, as Liang Ch'i-ch'ao suggested, constituted a basic intellectual source of K'ang's organic conception of *jen*, which was strongly reminiscent of the definition of *jen* as "organic oneness of the universe" in the Neo-Confucian moral philosophies of Chang Tsai, Ch'eng Hao, and Wang Yang-ming.[45] We

44. Ibid.
45. Wing-tsit Chan, "The Evolution of the Confucian Concept of *Jen*," *Philosophy East and West*, 4.4:295–319 (1955).

must not, however, think of K'ang's ideal of great unity as a simple outgrowth of the Neo-Confucian *jen*. In the first place, in K'ang's treatment of *jen* there is a tendency to view the world as infused with cosmic energy and power. The pseudo-scientific vocabulary which K'ang obviously borrowed from his study of Western learning to express this note of energy and power is vague and sometimes even confusing. Yet what Arthur Lovejoy calls metaphysical pathos is clear: *jen* was not only a life-giving and unifying moral-cosmic principle, but also a dynamic, energy-generating, natural force.[46] The resulting world view thus had a new element of robust dynamism seldom found in the traditional Chinese world view.

Aside from dynamism, there was also a new note of radical universalism in K'ang's concept of *jen* and its ultimate historical embodiment, the Age of Great Unity, which made K'ang's *jen* nearly incompatible with the same concept in Neo-Confucianism. K'ang suggested that the family must be included among the institutional barriers to be abolished so that a universal community could be created.[47]

46. Wing-tsit Chan, "K'ang Yu-wei and the Confucian Doctrine of Humanity," in Lo Jung-pang, ed., *K'ang Yu-wei*, pp. 355–374. For the concept of metaphysical pathos see Arthur O. Lovejoy, *The Great Chain of Being: A Study of the History of an Idea* (Cambridge, Mass., 1950), pp. 10–14. Lovejoy, in his discussion on the methodology to study the history of ideas, called attention to an influential cause in the determination of philosophical fashions and speculative tendencies, which he called metaphysical pathos. In his own words: " 'Metaphysical pathos' is exemplified in any description of the nature of things, any characterization of the world to which one belongs, in terms which, like the words of a poem, awaken through their associations, and through a sort of empathy which they engender, a congenial mood or tone of feeling on the part of the philosophers or his readers." I find this concept very useful in characterizing K'ang's thought which cognitively sometimes defies understanding.

47. K'ang, *Ch'ang-hsing hsüeh-chi*, p. 9; also Wing-tsit Chan, "K'ang Yu-wei," pp. 366–367; Laurence G. Thompson, tr., *Ta T'ung Shu*, pp. 226–227.

But Confucian *jen* was a characteristic combination of universalism and particularism. It is true that the ultimate fulfillment of Confucian *jen* requires the feeling of oneness among all beings across all kinds of distinctions and barriers. On the other hand, Confucianism had a basic and unalterable commitment to family values. In Confucian classics filial piety and brotherly love were often emphasized as the all-important initial requirement to be fulfilled for *jen* to prevail. Given this commitment, it is difficult to imagine that the realization of *jen* could be achieved at the cost of the institution of the family. Indeed, the realization of Confucian *jen* does not require the transcendence of family love so much as the extension of it. Obviously K'ang's willingness to see family values completely transcended in his utopian future implies that his interpretation of *jen* must have had some non-Confucian sources.

Although the element of radical universalism in K'ang's thought may have been influenced by the ideal of universal love in both Christianity and Mo-tzu's philosophy, it was mainly Buddhist in origin, for in the 1890's he drew upon the vocabulary of Mahayana Buddhism to describe his vision of great unity. According to Liang Ch'i-ch'ao, K'ang accepted the Mahayana belief that all beings derived from the same all-embracing Dharmatsaya and all human beings formed one brotherhood. Through ignorance, however, men had made a variety of distinctions and discriminations among themselves. The result was man's selfish love for his own person, his own family, his own group, and his own country. In K'ang's view, this was how struggle and warfare between human beings arose and also why the world was full of suffering. To transform this world into a world of bliss, man-made distinctions of whatever variety must be eradicated. Only then would the age of universal brotherhood and harmony dawn.[48] In this way, the radical universalism of Buddhism finally gained ascendancy over the particularism of Confucianism and thereby made K'ang's ideal of great unity something more than a mere outgrowth of the Neo-Confucian ideal of *jen*.

While K'ang's conception of self-cultivation was largely Confucian in character and origin, his ideal of practical statesmanship was deeply influenced by Western thinking. In the first place, there is no doubt that his interpretation of this ideal, as far as the present stage of human history is concerned, was permeated by Western values. As for his ideal of a society in the future, although it had its origin in the Confucian *jen* it also bore the clear imprints of Buddhist and Western thought. Finally, underlying his ideal of society was his over-all conception of history which was probably influenced by the Western idea of social progress. K'ang's ideal of practical statesmanship was thus Confucian in form but synthetic in character.

Such, in essence, were the ideas and doctrines which were the elements of K'ang's intellectual system in the 1890's. This system had its origin in the mainstreams of late Ch'ing thought. Han Learning, Sung Learning, the New Text School, and the School of Statecraft all contributed to the formation of K'ang's thought. Buddhism and Western learning also had a significant impact, transforming these developments of Confucianism into a system of ideas which not only had a profound effect on the intellectual world but became the fountainhead of a political reform movement as well. It was inevitable that such a system of thought would stir up furor and conquer minds, and one of the young minds it conquered was Liang Ch'i-ch'ao's.

48. Liang, "Nan-hai K'ang-hsien-sheng chuan," pp. 74–85.

3

Liang Ch'i-ch'ao's Early Life and Intellectual Background

Liang Ch'i-ch'ao was born into a lower class gentry family in a small village not far from Canton on February 23, 1873. During his childhood he received a good education and loving care from his family, especially from his grand-father. When very young he showed an intellectual pre-cociousness which, by age ten, had already earned him the reputation of a child prodigy.[1]

In traditional China such a promising child naturally found himself bound to take the civil service examinations. In 1889, when Liang was sixteen, he passed the provincial examination with high honor and so impressed the examiner that the official later gave him his sister in marriage.[2] However, this marked the last time he passed an examination. Henceforth the examination system barred his way to further traditional honors.

In addition to studying for the examinations, Liang was initiated at an early age into traditional Confucian scholar-ship. He was attracted by Han Learning and in 1887 en-tered the Hsüeh-hai t'ang at Canton, the citadel of Han Learning and a center of the late Ch'ing eclectic move-ment to combine Han and Sung Learning. For three years

1. *LNCC*, I, 2–9.
2. Ibid., pp. 10–13.

Liang remained there as a devoted and outstanding student.[3]

He might have grown up to become a master of "empirical research," had not destiny intervened. In the spring of 1890, after failing the metropolitan examination at Peking, he came into contact during a sojourn at Shanghai with a number of Chinese books on Western learning which gave him his first glimpse of the world outside China.[4] In the fall of the same year, through Ch'en T'ung-fu, who was his schoolmate at the Hsüeh-hai t'ang, Liang came to know K'ang Yu-wei. As Liang later recalled, the first long interview he had with K'ang proved to be an intellectual epiphany for him. K'ang's words shocked him out of his complacent acceptance of conventional learning and revealed a new intellectual world totally undreamed of before.[5]

Liang immediately quit his study at the Hsüeh-hai t'ang and henceforth considered himself to be K'ang's student. Considering that Liang was already a second-degree holder in the examination system, while K'ang had only received the first degree, this was indeed an outrage of convention in traditional China where both the degree difference and teacher-disciple relationship meant important status distinctions.[6] The year after Liang's interview with K'ang, the latter, at the request of Liang and Ch'en T'ung-fu, set up a private school called Wan-mu ts'ao-t'ang in Canton.[7] For four years Liang studied intermittently at K'ang's

3. Ibid., pp. 11–14.
4. Ibid., p. 15.
5. Ibid., p. 15; see also *YPSHC-WC*, ts'e 4, 11:16–17.
6. In 1890 when Liang who was already a *chü-jen* became K'ang's student, K'ang was still a *hsiu-ts'ai*. K'ang became *chü-jen* only in 1893. But in 1895 K'ang went on to win his *chin-shih* degree, while Liang never attained that degree. See Chao Feng-t'ien, "K'ang Ch'ang-shu hsien-sheng nien-p'u," *Shih-hsüeh nien-pao*, 2.1:187–191.
7. *LNCC*, I, 16.

private school. As he recalled, these were years of spiritual excitement and ferment, when the intellectual foundation for his whole life was laid.[8]

K'ang's teaching soon kindled Liang's political consciousness. He began to worry about the deepening national crisis and in his letters to friends even discussed the possibility of political action.[9] When K'ang went north to launch his campaign for reform in 1895, Liang left Canton and joined his teacher as a young political activist. In the spring of that year, when the Sino-Japanese War ended in a humiliating peace treaty with Japan, Liang went north to Peking to take the triennial metropolitan examination.[10] The defeat at the hands of the Japanese, who had long been despised by the Chinese as inferiors, naturally aroused the patriotic fury of the literati who had assembled at Peking for the examination. K'ang and Liang, sensing the significance of this occasion for their reform cause, persuaded the 1,300 examination candidates to join them in protesting the humiliating terms of the Shimonoseki Treaty and requesting "institutional reform" (*pien-fa*). As the representative of 190 Cantonese candidates, Liang petitioned the court on the current situation. This was the famous *Kung-chü* petition, which Liang later called, not without exaggeration, the first mass movement in Chinese history.[11]

Following the *Kung-chü* petition, K'ang and Liang stepped up the tempo of their reform movement, which now took on a broader scope than it had when K'ang first launched it single-handedly in 1888. At that time K'ang's reform efforts did not go beyond petitioning the emperor

8. *LNCC*, I, 16–17; see also *Hsin Chung-kuo wei-lai chi* (The future of new China), in *YPSHC-CC*, ts'e 19, 89:15.

9. *LNCC*, I, 21–23.

10. Chao Feng-t'ien, p. 186; Liang Ch'i-ch'ao, "Wu-hsü cheng-pien chi" (A recount of the coup d'état of 1898), in *YPSHC-CC*, ts'e 1, 1:1.

11. *LNCC*, I, 24.

and lobbying among high officials in the court. While continuing to advocate the fundamental principle of carrying out reform from above, K'ang and Liang made an important tactical change: they tried to petition the court and also endeavored to win the support of gentry-literati at large who, "because of their familiarity with the conditions of the people, can thus serve as the channel between the high and low." [12] They planned to accomplish this in two ways: by organizing study societies among the gentry-literati and publishing newspapers to publicize their cause. The study societies were to be organized on two bases: locality and intellectual specialty. They were to be set up first at Peking and Shanghai, with branch societies following later in every province, every county, every district, and every town. At the same time, for the purpose of studying the various new intellectual disciplines, societies which would serve to educate gentry-literati in the new knowledge throughout the country were planned and newspapers were to supplement those educative and integrative functions of study societies by facilitating communication and promoting consensus. In both undertakings Liang served as K'ang's chief assistant.[13]

The first result of this effort to organize study societies was the Ch'iang hsüeh-hui (The Self-strengthening Study Society) founded by K'ang and several other reform-minded gentry-officials at Peking in the summer of 1895. Later a branch society was set up by K'ang at Shanghai. Liang was appointed secretary of the society at Peking and also editor of a daily newspaper entitled *Chung-wai kung-pao* (The Chinese and foreign news), which was sponsored by the Ch'iang hsüeh-hui. This so-called newspaper contained no more than a few essays about current affairs in

12. "[Shang Ch'en Pao-chen] lun Hu-nan ying-pan-chih-shih," in *YPSHC-WC*, ts'e 2, 3:41–48.

13. T'ang Chih-chün, pp. 222–225.

each issue, written by Liang and his friend Mai Meng-hua. It soon became quite popular in gentry-official circles in Peking. At its height about three thousand copies were issued.[14] However, it was soon implicated in the factional struggles in the court at Peking and incurred hostility and interference from the government. Thus the Ch'iang hsüeh-hui came to an end only a few months after its founding, forcing the reformers to abandon their hopes for a nationwide network of similar study societies. For Liang personally, however, this experience was extremely fruitful, because it gave him his first taste of journalism and the opportunity to read translations of Western books belonging to the society.[15]

Meanwhile, besides helping K'ang organize study societies among gentry-officials, Liang also took on in the early summer of 1895 the publication of another edition of the *Compilation of Essays on Statecraft (Huang-ch'ao ching-shih-wen hsin-pien)*, a continuation of the original edition published by Ho Ch'ang-ling in 1826. In this projected new edition, Liang intended to publish a collection of essays written by his friends and himself about current affairs. The project, however, did not materialize immediately. When the new edition of *Huang-ch'ao ching-shih wen-pien* finally came out two years later, it was under the editorship of Mai Meng-hua.[16] In sponsoring this new edition, Liang clearly placed himself in the tradition of Confucian concern with practical statesmanship, which was the mainstream of late Ch'ing thought. Liang knew that current ideas on reform had gone beyond the administrative reform advocated by Ho Ch'ang-ling and Wei Yüan in the early nineteenth century. But, as he explained, he

14. *LNCC*, I, 25–26; see also T'ang Chih-chün, pp. 228–229.
15. *LNCC*, I, 26.
16. Ibid.; see also "Ching-shih wen-pien hsin-hsü" (A new preface to the compilation of essays on statecraft), in *YPSHC-WC*, ts'e 2, 2:46–48.

continued to use the old term *ching-shih* because he saw in the Confucian concern with practical statesmanship a good justification for channeling new ideals into China.[17]

Failure in their effort to establish study societies naturally led K'ang and Liang to try to carry on their campaign through the publication of another newspaper. When the branch society of the Ch'iang hsüeh-hui was banned at Shanghai, a number of reform-minded gentry-officials like Huang Tsun-hsien and Wang K'ang-nien proposed to use the remaining funds and some money from private sources to found a newspaper. The newspaper was set up in the spring of 1896, and Liang was invited to be the editor at the suggestion of Huang, who recommended him mainly because of his performance in the *Chung-wai kung-pao*. This was the beginning of the famous *Chinese Progress* (*Shih-wu pao*).[18] For two years Liang poured forth his ideas on the cause of reform, first in *Chinese Progress* and later also in the *Chih-hsin pao* (New knowledge), which was founded by K'ang and Liang and their associates at Macao in February 1897. Liang's stirring writings made *Chinese Progress* an immediate success and Liang's name soon became as familiar as K'ang's to the reading public.[19]

Before turning to Liang's activities in the period 1896–97, however, it is necessary to consider the intellectual influences he was exposed to after he left K'ang's school at Canton in 1895. Up to this time Liang's thinking had been almost completely dominated by K'ang, and his associations were also largely confined to K'ang's group. When Liang left Canton and went north to help K'ang

17. *LNCC*, I, 28.

18. "Ching-shih wen-pien hsin-hsü," pp. 31–32; T'ang Chih-chün, p. 231.

19. T'ang Chih-chün, pp. 239, 241. See also Hsü Chih-ching, "Pao-chien jent-ts'ai che," in Yeh Te-hui, ed., *Chüeh-mi yao-lu* (special series, 1905), 1:1.

campaign for reform in 1895, his intellectual contact naturally broadened. The new friends with whom he became acquainted, either at Peking or in the Yangtze valley, all seemed to share one or more of three interests: Western learning, the New Text doctrines, and Buddhism. Among them Yen Fu and T'an Ssu-t'ung stand out as the two who had the most significant impact on Liang's mind.

Yen Fu was not a close friend of Liang and their acquaintance was thus primarily an intellectual one. Since Yen was already well-known among enlightened literati for his knowledge of Western learning, Liang must have read the reformist essays Yen published in the Tientsin newspaper, *Chih-pao* in 1895.[20] He did not have any personal contact with Yen, however, until he went to Shanghai to edit *Chinese Progress* in 1896. Yen had just finished his translation of Huxley's *Evolution and Ethics* at the time, and Liang read the translation and Yen's commentaries before they were published.[21] Thus, as early as 1896, Liang was already introduced to Social Darwinism, which was to play a role in the development of his own thinking.

In the intellectual spectrum of the 1890's, Yen Fu represented a radical stance. He attacked the cult of the eight-legged essay and the vogue of textual criticism as K'ang and Liang also did; he also went further and dismissed all the current schools of Confucianism as intellectual waste. He sought the remedy to China's ills only in Western ideas and values.[22]

20. Wang Ch'ü-ch'ang, *Yen Chi-tao nien-p'u* (Shanghai, 1936), p. 28.
21. *LNCC*, I, 33; Liang Ch'i-ch'ao, "Yü Yen Yu-ling hsien-sheng shu" (A letter to Yen Fu), in *LNCC*, I, 33; *YPSHC-WC*, ts'e 1, 1:110.
22. Yen Fu said: "From the present-day standpoint, not only the eight-legged essay which stunts human talents should be abolished, all the Sung Learning, Han Learning and other trivial skills of fine style should be thrown into the discard." Yen Fu, "Chiu-wang chüeh-lun," in *Wu-hsü pien-fa*, III, 64. The following discussion of Yen Fu's thought is mainly based on Benjamin Schwartz's *In Search of Wealth and Power: Yen Fu and the West*, pp. 42–112.

For Yen in this period, Western learning meant primarily Social Darwinism. As Benjamin Schwartz has shown, he was particularly attracted by the Social Darwinian image of a dynamic cosmos and the view of history as an evolutionary process leading to a better future. The universe, as conceived in the West, was an "inexhaustible storehouse" of energy and force, manifested in the forms of matter and motion. Because of the persistence of energy and force, everywhere in the universe man observes a constant process of evolution from the homogeneous to the heterogeneous. The persistence of force and the inexorable flow of evolution are principles at work not only in the universe at large but also in the human world. Thus in Yen's view, basic to the development of Western civilization was a vision of reality which prized the ideals of dynamism and evolution.[23]

Emphasis on these two ideals also accounted for the exaltation of the value of struggle in the West. Given the world's limited resources and teeming life, the struggle for existence among human individuals was not just inevitable but desirable as well. For "it is the struggle for existence which leads to natural selection and the survival of the fittest — and hence, within the human realm, to the greatest realization of human capacities." [24]

Yen was interested in the Western values of vitality and struggle because, in his view, these values were the key to the wealth and power of Western nations. By the same token, Yen was led to believe that the lack of these animating values in the Chinese tradition accounted for the weakness of China. China was naturally weak because in the past the sages had done little to foster the energies and capacities of the people, and dynastic rulers had done

23. Benjamin Schwartz, pp. 52–56.
24. Ibid., pp. 46, 55, 59.

everything to suppress them.[25] It is little wonder that Yen became critical of both the cultural and political traditions of China.

The best remedy to strengthen China as a nation, as he saw it, was to develop the energies and capacities of the Chinese people. In the framework of Social Darwinism, the strengthening of the Chinese people was thought to depend upon the development of the capacities of the individual. But in Yen's view, which was apparently influenced by the historical development of England in the nineteenth century, the capacities of the human individual — intellectual, physical, and moral — could only thrive in the context of a free society. In this way Yen came to admire Western liberalism. Liberalism and the ethos of collective energy seemed to him to be the essential features of a single syndrome and were thus considered to be inseparably related.[26]

If Liang's friendship with Yen was primarily intellectual, his relationship with T'an Ssu-t'ung was intimate and personal, based on common intellectual interests as well as a shared political outlook. T'an, the son of a high-ranking official, from his early youth had been exposed to the influence of such traditional thinkers as Mo-tzu, Chang Tsai, Wang Fu-chih, and Huang Tsung-hsi, as well as to Western learning and Christian thought.[27] K'ang Yu-wei's reform activities in connection with the Ch'iang hsüeh-hui drew T'an's attention, and in the summer of 1895 he traveled to Peking to see him. Since K'ang had returned to Canton by that time, T'an met Liang instead and the two quickly became friends. Through Liang, T'an learned of

25. Ibid., pp. 56, 64–65, 70–71.
26. Ibid., pp. 59–61, 73–75.
27. Yang T'ing-fu, *T'an Ssu-t'ung nien-p'u* (Shanghai, 1957), pp. 28, 54, 57.

K'ang's ideal of practical statesmanship and New Text teachings and soon began to style himself K'ang's student even though he had not yet met him. Through Liang he was also introduced to the study of Buddhism. When Liang went to Shanghai to edit *Chinese Progress,* T'an also moved to Nanking and remained there studying with the famous Buddhist scholar Yang Wen-hui.[28] It was at this time that T'an started work on his provocative book, *The Study of Jen* (Jen-hsüeh). During the process of writing, T'an intermittently met Liang and discussed ideas with him.[29] Thus even though *Jen-hsüeh* was published after T'an's death, Liang was already familiar with its contents, and certainly its main ideas, long before that time. Along with *Ch'ang-hsing hsüeh-chi,* Liang later considered *Jen-hsüeh* as one of the books which had most strongly shaped his intellectual outlook.[30]

Even though T'an's philosophy was a syncretic system, drawing as it did upon Confucianism, Mohism, Buddhism, Christianity, and Western science, the central concept of his philosophy was the Confucian idea of *jen.* *Jen* was the controlling moral ideal in Confucianism. But in Neo-Confucianism, it also took on strong cosmological connotations. Apart from connoting the moral feelings of love and commiseration which grow out of natural familial affection, it also signified a cosmological principle, or rather force, which not only had the generative power but also the function of integrating the whole cosmos into an organic oneness. This Neo-Confucian view of *jen* was the base from which T'an developed his work.

Liang once maintained that T'an's philosophy of *jen*

28. Ibid., pp. 71–72, 76.
29. Ibid., pp. 78–79.
30. Liang Ch'i-ch'ao, "T'an Ssu-t'ung chuan," in T'an Ssu-t'ung, *T'an Ssu-t'ung ch'üan-chi* (Peking, 1954), pp. 521–526. See also *Hsin Chung-kuo wei-lai chi,* p. 15.

was an elaboration of K'ang's basic doctrine.[31] Both men centered their thought upon the ideal of *jen,* but T'an's interpretation of this ideal was far more radical than K'ang's, whose attitude toward Confucian moral order was at least that of a qualified acceptance. This was well illustrated in K'ang's ambivalent view of the problem of ethical universalism versus particularism in the interpretation of the ideal of *jen.* In the 1890's K'ang was ultimately committed to the ideal of a universal moral community. Yet the starting point for that ultimate ideal was still the Confucian value of filial piety. In other words, the ultimate realization of the universalistic aspect of *jen* must involve an essential ingredient of particularism in its process. T'an's moral *Weltanschauung* involved an unmitigated rebuttal of the core of Confucian moral order: the three sacred relationships of ruler-subject, father-son, and husband-wife embodied in the Confucian doctrine of the "three netropes" (*san-kang*). The characteristic Confucian particularism was refuted in favor of an out-and-out universalistic interpretation of the ideal of *jen.* This radical interpretation was hardly justifiable within the bounds of Confucianism, however extended.[32]

Although T'an's attitude toward the Confucian moral order differed significantly from K'ang's, one must not overlook the strong resemblance between the two men in terms of what Lovejoy has called metaphysical pathos. Two aspects of metaphysical pathos which were already more or less discernible in K'ang's thought seem to pervade T'an's moral philosophy of *jen:* the monistic pathos and the pathos of dynamism. The monistic pathos is most clearly

31. Liang Ch'i-ch'ao, "*Jen-hsüeh hsü*" (A preface to *Jen-hsüeh*), in *YPSHC-WC,* ts'e 2, 3:32.

32. T'an Ssu-t'ung, *T'an Ssu-t'ung ch'üan-chi,* p. 9. See also Wing-Tsit Chan, "K'ang Yu-wei and the Confucian Doctrine of Humanity", in Lo Jung-pang, ed., pp. 355–371.

reflected in the concept of *t'ung* (interpenetration), the central concept with which T'an tried to connote the cosmological function of *jen*. Despite the vague and sometimes esoteric language which T'an used, the concept of *t'ung* always connoted the tendency to, or the power of, combining and integrating things; it tolerated no antitheses, cleavages, or distinctions of any kind.

As a result of this central function of *jen,* all things which are disjointed or have the tendency to clash with each other are connected organically and bound together into one body. Nothing shows this monistic pathos more clearly than the fact that T'an repeatedly identified *jen* and *t'ung* with the concept of organic "oneness." [33] Aside from connoting an inexorable cosmic tendency to oneness, *jen* for T'an also meant an actuating and generating cosmic power or tendency. When this generating power works, "all kinds of things flourish and thus grow and mature." Indeed it was primarily because of this power of *jen* that the whole world was engaged in a universal and perennial process of changing, growing, and maturing, which T'an called "daily renewal" (*jih-hsin*).[34]

This concept of incessant growth was not original in T'an's thought; it reflected ideas which had deep roots in the Confucian and Neo-Confucian cosmologies. But in his thought these ideas were blended into a glorification of *tung* (dynamic) and *hsin* (new) which seldom appeared in traditional Chinese thought. It may be argued that T'an derived his fascination with the idea of dynamism from his study of Wang Fu-chih's philosophy.[35] Whatever its origin the important fact is that T'an saw the West as the great source of energy and ascribed the dominance of the

33. T'an Ssu-t'ung, *T'an Ssu-t'ung ch'üan-chi,* pp. 6–7, 11.
34. Ibid., pp. 38–39.
35. Hsiung Shih-li, *Tu Ching shih-yao* (Taipei, 1960), II, 133–136.

West in the modern world to the presence of this force.[36]

The prominence of monism and dynamism together in T'an's moral thought apparently represented an intellectual revolt against the traditional order of China, which, T'an felt, was beset with "distinctions" and "oppositions." These "distinctions" and "oppositions" were manifested in all kinds of moral and institutional cleavages and barriers which paralyzed traditional society. In modern terms what T'an revolted against was the cultural particularism of traditional China. Inhibited by these particularistic cleavages, the traditional order of China presented itself as an inert, fragmented world. In T'an's view, the problem for China was how to get rid of these burdensome distinctions; how to inject life and energy into society; how to make the world unified and harmonious. T'an Ssu-t'ung found the remedy in his radical interpretation of *jen*.[37]

Apart from the influences of T'an, Yen Fu, and a few others who shared more or less similar interests, Liang Ch'i-ch'ao was also exposed to the influence of Christian missionaries, which had become increasingly strong among Chinese gentry-literati in the late nineteenth century. When Liang studied with K'ang at Canton before 1895, he must have learned something about Christianity from K'ang, who had had a persistent interest in the translations and other activities of Christian missionaries for many years.[38] In 1895 when Liang traveled back and forth between Canton and Peking, the missionary publications of the SDK (Society for the Diffusion of Christian and Gen-

36. T'an Ssu-t'ung, *Jen-hsüeh* (The study of humanity), in *T'an Liu-yang ch'üan-chi* (Taipei, 1962), 1:24–24b.

37. T'an saw the Confucian idea of three netropes and five relationships (*san-kang wu-ch'ang*), which lies at the core of traditional Chinese moral order, as a kind of unbearably restraining net. Hence his famous catchword, "to break out of the net." Liang Ch'i-ch'ao, "Jen-hsüeh hsü," pp. 53–59.

38. Chao Feng-t'ien, pp. 181–184.

eral Knowledge in Shanghai), which enjoyed great popularity among the Chinese reading public at this time, must have caught his eye.[39] It is not known whether Liang had any personal contact with Christian missionaries until he worked for the Ch'iang hsüeh-hui in Peking in 1895, where he became acquainted with Timothy Richard and Gilbert Reid.[40] Nothing is known of Liang's relationship with Reid except that they often met each other at the Ch'iang hsüeh-hui.[41] As for Timothy Richard, it is known that Liang served as his secretary for several months in 1895. Although for some reason Liang never spoke at any length about his relationship with Richard, they must have met often during these months.[42] Doubtless Liang had a high regard for Richard for he praised Richard's observations and suggestions on current affairs in his famous "General Discussion on Reform" (Pien-fa t'ung-i), a serial published in 1896–97, and he commented favorably on certain of Richard's Christian tracts.[43]

Liang's attitude was less sanguine toward the other prominent missionary leader of that period, Young J. Allen, with whom he does not seem to have had any personal contact. Although Allen's observations about China did attract Liang's attention and Liang actually recommended Allen's *Wan-kuo kung-pao* (The globe magazine) as required reading for those who were interested in current affairs, Liang gave little credit to Allen's

39. W. E. Soothill, *Timothy Richard in China* (London, 1924), p. 183.
40. Liang Ch'i-ch'ao, "Chi Shang-hsien-t'ang" (On the worthy exalting Hall), in *YPSHC-WC*, ts'e 2, 2:31–32.
41. W. E. Soothill, p. 168; Timothy Richard, *Forty-five Years in China* (New York, 1916), p. 218.
42. Ibid.
43. Liang Ch'i-ch'ao, "Pien-fa t'ung-i" (General discussion on reform), in *YPSHC-WC*, ts'e 1, 1:6, 12; see also Liang, *Hsi-hsüeh shu-mu piao*, in *Chih-hsüeh ts'ung-shu ch'u-chi*, ts'e 9, 3:3b and *Tu hsi-hsüeh-shu fa*, in *Chih-hsüeh ts'ung-shu ch'u-chi*, ts'e 10, 1:4b, 2:2, 3, 6, 3:1b, 2, 3b.

Chung-tung chi-shih pen-mo (A history of the Sino-Japanese War), which he dismissed as worthless.[44]

Except for these three men, it is not known if Liang had any other personal contact with missionaries. It seems evident that Liang derived considerable knowledge about the West from missionary publications, for many of these were included in the *Hsi-hsüeh shu-mu piao* (Bibliography on Western learning) which he compiled in 1896.[45]

Thus by the time Liang went to Shanghai to edit *Chinese Progress* in 1896, he had been exposed to other intellectual influences, although K'ang was still unquestionably his most important mentor.

44. Liang, *Hsi-hsüeh shu-mu piao,* 1:1–7b, 2:1–9, 3:1–3b and *Tu hsi-hsüeh-shu fa,* 8b.

45. Ch'en Ch'i-yün, "Liang Ch'i-ch'ao's 'Missionary Education': A Case Study of Missionary Influence on the Reformers," *Papers on China,* 16:111–113 (December 1962).

4

The Foundation of Liang's Reformist Thought, 1896–1898

In discussing Liang's intellectual development in the two years prior to 1898, it must be remembered that his thinking, through the mediation of K'ang Yu-wei, had as its point of departure the late Ch'ing *ching-shih* tradition.[1] For Liang the ideal of *ching-shih* did not mean simply a commitment to political activism or a broad sense of social responsibility; it also implied more specifically an acceptance of institutional reform as indispensable to the realization of the ideal of practical statesmanship. In arriving at this definition he was influenced by K'ang's New Text teachings, an influence nowhere more clearly reflected than in Liang's provocative essay "Tu Ch'un-ch'iu chieh-shuo" (An interpretation of Ch'un-ch'iu), in which he upheld the central importance of the *Spring and Autumn Annals* among the Confucian canons.[2] This, Liang noted, "is the book in which Confucius set forth his ideas on changing and establishing institutions in order to instruct posterity."[3] He took particular care to point out, however, that *ching-shih* was not merely an ancient ideal but it had also inspired a long intellectual tradition in Chinese history. Liang pointed to Huang Tsung-hsi, Wang Fu-chih, and

1. "Tu Ch'un-ch'iu chieh-shuo" (An interpretation of Ch'un-ch'iu), in *YPSHC-WC*, ts'e 2, 3:14.
2. Ibid., pp. 14–17.
3. Ibid., p. 14.

Feng Kuei-fen as outstanding Confucian scholars in the recent past who had tried to realize the ideal of Confucian statesmanship by proposing institutional reformism.[4] The moral which Liang tried to drive home was obvious: if outstanding Confucian scholars in the past had espoused institutional reformism under the ideal of practical statesmanship, why should not modern scholar-officials do the same in a time of crisis?

Liang did not consider it sufficient to simply reaffirm the ideal of practical statesmanship. One also had to ask why this ideal had become obscured. If the Way had gone wrong, what was more urgent than the discovery of the causes? Though he accepted K'ang's idea that much of the blame should be placed on the Ancient Text School, a more convincing explanation was another of K'ang's favorite ideas, namely, the distinction between the school of Mencius and that of Hsün-tzu, which Liang, along with friends like T'an Ssu-t'ung and Hsia Tseng-yu, now espoused fervently.[5] As Liang emphasized in his controversial interpretation of Confucianism, the school of Mencius had inherited and developed the vital ideal of practical statesmanship articulated in the *Ch'un-ch'iu,* while the school of Hsün-tzu had been mainly oriented toward the scholasticism and ritualism of Confucianism. In accordance with K'ang's ideas, Liang called the former the School of Great Unity and the latter the School of Small Peace. In the Han dynasty, he explained, the School of Small Peace had begun to gain ascendancy over the School of Great Unity, for at that time all versions of the Confucian classics were handed down from Hsün-tzu. Ever since then, both the political and intellectual tradition had been dominated by the school of Hsün-tzu. Thus what had been taught in the

4. Ibid., p. 15.
5. *LNCC,* I, 22, 29.

past two thousand years was not the genuine Confucian tradition but the tradition of Hsün-tzu, which Liang passionately denounced as a disastrous degeneration of Confucianism.[6]

This scathing denunciation of the role of Hsün-tzu cannot be understood merely as an attempt to rationalize an emotional need to preserve cultural identity, as some modern historians would argue. Liang was also engaged in a revolt against certain dominant intellectual tendencies of Han Learning which he believed could all be traced to Hsün-tzu. In keeping with the *ching-shih* tradition of the late Ch'ing, Liang was rebelling against the scholasticism of Han Learning. And did not the scholasticism of Han Learning suggest a strong kinship with the intellectualism of Hsün-tzu's thought? Could Liang ignore the fact that Hsün-tzu's thought had in fact been a strong undercurrent in the School of Han Learning and that a contemporary master of Han Learning, Yü Yüeh, was an ardent advocate of Hsün-tzu's thought? [7] Was it not natural that he should see Hsün-tzu as the fountainhead of this much deplored late development of Confucianism? To be sure, Liang knew that in the late nineteenth century the halcyon days of Han Learning were already past. In scholarly circles, however, its influence was still considerable, especially among the Canton scholars connected with the Hsüeh-hai t'ang. Liang, who had been a devoted and outstanding student at the Hsüeh-hai t'ang for three years before studying with K'ang Yu-wei, was well aware of the intellectual attraction of Han Learning and its implied political indifferentism. By using Hsün-tzu as a symbol, he was endeavoring to discredit the whole scholastic tendency

6. "Tu Meng-tzu chieh-shuo" (Some interpretations of the Mencius), in *YPSHC-WC*, ts'e 2, 3:17–21; see also "Lun Chih-na tsung-chiao kai-ko" (On the religious reformation in China), in *YPSHC-WC*, ts'e 2, 3:56–57.
7. *CCHS*, I, 357–358; II, 453–522.

in Confucianism in the interest of the ideal of practical statesmanship.

In Hsün-tzu's thought Liang also saw the source of another powerful intellectual trend of the late Ch'ing, Sung Neo-Confucianism. Perhaps this is why he preferred to view Hsün-tzu rather than the more publicized Ancient Text School as the main cause of the degeneration of Confucianism, for the whole controversy between the New Text and Ancient Text Schools arose primarily over the problem of the nature of Han Learning, and hence was relevant only so far as the position and nature of Han Learning was in question. For Liang, however, it was not just Han Learning but also Sung Learning which tended to obscure the ideal of practical statesmanship. In this connection Hsün-tzu's significance lay in his strong emphasis on the centrality of *li* and the consequent authoritarianism of Confucianism, an emphasis which Liang interpreted as the intellectual forerunner of the ritualistic conformism and overconcern with self-cultivation which he also detected in orthodox Sung Neo-Confucianism.[8] It must be noted, however, that Liang's attack by no means implied a completely negative attitude toward Sung Neo-Confucianism. Liang had great respect for some of Chu Hsi's precepts concerning self-cultivation. What Liang deplored was not the value of the self-cultivation emphasized by Sung Neo-Confucianism, but rather its failure to relate self-cultivation to the larger concerns of the society and state.

In addition to the negative legacy of Han and Sung Learning, Liang also found in the examination system a no less important factor responsible for the atrophy of

8. "Lun Chih-na tsung-chiao kai-ko," p. 57; "Hsi-hsüeh shu-mu piao hou-hsü" (Epilogue to a bibliography on Western learning), in *YPSHC-WC*, ts'e 1, 1:127.

socio-political consciousness among gentry-literati. Liang's assault on the examination system was not entirely a response to Western impact; he was also continuing a long-standing convention of protest within tradition, for however Confucian an institution the examination system was, the coincidence of this institution with Confucian values was by no means complete and unproblematic. In fact, ever since the T'ang dynasty, the system had been continuously subjected to criticism by Confucian scholars.[9] Although the criticism had been broached from the standpoints of Confucian moral, political, and esthetic values, it was mainly because of his political concern for ordering state and society that Liang now felt the inadequacy of the system.

In Liang's view, the examination system originated in ancient times as an institutional device to recruit talent for public service. Thus in its origin the system embodied a very laudable ideal; its ideal of recruitment and advancement by talent and achievement represented a significant improvement upon the feudal hereditary system. But the important fact, Liang added, was that in antiquity the system did not stand alone; it was laid on the foundation of a country-wide school system.[10] Unfortunately, after the founding of the Han dynasty, although a recommendation system based on the ideal of recruitment by merit still existed it was no longer supported by a well-established school system. Furthermore, this system soon degenerated into the *chung-cheng* system by which recommendation of talent was made entirely according to family status. During the Sui and T'ang dynasties, the civil service examination system was for the first time formally in-

9. David S. Nivison, "Protest against Conventions and Conventions of Protest," in Arthur F. Wright, ed., *Confucianism and Chinese Civilization* (New York, 1964), pp. 227–251.
10. "Pien-fa t'ung-i," pp. 21–31.

stituted, but the standards used in the examination system mainly emphasized literary skill and rote learning, which, in Liang's view, were even more inappropriate than the recommendation system for detecting talent useful for public service. In brief, shorn of the concurrent support of the school system, the development of the examination system was seen as a continuous degeneration of the ancient ideal of public service by merit.[11]

However, the divorce of the examination system from the school system did not imply the decline of the ideal of government by talent; if based on a broad ideal of achievement and a greater variety of examination standards, an examination system could still perform some functions of tapping talent even without the support of a school system. In fact, this was true of the Han recommendation system and also of the examination system in its beginning. Initially, Liang noted, there were a great number of categories and a variety of standards for detecting and recruiting different talent into public service. Only in later times was the broad concept of talent and achievement gradually narrowed down until it was finally reduced to a mere competence in literary composition.[12]

Most disastrous of all was the fairly recent emergence of the eight-legged essay, a stereotyped form of writing which put a premium on the stylistic requirement of balance and antithesis, as the primary criterion for passing the examinations. As Liang emphasized, the composition of eight-legged essays was an entirely mechanical chore and consequently so easy that almost anyone with some practice could do it. Furthermore, it was so utterly devoid of useful content that its practice was not only a sheer waste of time and effort but also might have the grievous consequence of

11. Ibid., pp. 21–23.
12. Ibid., pp. 23–24.

debilitating minds and stunting talents. In short, the examination system as it had developed in Ming and Ch'ing times was nothing more than an embodiment of careerism and hence a complete negation of the Confucian ideal of contributing talent to the state and society by way of public service.[13]

What was to be done then, Liang asked, in order to establish a system which could perform the all-important function of "cultivating talents and strengthening China?" One remedy, he suggested, would be simply to add some practical subjects to the traditional repertoire required in the examination system. A better solution would be a radical renovation of the whole system in order to recruit a greater variety of practical talent and respond to current needs.[14] The best remedy, Liang emphasized, would be to abolish the examination system altogether and replace it with a nationwide school system. According to him "the central task of reform is to abolish the court examination system and establish school systems in the prefectures and districts." This was in fact the burden of the reform program spelled out in his popular serial "General Discussion on Reform," published in the *Shih-wu pao*.[15]

If the political rejuvenation of China hinged ultimately upon the education of its people, the problem then was who was going to educate the people. In a centralized bureaucratic state like China, could a country-wide school system be established without initiative and help from the government? Liang realized that this was not feasible, and in his "General Discussion on Reform" he appealed to the court to abolish the examination system and to take the lead in setting up a national school system.[16] A further

13. Ibid., pp. 24–26.
14. Ibid., p. 27.
15. Ibid., pp. 29–32, 8–76.
16. Ibid., pp. 9–31.

question arose: could the government undertake the education of the people without first being renovated itself? Liang, while emphasizing the education of the people as the foundation of political renovation, was at the same time busy campaigning for institutional reform from above. This was perhaps why, in his "General Discussion on Reform," he ended his program of educational reform by emphasizing the equivocal idea that even though China's political rejuvenation was dependent on the education of the people, the foremost task for the present was the institutional reform of the government.[17]

What we need to ask is whether this ideal of popular education was inspired by the Western concept or was simply a reflection of Confucian values. Education of the people had always been important in Confucianism, as reflected in the familiar ideal of *chiao-hua* (education and transformation). In fact, the concepts of "renovation of the people" (*hsin-min*) which Liang had started to use at this time for expressing his educational ideal, and which was to become the core of his later socio-political thought, was a central ideal in the Confucian classic, *Great Learning* (*Ta-hsüeh*).[18] But can Liang's program of educational reform be described as completely Confucian in origin and content? The nature and origin of his socio-political thought cannot be ascertained until the major elements of his educational program have been analyzed and the pattern formed by these elements made clear.

Liang's educational philosophy was scattered throughout many of his writings, but nowhere more clearly summa-

17. Ibid., p. 10.
18. Although Liang had not yet developed the idea of *hsin-min* (renovation of the people), he already touched upon this ideal in several of his writings of this period. See his "Pien-fa t'ung-i," p. 60 and "Ching-shih-wen hsin-pien hsü" (A new edition of essays on statecraft), *YPSHC-WC*, ts'e 2, 2:46–48.

rized than in the two syllabi which he drew up for teaching students at Shanghai and Hunan in 1896 and 1897. The layout of these syllabi consisted of two parts. The first dealt with those studies and disciplines in which students should engage in school and was generally further divided into cultivation of character and intellectual education. The second part outlined the goals which students should pursue after finishing school. This part was subdivided into the two categories of practical statesmanship and the propagation of faith.[19]

Significantly, both syllabi start with a number of categories all dealing with the cultivation of character, clearly indicating that while in Liang's view the ultimate goal of study was certainly practical statesmanship, the cultivation of statesmanship had to have its basis in, and hence begin with, the development of character. In other words, a kind of inner goal orientation and discipline of character was regarded by Liang as indispensable for the attainment of statesmanship in the outer realm of politics. For Liang this approach was undoubtedly rooted in Mencius' thought. In the *Mencius*, Liang noted that the ideas which centered around the ideal of practical statesmanship were in fact based upon what he called "inner teaching" (*nei-hsüeh*), which focused on the cultivation of an "unper-

19. "Hu-nan Shih-wu hsüeh-t'ang hsüeh-yüeh" (A syllabus for the Hunan School of Current Affairs), *YPSHC-WC*, ts'e 2, 2:23–29; "Wan-mu ts'ao-t'ang hsiao-hsüeh hsüeh-chi" (A syllabus for the Wan-mu ts'ao-t'ang primary school), *YPSHC-WC*, ts'e 2, 2:33–35. It was often the practice of traditional Chinese scholars to compile syllabuses and reading lists to indicate their intellectual outlook and general approaches to scholarship for the benefit of their students and later scholars. Hence such syllabuses and reading lists have particular value for a student of Chinese intellectual history in his effort to interpret the thought of a traditional Chinese scholar. For a discussion of these syllabuses and reading lists as materials for intellectual historians, see Ch'ien Mu, "Chin pai-nien-lai chu-ju lun tu-shu" (Some scholars' discussions on study in the past one hundred years), in his *Hsüeh-yüeh* (Hong Kong, 1958), pp. 81–136.

turbed mind" (*pu-tung-hsin*). According to Liang, "The cultivation of an unperturbed mind is the basic source of practical statesmanship and propagation of faith." [20]

Liang's emphasis on the priority of spiritual direction and character cultivation was Confucian in origin, but one may ask whether it was also Confucian in content. Spiritual direction and character cultivation are universal problems to which almost all advanced civilizations must provide some answers; since Liang lived in an age in which China was having increased contact with other civilizations, especially the modern West, Western cultural influences may also have influenced his approach to this problem. The resolution of these questions may lie in a careful examination of the categories included in his syllabi.

Liang began his syllabi with the ideal of "setting the life goal" (*li-chih*). Without question this derived from his Confucian education, for almost all Neo-Confucian scholars stressed this category as the essential first step in the pursuit of learning. This is hardly surprising in view of the basic premise of Neo-Confucian moral philosophy that all human beings had the innate moral potential to attain sagehood, and hence the choice of a goal was crucial in determining one's future. Apparently this Neo-Confucian concept remained axiomatic for Liang, who referred to Chu Hsi's famous analogy between the setting of the life goal and the sowing of seeds: the kind of fruit one reaps depends upon the kind of seed one sows.[21]

After this ideal, Liang discussed "cultivating the mind" (*yang-hsin*).[22] This concept also was distinctly Neo-Con-

20. "Hu-nan Shih-wu hsüeh-t'ang hsüeh-yüeh," pp. 23–25; "Wan-mu ts'ao-t'ang hsiao-hsüeh hsüeh-chi," pp. 33–35; "Tu Meng-tzu chieh-shuo," pp. 17–20.
21. "Hu-nan Shih-wu hsüeh-t'ang hsüeh-yüeh," pp. 23–24; "Wan-mu ts'ao-t'ang hsiao-hsüeh hsüeh-chi," pp. 33–34.
22. Ibid., p. 34; "Hu-nan Shih-wu hsüeh-t'ang hsüeh-yüeh," p. 24.

fucian, for in the Neo-Confucian scheme the mind needed constant care and cultivation so as to constitute an unfailing inner source of moral direction; otherwise man would be easily carried away by external distractions and the initial life goal would be upset. Liang laid particular emphasis on the Mencian idea of the "unperturbed mind" as indispensable for moral and social action. "The cultivation of mind," he noted, "is the primary source of managing affairs," but unfortunately this all-important concern was often overlooked by current scholars who were addicted to what he called "trivial and unfocused scholarship," by which he apparently meant Han Learning. Scholars of Han Learning, in their reaction against the idealistic philosophies of both the Lu-Wang School and Zen Buddhism and in their resultant excessive concern with book learning, usually went to the extreme of neglecting altogether the essential care of the mind.[23]

Liang offered two approaches to cultivating the mind: first, by the practice of quiet sitting (*ching-tso*); second, by accumulating life experiences. Young students could not be expected to have a broad experience of life, so he urged his students to follow the model of Ch'eng I and devote a certain amount of time every day to quiet sitting.[24] This sort of mental hygiene involved two processes: closing the mind to any kind of thought, so as to achieve a spiritual illumination; and either a wide-ranging speculation upon the vastness and the rationale of the manifold world or constant reflection on an extremely difficult task or life-situation.[25] Liang did not elaborate on these concerns, but these meditative practices were obviously an important part of what he took to be character cultivation.

23. Ibid., p. 24.
24. Ibid., pp. 24–25; "Wan-mu ts'ao-t'ang hsiao-hsüeh hsüeh-chi," p. 34.
25. "Hu-nan Shih-wu hsüeh-t'ang hsüeh-yüeh," pp. 24–25.

Liang called the final category "discipline of the self" (*chih-shen*). It required strict discipline of external behavior and manners. The core of this discipline was relentless self-examination of one's conduct and manners; this was to be done before bedtime each night and was to be taken as a basis for correcting one's behavior. As a model, Liang pointed to the practices of self-examination by Tseng-tzu, who was famous for his daily reflection upon three vital areas of moral conduct: sincerity in contact with people, trustworthiness in dealing with friends, and diligence in study.[26]

Such, then, were the methods and categories of spiritual direction and character cultivation which Liang recommended to his students. Years later, in reminiscing about the approach he used in these early instructions, he claimed that he followed the Lu-Wang School of Neo-Confucianism.[27] Unquestionably, there was a strong affinity between the moral activism of the Lu-Wang School and the activistic outlook that Liang was eager to impart. Furthermore, Liang's emphasis on the primacy of cultivating the mind did suggest a strong penchant for the "idealistic" approach of the Mencian tradition and the Lu-Wang branch of Neo-Confucianism. It must be noted, however, that Liang's claim cannot be taken to mean an exclusive advocacy of Lu-Wang moral philosophy and a rejection of the Ch'eng-Chu School. In drawing upon Neo-Confucian moral philosophy to explicate the categories of character cultivation, he made no distinction between the two schools. Liang's attitude can be further clarified by examining the reading list which he compiled at the suggestion of K'ang Yu-wei in 1893, in which writings of both schools were recommended as required reading in moral phi-

26. Ibid., p. 25.
27. *LNCC*, I, 42.

losophy. A number of writings of the Lu-Wang School were listed before those of the Ch'eng-Chu School, and the implication is that the former should be read before the latter.[28] Apparently Liang regarded the approach of the Lu-Wang School as more relevant to his view of character cultivation than the approach of Ch'eng-Chu School.

It seems impossible to determine at this point whether Liang's view of character cultivation can be identified solely with the Confucian concept of self-cultivation. Categories like "cultivation of the mind" and "discipline of the self" were undoubtedly part of Confucian self-cultivation, which in Confucian terms was called *kung-fu* (methods). But Confucian self-cultivation comprised other elements. Since Neo-Confucianism self-cultivation centered around the problem of "recovery of nature" (*fu-hsing*), it involved some specific psychological doctrines of human nature as well as metaphysical world views. Although according to his own testimony Liang was well read in the Neo-Confucian literature on moral philosophy, there is no way to tell whether he was still intellectually committed to these assumptions.[29] One may well doubt it in view of Liang's increasing acceptance of Western learning in its cognitive aspect.

What is most doubtful is whether Liang's view of character cultivation still retained the third important element of Confucian self-cultivation, the specific Confucian personality ideal of *jen* and its related ideal of sage-statesmanship. Liang's writings of this period do not contain any explicit rebuttal of this ideal, but it must be remembered that at this time he was associated with a number of radical intellectuals, including such iconoclastic thinkers as Yen Fu, Sung Shu, and T'an Ssu-t'ung. It is now well known

28. *Tu-shu fen-yüeh k'o-ch'eng*, pp. 1–15.
29. Ibid., pp. 1–15.

that T'an had grown so radical as to repudiate the whole Confucian *li* and its core — doctrine of the three netropes. Liang's radical spirit never went that far: he never joined T'an in launching an explicit and unreserved attack on the whole concept of *san-kang;* nor did he ever criticize an important element of *san-kang,* the moral value of filial piety. Closer examination, however, reveals that some of Liang's writings did add up to a partial rejection of the doctrine. Liang by the late 1890's had sloughed off the traditional unconditional loyalty to the dynastic monarchy. Furthermore, his writing on the necessity for women's education was a daring and unconventional assertion of women's capacity for an occupational contribution to society and hence of women's basic equality with men.[30]

Beyond this partial repudiation of the *san-kang,* Liang had also questioned or even rejected other important traditional values. In an interpretative commentary on "Sketches of the Rich" in the *Shih-chi* (The records of the historian), he accepted enthusiastically the ideal of profit-seeking commercialism and industrialism.[31] Liang tried to extend this ideal to include the kind of life view which he thought underlay and justified profit-making activities, epitomizing this in two concepts of happiness (*lo*) and luxury (*she*). In his view these two concepts provided cultural sanction for bodily desires and material wants and thereby also a motivational source of productive and profit-

30. T'an Ssu-t'ung, *Jen-hsüeh,* 1:7–7b. Sung Shu was a neglected thinker of the generation of the 1890's and a friend of Liang Ch'i-ch'ao and T'an Ssu-t'ung. His moral and social thought was almost as radical as T'an's in his attack against traditional *li-chiao* which he set forth in his little-known *Liu-chai pei-i* (Humble proposal from Liu-chai); see Li Che-hou, *K'ang Yu-wei T'an Ssu-t'ung ssu-hsiang yen-chiu* (Shanghai, 1958), p. 48. See also Su Yüan-lei, *Sung P'ing-tzu p'ing-chuan* (Shanghai, 1947), pp. 4–59. See also "Pien-fa t'ung-i," pp. 37–39.

31. "Shih-chi huo-chih lieh-chuan chin-i" (A modern interpretation of "Sketches of the Rich" in *Shih-chi*), in *YPSHC-WC,* ts'e 2, 2:35–46.

seeking labor. Unfortunately, Liang said, people in traditional China, misled by the negative Taoist approach toward life and the world, generally had an ascetic and inhibitive attitude to bodily desires and material needs. This attitude was most evident in the high valuation of thrift (*chien*) and deprecation of material affluence and enjoyment by traditional Chinese and was the reason why Chinese were often motivated to limit consumption and curb desires rather than to try to acquire and increase wealth. In contrast, Westerners had a receptive attitude toward material goods and placed a high premium on luxury. The result, Liang noted, was a paradoxical phenomenon which Chinese would do well to try to understand: "The more given to luxury Westerners become, the richer their nations become." [32]

This positive evaluation of the materialistic and acquisitive spirit indicated the gradual emergence in Liang's thought of a new personality ideal which found a striking reflection in the cult of dynamism. This cult was based on a particular world view which Liang spelled out in an essay entitled "On dynamism" (Shuo-tung). Its thesis was that the whole universe was infused by a kind of cosmic energy which he called dynamic force (*tung-li*). Myriad things — from the smallest particle of dust and drop of water to human lives, the whole earth, other planets, and even the whole universe — were all energized and kept alive by a dynamic cosmic force, whose functioning was rooted in the universal law of nature. For Liang, then, this was the source of the world, from which stemmed all electricity, heat, sound, and light. Without this force, the whole cosmos would atrophy; human bodies and souls would become numb, petrify, and wither away. Thus Liang viewed the whole world as engaged in a perennial process

32. Ibid., p. 37.

of what he called "daily renewal," and the mainspring of this "daily renewal" was an all-embracing dynamic force.[33]

This dynamic world view has a strong resemblance to T'an Ssu-t'ung's view of a cosmos constantly engaged in the process of self-renewal. The fact that Liang quoted T'an to support his articulation of this concept indicates that Liang must have been considerably influenced by T'an's thought in this regard. Significantly, however, in T'an's thought this cult of dynamism was still expressed in terms of the moral *Weltanschauung* of *jen*. In Liang's thought, this metaphysical pathos was differentiated from *jen,* which he did not mention in this essay, and had become a new world view, devoid of moral meaning.[34]

For Liang the cultural ideal of dynamism could be found in the Chinese tradition. It could be found in Confucianism, as reflected in the *Book of Changes* (*I-ching*) and in Wang Fu-chih's cosmological thought.[35] Furthermore this energizing concept can also be seen in Mahayana Buddhism. However, Liang saw the West as the prime locus of change and energy, citing the existence of these qualities as the reason that Western people were able to achieve so much and to "expand far and wide in the world." [36]

In contrast to this plethora of vitality in the West, Liang deplored the fact that the Chinese had long suffered from a lack of energy. It was because of the widespread acceptance of Taoism that such values as quiescence, passivity, and withdrawal were able to dominate people's minds. The result was that dynamic and energetic persons

33. "Shuo-tung" (On dynamism), in *YPSHC-WC,* ts'e 2, 3:37–40.
34. Ibid., p. 38.
35. Ibid.
36. Ibid., pp. 39–40; see also "Pien-fa t'ung-i," p. 6. Here Liang marveled at the sudden eruption of dynamism in Europe since the Napoleonic age. In his view it was this dynamism which provided the motive force for the modern transformation in Europe.

were generally frowned upon, and people were discouraged from being aggressive, assertive, and straightforward. Instead they were encouraged to be cautious, withdrawn, modest, and passive when confronted with problems and troubles. In sum, traditional Chinese society was viewed by Liang as an inhibitive order where dynamic activists withered but meek conformists thrived.[37]

Liang called the few activists who had existed in Chinese society *jen-hsia* or *chih-shih*.[38] Although he referred vaguely to certain famous Western figures in his discussion of dynamic personalities, it was mainly in the history of nineteenth century Japan, especially in the colorful and exciting period of the late Tokugawa and early Meiji, that he found concrete examples of such persons. The Japanese *shishi,* whom Liang called *tung-hsia,* seemed to him the perfect embodiment of modern man.[39] For thousands of years, he noted, both China and Japan had been "standstill countries" (*yung-ching-chih-kuo*). To move forward, both needed to be motivated by a new dynamism; for Japan in the nineteenth century the *shishi* provided this force. Initially only a few *shishi* appeared, but soon their spirit became contagious and many people in the late Tokugawa followed this model. Liang observed that even Buddhist monks, medical doctors, and women were *shishi,* and he

37. "Shuo-tung," p. 38.
38. "San hsien-sheng chuan" (The biographies of three gentlemen), in *YPSHC-WC,* ts'e 1, 1:115–118; "Chi tung-hsia" (A portrayal of some Japanese knights), in *YPSHC-WC,* ts'e 2, 2:29–31. In the former essay, Liang ascribed the rise of modern Japan as a great power to the emergence of several hundreds of dedicated and dynamic *shishi* like Sakamoto Ryōma and Nakayama Tadamitsu. In the latter he again ascribed the rise of modern Japan as a great power to the *shishi* spirit which prevailed in late Tokugawa Japan and animated the Japanese people, as described in Oka Senjin's *Sonjō Kiji* and Gamō Shigeakira's *Ijinden.* As illustrations of the spirit of what he called *tung-hsia* (Eastern knights), he gave biographical sketches of *shishi* like monk Gesshō, Saigō Takamori, Arimura Shunsai, Urano Bōtō and Komai Saian.
39. "Chi tung-hsia," pp. 29–31.

wrote several short biographies of examples of this new personality.[40]

The emergence of this ideal suggests that Liang's conception of character cultivation, although undeniably Confucian in derivation and in some of its elements, cannot be strictly identified with Confucian self-cultivation. The cultural transformation set in motion by the Western impact had finally penetrated the inner realm of Confucian concerns.

The categories dealing with character cultivation were followed in Liang's syllabi by discussions of intellectual education. This order of arrangement had the important implication that intellectual education could not stand alone but had to be oriented toward a moral-political goal. Neo-Confucian moral philosophy also occupied a prominent place in a reading list Liang had drawn up while serving as K'ang Yu-wei's teaching assistant at Canton three years earlier. Liang explained this order of priority by observing that moral philosophy served as a kind of guidepost for any kind of intellectual education; without it the latter would not only be meaningless but could conceivably lead to disaster if geared to immoral purposes.[41]

Despite its order of priority Liang regarded intellectual education as no less important than character cultivation. In fact, what distinguished Liang's educational program from those of many contemporary Confucian scholars was the tremendous significance he attached to intellectual pursuits. He was keenly aware that intellectual education was something the mass of Chinese people lacked and was a rarity in the Confucian cultural tradition. More important, Liang recognized that this lack of intellectual training lay at the root of China's humiliating encounters with the

40. Ibid.
41. *Tu-shu fen-yüeh k'o-ch'eng*, p. 3.

West. In this sense, he often urged intellectual enlightenment of the Chinese people as of the first order of importance for the revitalization of China. He spelled out the
significance of popular enlightenment in the framework of
K'ang's theory of "three ages." The whole progress of
human history could be understood in terms of competition through strength. In the Age of Disorder it was physical strength which determined the outcome of the struggle.
Thus in the past, Mongols and Moslems had conquered almost the whole world by dint of their superior physical
hardiness. And it was because of their superior intellectual
strength that the Caucasian races had lately been able to
conquer and rule the largest part of the world. And so
Liang argued: "The trend of the world is to evolve from
disorder to peace. The outcome of victory or defeat hinges
upon intellectual rather than physical strength. Therefore, nowadays, the first principle of self-strengthening is
to develop people's intellect." [42]

Behind Liang's fervent exaltation of knowledge and intellectual education remained the ideal of dynamism.
Knowledge was conceived as a sort of intellectual fuel
capable of producing energy. If, as Liang believed, the
weakness of China stemmed basically from a lack of energy,
then intellectual education had to be regarded as an essential ingredient in any plans for the rejuvenation of
China. [43]

It is significant that although Liang drew on the approach of the Lu-Wang School in developing his concepts
of character cultivation, in his notion of intellectual education he drew mainly on the approach of the Ch'eng-Chu
School of Sung Learning. In the latter case, the categories
he used coincided exactly with the central categories in

42. "Pien-fa t'ung-i," pp. 14–31.
43. "Lun Hu-nan Ying-pan-chih-shih," p. 41.

Chu Hsi's program for intellectual education: book study (*tu-shu*) and exhaustive exploration of principles (*ch'iung-li*).[44]

Liang's concept of book study, like K'ang's, consisted of five parts: Confucian classics, Chinese dynastic histories, non-Confucian Chinese philosophies, Neo-Confucian moral philosophy, and Western learning.[45] Although he often emphasized the necessity for conscientious scholars to balance the study of Western learning with the study of Chinese learning, there is no question that Western learning was central as far as intellectual education was concerned.[46]

The connotations of Western learning had undergone considerable evolution in the course of the nineteenth century as China's contact with the West broadened and its understanding of the West deepened. In the beginning Western learning was identified as no more than a sort of technological lore. Later it was discovered to be also a repository of useful knowledge about devices for increasing national wealth and promoting governmental effectiveness. In the late nineteenth century a handful of Chinese were even led to see it as a source of wisdom about the goals and organizational principles of polity.[47] This conceptual development of Western learning was naturally the basis from which Liang evolved his own view of the intellectual impact from the West. He summed up its contents in three categories: *i* (technical arts), *cheng* (polity), and *chiao* (religion).

When Liang spoke about *hsi-i* (Western technical arts)

44. "Hu-nan Shih-wu hsüeh-t'ang hsüeh-yüeh," pp. 25–27; "Wan-mu ts'ao-t'ang hsiao-hsüeh hsüeh-chi," pp. 34–35.

45. *Tu-shu fen-yüeh k'o-ch'eng*, pp. 1–15.

46. This can be seen in his compilation of the bibliography of Chinese books on the West and also in his fervent campaigns for collecting and publishing series of these books. See *LNCC*, I, 23–48.

47. See my discussion in Chapter 1.

he was referring to more than Western technology. As indicated in his discussion of the concept of *ch'iung-li*, he was aware of scientific theories as a body of universal principles (*li*) which were distinct from technology but were the source of its applications. In Liang's mind, then, Western learning was the source of technological lore as well as of knowledge of the organizing principles of the natural world.[48]

In Liang's syllabi the concept of *ch'iung-li* was applied exclusively to the study of the natural world. In Chu Hsi's thought, however, *li* was both the law of nature and the law of ethics. In other words, *ch'iung-li* was intellectual search and moral cultivation. Liang's restrictive use of *ch'iung-li* for the intellectual investigation of the natural world clearly implied an awareness of the uniqueness of that world. Thus the Neo-Confucian concept of *li* was now completely stripped of ethical connotations. Western learning must have initiated in Liang's mind a process of differentiation between the principles of ethics and those of nature, or more broadly, between virtue and knowledge. This differentiation eventually culminated in a distinction between moral education (*te-yü*) and intellectual education (*chih-yü*), which previously had not been distinct in the Confucian tradition.[49]

For Liang, beyond the category of *hsi-i*, Western learning encompassed the categories of polity and religion. To see how far Liang's conceptions of polity and religion were affected by Western learning, we must turn to a detailed analysis of the two categories next to those of cultivation of character and intellectual education in his syllabi, namely, practical statesmanship and the propagation of the faith.

Ching-shih was a complex concept and included three

48. "Hu-nan Shih-wu hsüeh-t'ang hsüeh-yüeh," pp. 25–27.
49. Ibid.; "Nan-hai K'ang-hsien-sheng chuan," p. 65.

meanings as it evolved in late Ch'ing. The first two — the willingness to become involved in the world and the political commitment to public service — were clearly assumed in Liang's political activism. But what he really intended to accentuate in the ideal of *ching-shih* was the third meaning, namely, political renovation *(hsin-cheng)*. This intent found expression in his plan to publish a new edition of the *Compilation of Essays on Statecraft,* in which he planned to collect all the current writings on institutional renovation.[50]

This stress on political renovation as the core of the *ching-shih* ideal was evidently inspired mainly by the West, for he fervently endeavored to publicize the Occident as the source of political wisdom and as a sort of laboratory of political experience. Important as Western sciences and technology were, he noted, it was more urgent for China to study Western political experience. It was the latter that might lead to a renovation of Chinese polity; and given the existence of a sound polity, the acquisition of Western science and technology would then be a rather simple matter. Without sound political institutions, however, whatever technological expertise China acquired would very likely be wasted. This priority of *hsi-cheng* (Western political experience) over *hsi-i* on the scale of China's needs was in fact a lesson Liang drew from the failures of the Self-strengthening Movement and the success of the Meiji reforms. Both China and Japan had tried to develop a modern navy, he observed, but China failed and Japan succeeded. Why? The basic reason was that the statesmen of Meiji Japan, unlike the statesmen of the Self-strengthening Movement, stressed the priority of po-

50. *LNCC,* I, pp. 28–29; see also "Hsi-hsüeh shu-mu-piao hsü-li" (Preface to a bibliography on Western learning), in *YPSHC-WC,* ts'e 1, 1:122–126. "Hsi-cheng ts'ung-shu hsü" (A preface to a collection of books on Western government), in *YPSHC-WC,* ts'e 2, 2:62–64.

litical over technological studies. The success of their political renovation ultimately insured their technological advance and their victory in military competition with China. It was in this sense that Liang argued: "Present-day schools should take political studies as their major concern and technological studies as a secondary concern . . . Political studies have broad use and technological studies have limited use." [51]

How Liang's idea of political renovation as the core of the *ching-shih* ideal was shaped by Western political experience can be seen most clearly in the protean but vital concept of *ch'ün* (grouping), around which most of his socio-political thinking revolved. In an article entitled "On grouping" (Shuo-ch'ün), written in 1897, Liang proclaimed that the basic principle for giving order to the world, as he had learned from K'ang Yu-wei, lay in regarding grouping as the basis and transformation as the means (*i ch'ün wei t'i, i pien wei yung*). Liang immediately made it clear that all the changes he advocated were intended to serve his central ideal of *ch'ün*. In the same article, Liang announced his intention of writing a large work to develop his ideas on this concept, drawing also on the thought of T'an Ssu-t'ung and Yen Fu, but this ambitious project never materialized. Because grouping was so integral to Liang's ideal of *ching-shih*, however, almost all his socio-political writings touched on it in one way or another.[52]

51. "Pien-fa t'ung-i," pp. 62–64; see also "Shang Nan-p'i Chang-shang-shu shu" (A memorial to Chang Chih-tung), in *YPSHC-WC*, ts'e 1, 1:105–106; "Yü Lin Ti-ch'en t'ai-shou shu" (A letter to Lin Ti-ch'en), *YPSHC-WC*, ts'e 3, 3:2–3; "Fu Liu Ku-yü shan-chang shu" (A reply to Dean Liu Ku-yü), *YPSHC-WC*, ts'e 3, 3:13–14. Liang's emphasis on political study is apparent from the fact that he often urged friends who held positions of public responsibility to set up an academy of political study (*cheng-chih hsüeh-yüan*) on the model of such institutions in the West.

52. "Shuo ch'ün hsü" (The preface to a treatise on group), in *YPSHC-WC*, ts'e 2, 2:3–7. *Ch'ün* must not be seen as a concept derived from the traditional ideal of organic harmony and moral solidarity. It is rather a

Liang's expression of *ch'ün* was often couched in vague, confusing language. The blame was not entirely his, for within this single concept he tried to cope with several new problems, and as is not uncommon in a transitional generation, the vocabulary and concepts at his disposal tended to be inadequate for the formulation of these new concerns.

Three problems were implicit in Liang's concept of *ch'ün*. The first of these, which might be called the problem of integration, was most manifest where *ch'ün* was used as a verb or gerund, connoting "to group" or "grouping." Liang was concerned with the problem of how to group or integrate the Chinese people into a cohesive and well-knit political community. Closely connected with this concern was the organization of the community's political system. At issue was the critical question of whether China should remain a monarchy or adopt a new system of government organized on the principle of popular participation. This second consideration might be called the problem of political participation. Finally Liang turned his attention to the scope of the new political community. Should China remain an empire or become a nation-state?

The significance of Liang's concept of *ch'ün* can hardly be overstated, for it involved the vital problems of political integration, political participation and legitimation, and the scope of the political community. His posing of these very questions signified that China was undergoing a crisis

---

new concept inspired primarily by the Western example of capacity for associational organization and political cohesion. That *ch'ün* is a new concept can be seen in the vehement denunciation the conservative Confucian scholar, Wang Hsien-ch'ien, made of the concept *ch'ün*. *Ch'ün*, he noted, is a foreign-inspired concept which receives no sanction in Chinese cultural tradition. More important, it is injurious to the interest of Chinese state and society as a flood. As he said, *"ch'ün* is a great trouble in the world," *"ch'ün* is a plague to scholarship." See Wang Hsien-ch'ien, "Ch'ün-lun," in *Hsü-shou-t'ang wen-chi*, 1:13–14b.

of polity, which in a sense was unprecedented in her long political tradition.

When Liang used *ch'ün* in the sense of grouping or integrating, he regarded it not merely as a socio-political principle, but also as a cosmological principle. In fact, he took the view that the socio-political principle of integration was rooted in the very nature of the process of cosmological evolution, for inherent in the nature of the universe was a tendency for things to combine, to be integrated into groups. Hence it seemed to Liang that all processes of change and evolution in the universe were governed by the all-inclusive principle of grouping. Everything in the universe, whether animate or inanimate, was made of diverse constituent elements, and the existence of everything depended upon the principle of grouping and holding together these constituent elements. Apparently the principle of grouping was conceived here as the constitutive law of nature governing the existence and extinction of myriad things in the universe. Liang said: "Throughout the universe and history, from the biggest to the smallest and most indivisible, anything with magnitude or capacity to feel and move depends upon the principle of grouping for its existence and endurability." [53]

This principle assumed increasing importance on the scale of natural evolution, in which the heterogeneous was more advanced than the homogeneous and the complex is more advanced than the simple. As a corollary, grouping was of greater relevance in the animate world than in the inanimate world; in the human world than in the rest of the animal kingdom; among civilized people than among primitives.[54]

53. "Shuo ch'ün i: Ch'ün-li i" (The first section of the treatise on group: The first section of the theory on group), in *YPSHC-WC*, ts'e 2, pp. 4–6.
54. Ibid., pp. 5–6.

It was a fact, Liang further noted, that the myriad things in nature were not equally endowed with the capacity to form groups. Since competition was inevitable in nature, the capacity of a certain kind of entity for forming a group determined its survival or demise. In other words, it was the principle of grouping which governed the universal competition for survival in nature. Human beings, being endowed with greater capacity for grouping, naturally emerged triumphant in the struggle for survival and hence proliferated. By the same token, when different human groups became locked in struggle, the civilized people who were better endowed with the capacity for cohesive grouping would prevail over the barbarians. As history developed, the tendency and also the need for grouping increased. Failure to keep up with this tendency and to satisfy this meant extinction.[55]

Three aspects of this world view of universal integration are worthy of attention. First, the universe and human society were seen as being engaged in a process of evolutionary change. Second, to illustrate this universal trend of integration Liang used the organistic model of plants and the human body. The Darwinian concept of biological organism probably was already very much in Liang's mind and had begun to serve as an analogy which he would make increasing use of in conceptualizing the emerging new world. Finally, in both the human world and the animal kingdom, struggle, especially intergroup struggle, was regarded as endemic and universal. The conclusion may be drawn that Liang's view of *ch'ün* as a cosmic and social trend toward group integration and cohesion was saturated with Darwinian concepts, images, and metaphors, most probably because of the mediation of Yen Fu, whose in-

55. Ibid.

fluence Liang had acknowledged at the beginning of his treatise on ch'ün.[56]

With this view of ch'ün as a socio-political organism, Liang's thought evinced a notable tendency to drift away from the moral ideal of jen which had played such a prominent role in his intellectual background. We have noted that jen was the central ideal of Confucian moral idealism and as such had become a primary source of inspiration to K'ang Yu-wei and T'an Ssu-t'ung. In their thought, however, jen represented primarily a moral revulsion against the particularism of the prescriptive Confucian order which prevented the traditional society from becoming one of universal and organic harmony. In the thought of both men, jen suggested a strong yearning for a kind of moral Gemeinschaft where people were drawn toward each other by the force of love, without any discrimination, and formed an organic and harmonious society. Such a view of jen may still be seen as the culmination of an inherent and long-standing tension between the spiritual jen and prescriptive li within the Confucian tradition.[57] But it is of highest significance that in Liang's thought of this period jen seems to have receded into the background, leaving little trace in his writings. What retained Liang's intense interest instead were the two kinds of metaphysical pathos prominent in the moral philosophy of jen put forward by K'ang and T'an. We have already seen how the pathos of dynamism, once free of its moral overtones, had shaped Liang's new personality ideal. Now we see how the other metaphysical pathos, the monistic, or a corporate feeling of oneness, was differentiated by Liang from the moral ideal of jen and developed into a political

56. "Shuo-ch'ün hsü," p. 3.
57. Wei-ming Tu, "The Creative Tension between Jen and Li," in Philosophy East and West, 18.1 and 2:29–39, (January–April 1968).

ideal of communal cohesion and integration. With the concept of *ch'ün* Liang was moving from the Confucian cultural ideal of moral *Gemeinschaft* toward an incipient idea of national community. This attitude was clearly suggested in his view of how a state is constituted: "It is not merely to have rulers, officials, students, farmers, laborers, merchants, and soldiers, but to have ten thousand eyes with one sight, ten thousand hands and feet with only one mind, ten thousand ears with one hearing, ten thousand powers with only one purpose of life; then the state is established ten-thousandfold strong . . . When mind touches mind, when power is linked to power, cog to cog, strand around strand, and ten thousand roads meet in one center, this will be a state." [58]

Liang's fervent campaign for socio-political integration did not necessarily imply that this ideal was somehow lacking in China's cultural tradition. One is immediately reminded of Hsün-tzu's thought, where *ch'ün* also occupied a prominent place, being understood as human community and seen as the defining characteristic of human beings as distinguished from the rest of the animal kingdom. By dint of his ability to form a community, Hsün-tzu asserted, man had become master of the other animals, which were otherwise greatly superior in strength. The very organization of a human community required distinctions and thus prescriptive norms for such distinctions. The prescriptive norms in turn necessitated the institution of a ruler for their maintenance and operation, or more specifically, a kingship. Thus in Hsün-tzu's thinking, the institution of kingship became inseparable from

58. "Nan-hsüeh-hui hsü" (The opening statement on the Southern Study Society), in *YPSHC-WC*, ts'e 2, 2:64–65; part of it was translated by Timothy Richard later for the *North China Herald*; see *North China Herald and Supreme Court and Consular Gazette* (April 18, 1898), p. 676.

any human community. In his own words, he identified what he called the "way of man" (*jen-tao*) with what he called the "way of kingship" (*chün-tao*), because *chün-tao* was the only way of forming a human community.[59]

Liang's ardent espousal of *ch'ün* differed greatly from Hsün-tzu's. In fact Liang must have been very conscious of the vast difference between his view and that of Hsün-tzu, for it was during the 1896–1898 period that Hsün-tzu became the main target of Liang's violent attack against the political tradition of China. Their differences revolved around the problem of kingship. Hsün-tzu saw this institution as implicit in the concept of *ch'ün*, but Liang regarded it as the very source of the degeneration of *ch'ün* and hence something which had to be dissociated from Chinese polity. Liang saw traditional kingship as no more than an embodiment of the ruler's inveterate egoism; as such it was primarily oriented to self-maintenance rather than to the ideal of public service. This was what Liang really meant when he emphasized that the goal of traditional polity was "to prevent troubles" (*fang-pi*) rather than "to manage affairs" (*chih-shih*), with the result that traditional polity had been characterized by all kinds of irrationalities, which paralyzed the whole system. It had become a purely repressive order which not only inhibited the vitality necessary for rejuvenating China but would also inevitably result in its own destruction: "Throughout the past two thousand years, from the Ch'in dynasty to the Ming dynasty, the law became increasingly more meticulous and elaborate; politics and education deteriorated increasingly; the monarchical power became daily more exalted and national prestige daily plummeted. From the officials on top to the mass of people below, all were caught in an intellectual net. They were so inured to it and complacent about it, so tamed

59. See Mou Tsung-san, *Hsün-hsüeh ta-lüeh* (Taipei, 1953), pp. 1–46.

and harassed by it, that they were immobilized, stupefied, and unable to think. The oppressors of the people in the past, priding themselves on this situation, intensified their abuse of the people. Ultimately two emergencies developed, which were out of their control and beyond their ability to guard against — foreign incursions and roving bandits — and the extinction of those oppressive rulers followed. Thus all the steps and measures which they took to forestall trouble only served to work against them." [60]

In his ringing denunciation of traditional despotism, Liang was by no means blazing a completely new path. An important impetus was provided by the heritage of protest against despotism, which had existed for centuries within the Chinese cultural tradition. This passionate indictment of traditional monarchy as an embodiment of the ruler's selfishness was strongly reminiscent of Huang Tsung-hsi's anti-despotic thought as presented in his famous *Ming-i tai-fang lu* (A plan for the prince), and Liang later acknowledged that Huang's thought was an important source of inspiration for his own diatribes against despotism.[61]

Aside from Huang Tsung-hsi's thought, an even more significant influence can be traced to the Mencian doctrine of benevolent government. Although the kingship as an institution was never questioned in the Mencian tradition, there remained a prominent tendency to see concern for the people's welfare as the ultimate sanction for any individual monarch's personal authority. In one of

60. "Lun Chung-kuo chi-jo yu-yü fang-pi" (On China's weakness is due to prevention of troubles), in *YPSHC-WC*, ts'e 1, 1:96.
61. W. T. de Bary, "Chinese Despotism and the Confucian Ideal: A Seventeenth Century View," in John K. Fairbank, ed., *Chinese Thought and Institutions* (Chicago: University of Chicago Press, 1957), pp. 163–203. See also Liang Ch'i-ch'ao, *Intellectual Trends in the Ch'ing Period*, p. 38.

Mencius' famous dicta, the people were held to have primacy over the gods and the Son of Heaven, suggesting that the people were the source of legitimation for the authority of the monarch. It is no wonder then, that in developing his political outlook of anti-despotism Liang accentuated the Mencian strain in Confucianism and maintained that it represented the genuine political heritage of Confucianism. Those facets of Confucianism which had become closely bound up with the absolutism of traditional monarchy Liang dismissed as grievous distortions bequeathed by Hsün-tzu.[62]

It is of the highest importance, however, that Liang's political ideal had developed beyond the level of traditional anti-despotism and was tending toward a concept of popular participation. The decisive influence was doubtless the Western democratic ideal, for the most Liang could derive from the anti-despotism of Mencius or Huang Tsung-hsi was a view of the people as the source of the individual monarch's legitimacy. With the institution of monarchy taken for granted, this line of thought could only center around the ideal of "government for the people." This was still a far cry from the Western "government by the people." A close examination of Liang's thought during this period reveals that consciously or unconsciously he had definitely made the transition from the Mencian ideal of benevolent government to the Western ideal of political participation. In Liang's popular political writings the people had become the standard of legitimation for universal kingship as an institution. Thus when Liang attacked traditional despotism, it was no longer the egoism of the individual monarch that he deplored, but rather the political system of monarchy itself, which he

62. "Tu Meng-tzu chieh-shuo," pp. 17–21; see also "Lun Chih-na tsung-chiao kai-ko," pp. 56–59.

excoriated as the institutional embodiment of egoism.[63] Unquestionably this upgrading of the people from a standard for political legitimation within the institutional framework of monarchy to the ultimate standard for the political legitimation of the monarchy as an institution was due to Western intellectual influence. For only in Western political experience could Liang find different types of political systems which would be an alternative to the institution of monarchy.

This transition can be seen clearly in the distinctions he made between the moral value of public-mindedness (*kung*) and the moral vice of selfishness (*ssu*), and between what he called "egoistic methods" (*tu-shu*) and "collectivistic methods" (*ch'ün-shu*). The concepts of *kung* and *ssu*, one must recall, like those of *i* (righteousness) and *li* (profit), were cardinal moral categories by which traditional political actions were judged. Influenced by K'ang Yu-wei and T'an Ssu-t'ung, Liang's writings were also marked by a strong moral revulsion against traditional society. In his words, this society worked by "egoistic methods," but Liang was looking toward a new society which would be based on the ideal of public-mindedness and would work by "collectivistic methods." [64] It was in his treatment of the ideal of *kung*, however, that Liang went beyond the traditional meaning of altruism to suggest subtly the connotations of popular sovereignty. Public-mindedness meant that everyone in the group had the right to govern himself; the right of self-government meant that everyone did what he should do and was entitled to the profits he deserved. In Liang's words, "What is called monarchy is nothing but selfishness; what is called de-

63. "Lun Chung-kuo chi-jo yu-yü fang-pi," pp. 96–100.
64. "Shuo ch'ün hsü," p. 4.

mocracy is nothing but public-mindedness." [65] One may conclude that Liang's concept of *ch'ün* also involved democratic connotations of popular sovereignty, because the kernel of the concept of "collectivistic methods" was the moral ideal of public-mindedness, which Liang identified with the ideal of democracy.

We may pause for a moment to consider the implications of the conceptual fusion of *ch'ün* and democracy in Liang's thought. In the first place, this meant an all-important change of the standard of legitimation of political authority, thus opening the possibility of organizing Chinese polity on a different basis from that of universal kingship. We have already noted the significant differences between Mencian political doctrine and the Western ideal of democracy. But Mencian ideals of anti-despotism were at best a sidestream in the Confucian tradition. If we take into account the orthodox tradition of Chinese political culture, the change of values involved in the emergence of the ideal of *ch'ün* was even greater, for in the orthodox political tradition the ultimate source of political legitimation had always been the mandate of heaven. The people's will *per se* had never been considered sufficient for the legitimation of political authority; it was an effective sanction for political authority only as a reflection of the will of heaven. In other words, its validity as a standard of political legitimation was only derivative. For Liang, however, the concept of the people (*min*), although not yet as well-defined as his later idea of citizen (*kuo-min*), had a subtle but vital difference from the traditional idea of people in that it replaced the mandate of heaven as the ultimate standard of political legitimation: all political ac-

65. "Yü Yen Yu-ling hsien-sheng shu," in *YPSHC-WC*, ts'e 1, 1:109.

tions of the state had to be justified with reference to the collective will of people alone.[66]

To be sure, Liang had not necessarily become completely disillusioned with the monarchy as a political institution nor had he advocated its immediate replacement by a democratic form of government. As he told Yen Fu, although democracy was an admirable political system, the ideal of popular sovereignty was not yet well developed or widely accepted in China, and thus the monarchy remained useful for the period of transition.[67] In the framework of the "three-age" formula, the value of monarchy was still admitted for the Age of Approaching Peace, while the rule of the people could only be realized in the future Age of Universal Peace.[68] The important point is that in Liang's view the monarchy as a political institution was bound to pass away and yield its place to popular rule when conditions matured. The traditional mystique of the monarchy was gone and was not so much valued on its own terms as tolerated on the ground of expediency. It is in this sense that Liang's popular political writings, along with those of some of his contemporaries, can be said to have paved the way to the ultimate demise of the monarchy in 1911.

Aside from transforming the standard of political legitimation, the fusion of *ch'ün* and democracy also implied that political participation had the function of promoting group cohesiveness. This collectivistic idea of the function of democracy was in fact in keeping with the general trend among such late nineteenth-century scholars as Wang T'ao,

66. Joseph R. Levenson, "The Suggestiveness of Vestiges: Confucianism and Monarchy at the Last," in David S. Nivison and Arthur F. Wright, eds., *Confucianism in Action* (Stanford, 1959), pp. 248–249.

67. "Yü Yen Yu-ling hsien-sheng shu," p. 110.

68. "Lun chün-cheng min-cheng hsiang-shan chih-li" (On the principle of succession of monarchy by popular rule), in *YPSHC-WC*, ts'e 2, 2:7–11.

Ch'en Ch'iu, Ch'en Chih, and others.[69] Thus in one instance Liang treated the idea of people's rights (*min-ch'üan*), almost solely as a kind of mechanism which could generate collective dynamism in China;[70] in another context, discussing the idea of a national assembly, he emphasized that this could serve to facilitate communication between ruler and ruled and thus promote national solidarity.[71] Underlying this concept of democracy was an image of the state as a sort of socio-political organism.

From this collectivistic and organismic view Liang came to an appreciation not only of democracy but also of several other modern Western institutions. For example, he viewed the newspaper primarily as an institutional channel to facilitate intellectual communication between different parts of the country. In this way the newspaper was prized as a means to promote national solidarity.[72] More or less the same reasoning led Liang to an awareness of the social significance of law. Any group, he noted, needs law, for this was what bound a group together and gave it order. The more intellectually advanced a group becomes, the more complicated and varied become the rules and regulations which the group needed. Thus one important method for attaining national cohesion and strength was to learn the legal knowledge of the West.[73]

Along with newspapers and the law there were voluntary associations, which Liang recommended as an important

69. Onogawa Hidemi, pp. 71–111; Lloyd E. Eastman, "Political Reformism in China Before the Sino-Japanese War," *Journal of Asian Studies,* 27.4:695–710 (August 1968).

70. "Lun Chung-kuo chi-jo yu-yü fang-pi," pp. 99–100; "Ku i-yüan k'ao" (A study of the parliamentary system in ancient China), in *YPSHC-WC,* ts'e 1, 1:96.

71. Ibid., p. 94.

72. "Lun pao-kuan yu-i-yü kuo-shih" (A discussion on the usefulness of newspapers to national affairs), in *YPSHC-WC,* ts'e 1, 1:100–101.

73. "Lun Chung-kuo i chiang-ch'iu fa-lü-chih-hsüeh" (On China's necessity for studying law), in *YPSHC-WC,* ts'e 1, 1:93–94.

means for integrating the Chinese people into a unified state. He specifically emphasized three forms of voluntary association. To unite the whole country into a cohesive group, said Liang, a national congress would be best; to unite the business world, a corporation would be best; to unite the gentry-literati a study society would be best. Among these three, however, Liang singled out the study society as the most fundamental type of association upon which the other two would ultimately rest.[74]

There are two main reasons why Liang regarded the study society as the pivotal organization in his reform program. First of all, since the Chinese people in general had not attained the intellectual level necessary for political participation, the gentry-official class necessarily had to play a guiding role in giving political training to the people and leading them gradually to popular rule. This was why in planning for the self-government of Hunan, Liang regarded the political participation of the gentry-official class as the prerequisite for investing the Hunanese people with popular rights. But as a preliminary step, the gentry-officials themselves first need to be enlightened and to achieve intellectual accord through close exchanges of opinions and information. Liang saw the study society as the best means to serve these purposes.[75]

An even stronger reason for attaching so much importance to the study society was that for Liang it formed a kind of constitutive link in the formation of a state — and a state, he specified, was formed only "when mind touches mind, when power is linked to power, cog to cog, strand around strand, and ten thousand roads meet in one center." [76] Even if the members of the country's various

74. "Pien-fa t'ung-i," p. 31.
75. "Lun Hu-nan ying-pan chih-shih," pp. 41–48.
76. "Nan-hsüeh-hui hsü," p. 64.

status and occupational groups were all intellectually enlightened, they would not add up to a nation if they did not share certain views in common. It was only through study societies that the people could attain a common view, or as Liang said, "ten thousands be made into one." [77] The study society, then, was the indispensable organizational link which would unite the otherwise variegated and loosely knit Chinese society into a unified and cohesive state. This point of view lay behind the feverish activities of K'ang Yu-wei and Liang Ch'i-ch'ao in organizing study societies in the two years prior to 1898.

The fact that Liang's ideal of *ch'ün* entailed the concept of socio-political integration and democratization led to a third problem, namely, the territorial scope of the new political community. The focus of Liang's socio-political thought on the idea of *ch'ün,* his zealous search for power and wealth for China, and his strong consciousness of the world as an arena of struggle among many nation-groups may have seemed to signal his commitment to the ideal of the Western nation-state. But it is curious that his acceptance of nationalism at this time was qualified and often more implicit than explicit. While some of his socio-political writings suggested the idea of the nation-state, others still reflected his commitment to the idea of a universal community in the future, which was more or less a reflection of K'ang's ideal of an age of "great harmony." Liang's simultaneous commitment to these two ideals is reflected in the distinction he made between what he called the nation-group (*kuo-chia ch'ün*) and the universal group (*t'ien-hsia ch'ün*). While the West excelled in building up nation-groups, he once said, it was deficient in developing the ideal of a universal community. Evidently Liang was looking beyond the nation-state to some sort of

77. Ibid., p. 66.

universal community as the ultimate locus of his political loyalty.[78]

From his standpoint there was not necessarily a contradiction in the simultaneous acceptance of the nation-state and the universal community, for by invoking the Kung-yang doctrine of "three ages," he placed the nation-state in the Age of Approaching Peace and reserved the universal community for the Age of Universal Peace.[79] However the latent resistance in Liang's mind to a full and exclusive commitment to the nation-state was not really capable of being reconciled with the formula of "three ages"; we can detect in Liang's thought, over and above K'ang Yu-wei's ideal of universal harmony, an ambivalence which he did not shed until his exile in Japan. This ambivalence stemmed from Liang's continued commitment to what might be called vestigial culturalism and his qualified acceptance of nationalism. This vestigial culturalism is evident in a preface he wrote for a book by a very close friend, Hsü Ch'in, who tried to develop the idea of culturalism as it appeared in the *Ch'un-ch'iu*. In this preface, Liang commended Hsü Ch'in's rejection of the idea of distinguishing China from barbarian countries according to racial or geographical criteria, for in the *Ch'un-ch'iu* the distinction between Chinese and barbarians had no such reference. "What is called 'barbarian' in the *Ch'un-ch'iu* is very different from later ages," Liang wrote, "In later ages, the name 'barbarians' refers to geographical and racial differences. In the *Ch'un-ch'iu* the term 'barbarian' refers to politics, customs, and behavior." [80] Thus, Liang argued, those who behaved like barbarians, even

78. "Shuo ch'ün hsü," p. 123.
79. "Lun chün-cheng min-cheng hsiang-shan chih-li," p. 11.
80. "Ch'un-ch'iu Chung-kuo i-ti-pien hsü" (A preface to the distinction between China and barbarians in *Spring and Autumn Annals*), in *YPSHC-WC*, ts'e 2, 2:48.

though they were Chinese, should still be counted as barbarians, and those who did not behave like barbarians,
even though they were barbarians, should be respected as
gentlemen. Strictly judged by this cultural standard, many
Chinese had to work hard before they could free themselves from the pejorative title "barbarian"; such being
the case, how could the Chinese condemn foreigners as
barbarians?[81] A man fully committed to nationalism
would not put forward such ideas, which are strongly
reminiscent of traditional culturalism.

In sum, then, Liang's ideal of *ching-shih* centered around
the involute concept of *ch'ün,* which signified three predominant tendencies in his socio-political thinking: political integration, democratization, and an implicit but ambivalent acceptance of the ideal of the nation-state. *Ch'ün*
as the synopsis of these three tendencies was doubtless
something new in the thought of late Ch'ing — indeed,
something unique in the generation of 1890 — although
some of the tendencies it represented had been foreshadowed in the thought of a few thinkers of previous generations. Furthermore, *ch'ün,* as the core of the ideal of *ching-
shih,* was unquestionably a radical departure from the
traditional connotations of this ideal. Liang was conscious
of this fact, because, as he wrote in letters to his friends,
ching-shih was already an *old* ideal for him, implying that
it was inadequate as a synopsis of his political thinking.
But as he further explained, he had to use it for the
propagandist reason that as a dominant traditional ideal
it still carried weight with most of the Chinese people.[82]
Liang's attitude was a very important symptom of the fact
that *ching-shih,* drained of its intrinsic intellectual appeal
and left only with propagandist value, was close to the end

81. Ibid., p. 49.
82. *LNCC,* I, 28–29.

of its career as the dominant ideal of the Chinese political tradition. Very soon it was to fall into disuse, and the Chinese political culture, driven by a need for new ideals and values to replace this central concept, was to be engulfed by the ideologies of the modern West.

Thus far we have seen that even though the primary categories in Liang's educational program remained largely Confucian in form and provenance, their content was influenced markedly by the West. Can we then subscribe to Joseph R. Levenson's assertion that in this period Liang was intellectually alienated from his Chinese tradition but still emotionally tied to it?[83] In view of the foregoing analysis, this assertion seems to be rather simplistic. While certain Western values certainly contributed to the realm of self-cultivation and change considerably Liang's personality ideal, he by no means completely lost confidence in all the Confucian moral values, especially those values which centered around family ethics. Furthermore, on problems of character discipline Liang still turned to certain Neo-Confucian doctrines and precepts for direction. Finally, no matter how much the specific content of his educational categories had changed, he was still deeply committed to the Confucian ideal reflected in the overall pattern of his educational categories, namely, that the central orientation of human life must be both moral and political.

Basically Levenson's characterization derives from his often implicit assumption that Liang looked upon the Chinese tradition as a monolithic entity and thus felt able to judge it as an undifferentiated whole. While this view of tradition may have been held by the post–May Fourth

83. Joseph R. Levenson, *Liang Ch'i-ch'ao and the Mind of Modern China* (Cambridge, 1959), p. 1.

generation, it was very unlikely to have been taken by the generation of those who came into intellectual adulthood in the 1890's, who were primarily brought up within the traditional culture. For Liang, who received a traditional education and was thoroughly familiar with the inner complexities of the tradition, the manifold facets of the culture would be apparent. In his mind Chinese cultural tradition was by no means identified solely with the Confucian tradition. In fact, from the time he studied with K'ang Yu-wei at Canton, Liang was influenced by the late Ch'ing revival of non-Confucian classical philosophies and found a profound and sustaining interest in them.[84]

It is very difficult to say that Liang's interest in these philosophies was not genuinely intellectual, for some of the ideals he found here, such as the concepts of wealth and power in ancient Legalism and the ideal of universal love in Mohism, have as much universal value and contemporary significance as Western ideals. When it came to the Confucian tradition itself, Liang was only too familiar with the various schools of thought. Some of the problems over which these schools were divided and had carried on long-standing controversies doubtless continued to have deep significance for him. While on certain points Liang was very critical of the scholasticism of Han Learning and Ch'eng-Chu Neo-Confucianism, elsewhere he was deeply appreciative of certain doctrines of Lu-Wang Neo-Confucianism and Mahayana Buddhism. In short, while Liang may have rejected certain aspects of traditional thought, he remained intellectually committed to others. To maintain without reservation that Liang was at this time intel-

84. About the revival of interest in the pre-Ch'in Chinese philosophies in the late Ch'ing see Liang Ch'i-ch'ao, *Chung-kuo chin san-pai-nien hsüeh-shu shih* (Taipei, 1955), pp. 224–234; see also Liang, *Ch'ing-tai hsüeh-shu kai-lun*, pp. 56–57.

lectually alienated from Chinese tradition is to overlook the subtlety of his mind and to do injustice to the complexity of the Chinese culture heritage.

In contrasting Levenson's image of the traditional culture with a more complex picture of it, I do not intend to obscure the important fact that Liang had been profoundly affected by Western thought; as we have seen, certain Western ideas and values not only dominated his sociopolitical thinking but also impinged on his moral outlook and personality ideal. For a Chinese scholar deeply grounded in a tradition that had always prided itself on being the center of civilization, such an intellectual impact from outside inevitably had shocking effects and gave rise to the problem of cultural identity. It is in this connection that I will discuss Liang's concept of "preserving the faith" (*pao-chiao*) or "propagating the faith," which was the fourth and also the final category of his study schedule.[85] It is also in this connection that Levenson's approach provides insight into Liang's mind.

The very conceptualization of *pao-chiao* or *ch'uan-chiao* implied a strong awareness that China was caught in a deep cultural crisis, for in traditional China religion and politics were closely fused and the concept of *ch'uan-chiao* was implicit in the concept of *ching-shih*. No distinction needed to be made between *ching-shih* and *ch'uan-chiao*, because it was taken for granted that Confucian statesmanship involved primarily the task of propagating the Confucian moral faith to "educate and transform" people. Thus the differentiation of the concept of *ch'uan-chiao* from the ideal of *ching-shih* meant not only that the traditional fusion of politics and Confucianism could no longer be maintained; it also signified a consciousness on the

85. "Hu-nan Shih-wu hsüeh-t'ang hsüeh-yüeh," pp. 28–29; "Wan-mu ts'ao-t'ang hsiao-hsüeh hsüeh-chi," p. 35.

part of some Chinese scholar-officials that the challenge
China faced in the late nineteenth century was not merely
a socio-political one but a religio-cultural one as well.
Thus inevitably, over and above the problem of defending
China as a socio-political entity there arose the problem
of how to preserve the cultural identity of China.

In exploring the reasons behind Liang's advocacy of
Confucianism as a faith, it must be assumed that he did this
from a complex of motives rather than from a single one.
Thus various statements he made suggest that his advocacy
of "preserving the faith" may have stemmed partly from
a practical concern to promote socio-political renovation.
His awareness, for instance, that the revival of classical
learning during the Renaissance and Reformation contributed to the intellectual advancement of European
countries led him to expect the exaltation of Confucianism to produce similar results in China. "The reason why
the West has such a civilization as it has now is the oc-
currence of a religious revolution and the revival of classical learning [in her past]. This is because religion is the
medicine which can make over the human mind," he once
said.[86]

On occasion he also referred to the normative and integrative functions of religion for a society. In defense of
his position on the problem of "preservation of the faith,"
he once wrote to a friend that, "just as no people can be
governed without a creed, no country can be established
without a creed, and the state is subject to normative control by the creed."[87] When Yen Fu in a letter to Liang
advised against the idea of preserving the faith on the
ground that it would have an inhibiting effect on the

---

86. "Lun Chih-na tsung-chiao kai-ko," p. 55.
87. "Yü yu-jen lun pao-chiao shu" (A letter to a friend discussing
preservation of faith), in *YPSHC-WC*, ts'e 2, 3:9–10.

intellectual development of the country, Liang replied in the same pragmatic vein, maintaining that the Chinese people were intellectually undeveloped and lacked unity of mind and sentiment. This unity was particularly needed in a time when the state was threatened by alien religion and ideology, he said, and there was no better means to achieve this unity than the exaltation of the Confucian faith.[88] These statements point up Liang's disposition to view religion as a sort of handmaid to the state.

But the pragmatic motive cannot serve as the complete explanation of Liang's campaign for the preservation and propagation of the faith; it would not account for the fact that in the midst of the reform movement during this period, Liang on a few occasions felt obliged to remind K'ang Yu-wei that preserving the Confucian faith was their ultimate purpose. In fact, he once went so far as to suggest that they should temporarily withdraw from political activities and devote themselves completely to study, even if it meant sacrificing the goal of preserving the state. After all, Liang said, such activities were secondary to their ultimate purpose of propagating the faith.[89]

The explanation of his attitude must be sought in that subtle and imponderable realm of cultural identity, for China was not just a state, a political entity; it was also a civilization, a repository of cultural ideals and beliefs. Liang regarded himself as a member of China the state, but he also regarded himself as a participant of civilization, a bearer of a unique set of cultural values and beliefs. Similarly, in Liang's mind the West was divided into numerous states but was also somehow a cultural whole, a civilization in which Christianity was a notable compo-

88. "Yü Yen Yu-ling hsien-sheng shu," pp. 109–110; Wang Ch'ü-ch'ang, *Yen Chi-tao nien-p'u*, p. 29.

89. *LNCC*, I, 34–35.

nent. The problem for Liang lay in his conviction that China had to make rapid and drastic changes in cultural value and belief if she were to survive as a state amidst the Western powers which dominated the world situation at the end of the nineteenth century. Under the strain of convulsive cultural changes, it was almost inevitable that he felt a need to maintain his emotional balance and make the drastic changes still meaningful and coherent in terms of his own memory and experiences. What was at stake was Liang's own cultural identity, his own sense of confidence and dignity.[90]

Liang's campaign for the preservation and propagation of the faith must be considered largely in the light of the foregoing. In a narrow sense it may be understood as a specific defensive response to the proselytizing activities of Christian missionaries in China. To Liang there seemed to be no better way to reassert his cultural confidence than to assert the role of Confucianism as a world religion vis-à-vis Christianity; even if there were definite grounds on which Chinese culture compared unfavorably with Western secular learning, this did not mean that similar grounds could also be found for denigrating Confucianism as a moral-religious system in comparison with Christianity. This is perhaps why, in discussing the source of the power and glory of the modern West, Liang and his friends sometimes made a distinction between the secular culture of ancient Greece and Rome on the one hand and Christianity on the other. They argued that the power and wealth of the modern West stemmed solely from the Greco-Roman heritage and had nothing to do with Christianity. In the same vein Liang also argued that the ex-

90. For a discussion of the concept "cultural identity," see Soedjatmoko, "Cultural Motivations to Progress: The 'Exterior' and 'Interior' Views," in Robert N. Bellah, ed., *Religion and Progress in Modern Asia* (New York: The Free Press of Glencoe, 1965), pp. 1–14.

pansion of Christianity as a world religion was not due to its own merit but was dependent on the power of the Western nations.[91] Of course Liang was not unaware of the elevating effect of Christianity on the cultural development of the West in the past, and the model of Christianity did provide some inspiration for his campaign for the propagation of Confucianism as a world religion. In view of this fact, his contradictory attempt to dissociate Christianity from the power and glory of Western civilization suggests an intention to make Christianity an easy target for Confucianism and an urge to preserve cultural confidence and to get back at the West.

Liang's campaign for the propagation of the faith, however, was not the only place where he revealed a need to maintain cultural identity. This quality was also reflected in his affirmation of the Chinese cultural tradition as a whole, as opposed to Western learning. Liang was still intellectually committed in considerable measure to the Chinese cultural heritage with regard to both moral values and socio-political thought; what he claimed for Chinese learning, however, often seemed to exceed by far what his genuine intellectual appreciation warranted. This was typified in Liang's notable tendency to find many modern Western values and institutions in the Chinese cultural tradition. For example, in his famous "Epilogue to a Bibliography on Western Learning," he claimed that the Chinese cultural tradition had anticipated many of the modern Western values and institutions and had also developed some of them to a higher degree than had yet been attained in the West.[92] It is possible that to some degree Liang may have been motivated to make this claim simply to facilitate cultural borrowing. Indeed, once when

91. Liang Ch'i-ch'ao, *Tu hsi-hsüeh-shu fa*, pp. 14b–16.
92. "Hsi-hsüeh shu-mu piao hou-hsü," pp. 127–128.

Yen Fu took him to task for making this sort of remark, he explained that he did it for the sake of didactic expediency. Still, one suspects this is not the whole explanation. Many Chinese felt the need to make this sort of assertion; why should Liang have been an exception?

In any case, when confronted with some of the excessive claims Liang made for the Chinese cultural heritage, one must take into account his need for cultural identity and confidence. There appears no better explanation for Liang's insistent pleading for the importance of studying Chinese learning than what he emphasized in his "Epilogue to the Bibliography on Western Learning." In this essay, surprisingly, instead of recommending the virtues and advantages of Western learning, Liang sounded an urgent warning about the imminent extinction of Chinese learning. A mere pursuit of Western learning without the framework of Chinese learning, he cautioned, might very well lead, as it had already, only to the emergence of Chinese compradors and business go-betweens working slavishly for the Westerners. Liang perceived in the widespread acceptance of Western learning the danger of an erosion of China's cultural identity. This was perhaps the basic reason why he concluded his essay with the following pronouncement: "Chinese learning divorced from Western learning is bound to be useless while Western learning detached from Chinese learning will have no basis." [93]

Having explored the meanings of each of the primary categories in Liang's educational program, it is now possible to see in perspective the general pattern. The preceding analysis has indicated the Confucian lineage of these syllabi; their direct predecessor was doubtless an educational syllabus widely accepted by Confucian scholars

93. Ibid., pp. 126–127, 129; "Pien-fa t'ung-i," p. 19.

in the nineteenth century. That syllabus was divided into four cardinal categories: practical statesmanship, moral philosophy of self-cultivation (*i-li*), poetical literature (*tz'u-chang*), and textual criticism (*k'ao-cheng*). In K'ang Yu-wei's *Ch'ang-hsing hsüeh-chi* the last two categories were reduced to peripheral significance and the first two were reinterpreted as the central concerns of Confucianism. Furthermore, in K'ang's case, even though his thoughts concerning self-cultivation remained largely intact in the face of "Western impact," his view of practical statesmanship clearly reflected Western influence. In Liang's own syllabus we see the Confucian educational program subjected to even greater change. In the first place, though the categories of self-cultivation and practical statesmanship remained central, definite changes were apparent in their contents. Second, the categories of poetic literature and textual criticism, though still cloaked in a Neo-Confucian form, had almost completely yielded their places to the Western intellectual disciplines. Finally, the appearance of the completely new category of *ch'uan-chiao* suggests not only a clear awareness of the religio-ideological challenge involved in the Western impact but also the existence of a need to defend a threatened cultural identity. Taken together the whole pattern of Liang's educational syllabus pointed definitely to a radical erosion of the Confucian personality ideal of sage-statesmanship which lay at the core of the doctrine of moral renovation of people (*hsin-min*) in the Confucian classic, *Great Learning*. It is true that in his campaign for reform he still recommended the relevance of the Confucian ideal of *hsin-min*. But by now in his mind this ideal had taken on a new meaning which was to dominate his thought: the propagation of new civic virtues for the education of a modern citizenry.

5

Liang in Exile

The circles of K'ang, Liang, and their associates in the years around 1895 were deeply affected by intellectual change. This change involved a basic transformation of societal values as well as of personality ideals and moral values. In sum, people were beginning to question and even challenge some of the central cultural values and institutions of the traditional order. More important, these intellectual changes were no longer confined to what went on in the minds of a few isolated intellectuals; now, through the establishment of newspapers, schools, and study societies, fresh shock waves of intellectual change spread to wider and wider circles of the Chinese gentry-literati and finally led to the creation of a full-scale intellectual movement in the late 1890's.

Although by no means well planned or well coordinated, this movement was of a truly surprising magnitude, a magnitude which has often been underestimated. Its exact scope still awaits monographic assessment; however, available studies indicate that it comprised a large number of study societies and a significant number of newspapers and schools.[1] Mediated through such institutional channels,

1. T'ang Chih-chün, "Wu-hsü pien-fa shih ti hsüeh-hui ho pao-k'an" (The study societies and newspapers during the period of the reform movement of 1898), in *Wu-hsü pien-fa shih lun-ts'ung*, pp. 220–270.

this intellectual movement doubtless had nationwide impact.

Its most significant long-range effect was the ideological split within the hitherto unitary elite group of gentry-literati. To be sure, over the centuries there had been no lack of intellectual dissension within their ranks: conflicting schools had been formed on the basis of different interpretations of Confucian classics; contending cliques and factions had appeared in the court wrangling over the enactment of certain Confucian rituals and the establishment of specific government policies. But seldom had such disagreement extended to the basic moral and societal values of the traditional order. Indeed one of the striking characteristics of the traditional gentry-literati was their general and enduring consensus on the central values and institutions of the traditional order. The writings of Liang and others had gone so far as to challenge in one way or another the center of this order. These challenges naturally led to vehement reactions from the ranks of conservative gentry-literati in defense of threatened values and institutions. The resulting cleavages threatened to split the class of gentry-literati apart.

It was a split that marked the emergence of a very important new social group, the Chinese intelligentsia. The modern Chinese intelligentsia had drawn a few isolated members, Wang T'ao and Cheng Kuan-ying, for example, from among comprador-intellectuals in the treaty ports even in the 1880's and 1870's; it did not emerge as a significant group at that time, however. Their emergence as a social group must be placed in the late 1890's when a significant number of gentry-literati became differentiated from the traditional group. These men were bearers of new ideas and values so different from the traditional outlook that they could no longer be accommodated within the ranks of the gentry-literati. The latter group, it must be recalled, was an elite group that had been closely linked to the center of traditional order both in terms of ideological outlook and realistic interest. To be sure, over the centuries there had always been elements of protest and alienation within that group, but protest had usually been directed against certain specific policies or certain specific acts of individual monarchs or officials and had been carried on in the name of the sacredness of central traditional values and institutions. In this sense the gentry-literati can be seen as the custodians of traditional order. In view of this characterization, the new intellectuals of the 1890's are best described as Chinese intelligentsia in possession of a new ideological outlook that tended to make them more or less critical of a part or even the whole of the central traditional values and institutions.

Heated ideological conflicts marked the advent of these intelligentsia. Liang, as K'ang's chief assistant, was in the thick of the battle. The publication of Chang Chih-tung's well-known *Exhortation to Learning (Ch'üan-hsüeh p'ien)* in 1898 was intended as a repudiation of the K'ang-Liang heresy and was an attempt to redefine the position of Confucianism vis-à-vis the new intellectual situation.[2] But more indicative of the significance of the ideological conflict was the Hunan reform movement in which Liang played an active role in late 1897.

Liang left the *Shih-wu pao* in the fall of 1897 because of official pressure from the outside and because of his disagreement with the manager, Wang K'ang-nien, over editorial policy.[3] Just at this juncture a reform movement was in the making in Hunan. Ever since 1895 that province had

2. Liang Ch'i-ch'ao, *Chung-kuo chin-san-pai-nien hsüeh-shu-shih* (A history of Chinese thought in the past three hundred years), in *YPSHC-CC*, ts'e 17, 75:29.
3. T'ang Chih-chün, pp. 231–234.

been under the rule of a reform-minded governor, Ch'en Pao-chen, who was interested in bringing about change on a provincial scale. In the course of two years, Ch'en had been able to gather around himself a galaxy of young enlightened scholar-officials including Chiang Piao, T'ang Ts'ai-ch'ang, T'an Ssu-t'ung, and Huang Tsun-hsien. From the cooperation of these people and other enlightened Hunan gentry, a spate of institutional innovations resulted which included the setting up of new schools, newspapers, study societies, manufacturing companies, and steamship enterprises. One of the country's most conservative provinces had now become the center of innovation.[4]

A cornerstone of the Hunan reform was the establishment of Shih-wu hsüeh-t'ang (School of Current Affairs), which was first suggested by a group of Hunanese gentry. With the support of local gentry and under the sponsorship of the educational commissioner, Chiang Piao, the new school was inaugurated in the fall of 1897.[5] On the recommendation of Huang Tsun-hsien, who now held the post of salt commissioner in Hunan and played a leading role in the reform, it was decided to invite Liang Ch'i-ch'ao to be the chief lecturer on Chinese studies at this new school.[6]

Liang Ch'i-ch'ao's reformist efforts had been repeatedly frustrated by the Ch'ing central and provincial governments. For him the invitation to participate in the reform movement in Hunan, which had been blessed with the zealous patronage of Hunan provincial authorities and had already engaged the enthusiastic support of so many of his

4. *LNCC*, I, 42–43; Teng T'an-chou, "Shih-chiu shih-chi mo Hu-nan ti wei-hsin yün-tung," *Li-shih yen-chiu*, 1:17–34 (1959); Charlton M. Lewis, "The Reform Movement in Hunan (1896–1898)," *Papers on China*, 15:62–86 (December 1961); Onogawa Hidemi, pp. 276–342.

5. *LNCC*, I, 42–43.

6. Ibid.; see also Onogawa Hidemi, pp. 281–286; see also P'i Lu-men, *Shih-fu-t'ang wei-k'an jih-chi*, in *Hunan li-shih tzu-liao* (Hunan), 4:68.

friends, must have appeared as a godsend. According to one record, before Liang went to Hunan, there was some discussion within the K'ang-Liang group as to the approach Liang should take to advance the cause of reform in Hunan. Was Liang to continue his gradualist approach or give it up in favor of a radical one? Would Liang aim for constitutionalism or for thorough-going renovation by way of popular education and racial revolution? Liang, along with some other disciples of K'ang Yu-wei who were also invited to teach at Shih-wu hsüeh-t'ang, was said to have favored the radical approach; K'ang, though hesitant for some time, nevertheless did not show overt disapproval of these disciples.[7] Vague as it is, the record suggests that Liang went to Hunan in a radical mood.

Very soon after he started to lecture at the Shih-wu hsüeh-t'ang at Ch'angsha in the fall of 1897, Chiang Piao, as the educational commissioner, was replaced by Hsü Jen-tsu, a close friend of Liang and a fervent admirer of K'ang Yu-wei's Kung-yang doctrines.[8] With Hsü's full support, Liang felt free to propagate his ideals and teachings among the students at the Shih-wu hsüeh-t'ang. Liang's lectures, as he himself recalled later, consisted mainly of two parts: the moral philosophy of the Lu-Wang School regarding self-cultivation; and socio-political ideals based on the Kung-yang doctrines and the *Mencius*. Liang also required his students to submit notes on their readings for his comments.[9] In his written comments as well as in his lectures, Liang presented to those young Hunanese something they had never heard of before: moral diatribes against Chinese political tradition mixed with a romantic cult of the dimly understood ideal of popular rights as a

7. *LNCC*, I, 44.
8. Onogawa Hidemi, pp. 286–287; Su Yü, 4:1–1b.
9. *LNCC*, I, 42–44.

political panacea. Liang also tried to disseminate such teachings to the outside world by surreptitiously reprinting and passing around many thousands of abridged editions of Huang Tsung-hsi's *A Plan for the Prince,* supplemented with interpretive comments by himself and his friends. According to Liang, this produced an enormous impact on the intellectual climate of the closing years of the nineteenth century.[10]

What made Liang's teachings even more provocative was a discernible note of anti-Manchu racialism. In his comments on the students' notes he sometimes made explicit references to the strictly taboo fact that the Manchus had committed heinous atrocities during their conquest of China in the seventeenth century. Furthermore, he and his friends also reprinted and distributed thousands of copies of Wang Hsiu-ch'u's *An Account of Ten Days at Yangchow (Yang-chou shih-jih chi),* which was a lurid description of the outrageous brutalities that the Manchus had allegedly perpetrated at Yangchow when they took the city.[11] This work, along with Huang Tsung-hsi's *A Plan for the Prince,* was later also used by the revolutionists as their major propaganda literature before the publication of Tsou Jung's *Revolutionary Army (Ko-ming chün)* and Ch'en T'ien-hua's pamphlets on revolution.[12]

Liang's radical attitude was further evidenced in a memorial he submitted to Governor Ch'en Pao-chen; he suggested that Hunan, if necessary, should declare independence from the central government at Peking. This proposal was a reflection of Liang's exasperation over the ineptitude of the Ch'ing court in coping with the aggression of foreign powers. If the central government could

10. *LNCC,* I, 43; see also Liang, *Ch'ing-tai hsüeh-shu kai-lun,* p. 62; Su Yü, 5:8b; Liang, "Lun Chung-kuo chi-jo yu-yü fang-pi," p. 96.

11. Su Yü, 5:8; *LNCC,* I, 43.

12. Ibid.; Feng Tzu-yu, *Ko-ming i-shih* (Chungking, 1943), I, 10.

not be motivated to carry out reform, Liang argued, then the only way to prevent subjugation by foreign powers was to secede from the central government. After secession it would then be possible to carry out reforms and thoroughly renovate an independent Hunan; later Hunan might even be made the base for the eventual recovery of all China from foreign aggression and subjugation.[13]

This passionate advocacy of popular rights, the racist condemnation of the Manchu lineage of the Ch'ing court, and the suggestion that Hunan secede from the central government make the political program of Liang and his friends during their stay at Hunan well-nigh indistinguishable from that of the then burgeoning revolutionary movement. So far as ideology was concerned, the reform movement may best be regarded as a spectrum. At one pole were mild reformists; at the other, such radicals as T'an Ssu-t'ung and Liang Ch'i-ch'ao and their associates when they were engaged in the Hunan reform. In this perspective, K'ang Yu-wei's political program, although the most publicized, probably occupies only a middle position.

Liang's radical teachings and the ideas of such friends as T'an Ssu-t'ung, T'ang Ts'ai-ch'ang, and others were published in newspapers like *Hsiang-pao* (Hunan news) and *Hsiang-hsüeh pao* (Hunan journal) and expounded in the auditorium of the study society, Nan hsüeh-hui.[14] All of this was a powerful stimulus to the intellectual ferment created among the Hunan youth. When this controversy gradually gathered momentum and affected an ever widening sphere, it caused shock and alarm among Hunan gentry-literati at large, a reaction that eventually culminated in a concerted ideological counterattack from a

13. *LNCC*, I, 45–46; see also Liang, "Shang Ch'en Chung-ch'en shu" (A memorial to Governor Ch'en) in Su Yü, appendix, pp. 1–3b.
14. Onogawa Hidemi, pp. 294–295.

group of locally influential Hunanese bent on smothering the heretical and pernicious ideas of K'ang and Liang.

These Hunanese were not entirely conservative in outlook; in fact they included some moderate elements who could, in a sense, be regarded as enlightened. Some of them, like Wang Hsien-ch'ien, had even been among the supporters of the reform movement in the beginning.[15] Initially sympathetic to most of the institutional renovations that were being attempted at that time in Hunan, they withdrew their support as soon as they realized the actual or potential threat of some of the ideas of Liang and his associates to the central institutions and values of the traditional order; thereupon they joined other conservative gentry-literati in launching a violent campaign against the reformist group. In refutation of what they regarded as heretical teachings, they issued a large amount of polemical literature later collected in two compendia, attacking the radical writings of K'ang and Liang: *The Collection of Writings for Promoting the Sacred Teachings* (*I-chiao ts'ung-pien*) and *The Essential Writings for Awakening the Misled* (*Chüeh-mi yao-lu*).[16]

Ideological denunciations were also accompanied by riots instigated by the conservative gentry against the reformists. Thus was inaugurated the first large-scale ideological conflict within the ranks of gentry-literati, the intensity and scope of which reminds one of the struggle between gentry-literati and foreign missionaries in the nineteenth century. Although this conflict soon ended in the total defeat of the reformist group, it revealed the deep ideological split within the world of gentry-literati, a split

---

15. Ibid., pp. 281–285.

16. *LNCC*, I, 77–79; for a detailed account of the conservative reaction against the reformist group, see Su Yü, ts'e 5 and ts'e 6; Yeh Te-hui, *Chüeh-mi yao-lu*.

that led to the emergence of the Chinese intelligentsia as a new social group.

But before the ideological conflict developed into a disastrous storm for the reformists, Liang had already made his exit. In the early spring of 1898, cut down by a serious illness, he was forced to stop teaching and go to Shanghai for medical treatment.[17] By this time, Peking had once more become the center of the reform movement. This time the Russian demand to lease Dairen and Port Arthur provided the impetus for the resurgence of the reform movement at the capital. Coming on the heels of the German seizure of Kiaochow Bay, this move sent another wave of alarm throughout China. Liang, after convalescing for a short time at Shanghai, again plunged into the midst of the reform campaign, helping K'ang mobilize and organize gentry-literati in support of appeals for institutional reform.[18] By now, however, the general prospects of the reform movement did not look bright.

The campaign had been repeatedly thwarted by both the central government at Peking and provincial authorities at Shanghai. In Hunan, though blessed with the auspices of the provincial government, it was nonetheless hamstrung by the conservative gentry-literati. Now even under the threat of imminent dismemberment by the foreign powers, the Ch'ing court failed to pay any heed to the urgent appeal of the reformists. Although the reform movement seemed to be doomed, a development that had been an undercurrent for years now came to a head and for a time the movement almost succeeded.

This development had taken place within the Ch'ing court. In the course of the last decade of the nineteenth

17. *LNCC,* I, 48.

18. *LNCC,* I, 49–54; see also John Schrecker, "The Pao-kuo Hui: A Reform Society of 1898," in *Papers on China,* 14:50–64 (December 1960); T'ang Chih-chün, pp. 256–260.

century, a covert power struggle had developed between the faction centered around the young Emperor Kuang-hsü (who had become increasingly restive in his figure-head position) and the faction centered around the aging Empress Dowager who, though in retirement, still maintained an effective grip on her power. This latent power struggle between the two factions provided an unexpected avenue through which K'ang and Liang could gain a foothold in the establishment. For although the emperor's faction was not necessarily more enlightened than the Empress Dowager's, their weaker position made them more willing to make alliances with new elements and less averse to change in the status quo.[19]

Perhaps this struggle explains why Weng T'ung-ho, the emperor's tutor and also his closest advisor at the time, even though he was by no means very sympathetic to K'ang's radical interpretation of Confucianism, appreciated K'ang's views on political reform and recommended K'ang to the emperor.[20] Once in personal contact with the young emperor, K'ang very easily won the latter's trust and thus inaugurated the dramatic One Hundred Day Reform of 1898, the details of which have been recounted amply elsewhere.[21] After the reformist group gained favor with the emperor, Liang received nothing more than an apparently minor post as head of the Translation Bureau (I-shu chü). Whatever the explanation, the important fact is that during that eventful summer, when the young emperor tried to initiate the so-called "new policies" *(hsin-cheng)* based on K'ang Yu-wei's reform program, Liang does not seem to have played the prominent role which might have been expected in view of his important posi-

19. Hsiao Kung-ch'üan, "Weng T'ung-ho and the Reform Movement of 1898," in *Ch'ing-hua hsüeh-pao* (new series), 1.2:136–149 (April 1957).
20. Ibid., pp. 149–179.
21. Ibid.

tion in the reformist group.[22] It is interesting, however, that during these months Liang seems to have had forebodings of the eventual futility of their efforts. He knew that all the power was in the hands of the Empress Dowager. He felt disillusioned and intended to leave Peking. When the reform movement finally ended in the tragic coup in September, Liang took asylum in the Japanese embassy and, through the help of Japanese agents, fled to Japan where he was later joined by K'ang Yu-wei and other members of the reformist group.[23]

Liang's exile to Japan coincided with a development of tremendous significance, namely, the increasing influx of Chinese students into Japan. This was not, of course, the first time Chinese students had gone abroad to study; in the 1870's students had been sent to America and Europe to study Western sciences and technology.[24] What had happened in the years following the late 1890's, however, was very different from the experience of the 1870's. In the first place, Japan had replaced America and Europe as the primary destination of Chinese students who wanted to go abroad. The geographical and cultural propinquity of Japan to China made it possible for Chinese students to go there in larger numbers. More important, the movement to Japan in the late 1890's and the early 1900's took place in an intellectual context very different from that of the 1870's. In the 1870's the student mission took place largely as a result of the government's need for some expertise on Western sciences and technology. It was not accompanied by any widespread serious interest in Western learning on the part of gentry-literati. But in the decade around 1900, although the movement to study in Japan

22. *LNCC*, I, 61–62, 65–67.
23. *LNCC*, I, 57–58.
24. C. Y. Wang, *Chinese Intellectuals and the West, 1872–1949* (Chapel Hill, N.C., 1966), pp. 41–50.

was still mainly government initiated and government sponsored, students left in the intellectual climate of the reform movement and were full of interest in new learning and experiences.

As a consquence, the flow of Chinese youth to Japan, which in the beginning involved only a very small number, in the course of a few years had developed into a sustained intellectual movement which eventually involved more than ten thousand students. This remarkable increase in the number of students is indicated by the fact that in 1899 they were estimated at about 200 but at 13,000 or more in 1906. Obviously the turn of the century was an era when Tokyo–Yokohama attracted an increasing flow of Chinese youth and became the center of the burgeoning Chinese intelligentsia.[25]

Not all these Chinese intellectuals were students in the strict sense; in fact, very few of them engaged in serious studies there and even fewer were graduates of Japanese schools. According to one estimate, at the most there were only 700 Chinese graduates in any one year and the majority of these had only gone through cram courses.[26] And yet most of these young Chinese developed one burning interest during their foreign sojourn — politics. The various student associations and provincial guilds they formed in Japan were all politically oriented, and the newspapers and journals they published were all ideologically charged.[27]

Liang was unquestionably one of the few most active and influential leaders among the Chinese intelligentsia at the beginning of this century. To begin with, Liang's

25. Liang, *Chung-kuo chin-san-pai-nien hsüeh-shu-shih*, p. 31; Sanetō Keishū, *Chūkokujin Nihon ryūgaku shi* (Tokyo, 1960), pp. 35–110.

26. Liang, *Chung-kuo chin-san-pai-nien hsüeh-shu-shih*, pp. 30–31.

27. Harold Z. Schiffrin, *Sun Yat-sen and the Origins of the Chinese Revolution* (Berkeley, 1968), pp. 255–299.

involvement in the dramatic events of the reform movement in the late 1890's made his name almost as renowned as that of K'ang Yu-wei. His importance was even further enhanced when K'ang Yu-wei was forced to leave Japan in 1899 because of diplomatic pressure from the Ch'ing government.[28] K'ang's departure inevitably left Liang as the most influential figure among the Chinese reformists in China and Japan.

Liang resumed his intellectual activities almost from the beginning of his exile. Even before his arrival in Japan he had started to learn the Japanese language en route and to try his hand at translating Shiba Shiro's *Kajin Kigu* (The strange encounters of elegant females).[29] Scarcely two months after he had settled in Japan he managed to publish a journal at Yokohama with funds pooled from the local Chinese merchants. This was the famous *Journal of Disinterested Criticism (Ch'ing-i pao)*.[30] After this journal ceased publication because of a fire in 1901, Liang managed to start in the early spring of 1902 a fortnightly titled *New Citizen Journal (Hsin-min ts'ung-pao)*. Almost at the same time, he established another journal called *New Novel (Hsin hsiao-shuo)*.[31] The *New Novel*, like many other publications in this period, was short-lived, but the *New Citizen Journal* had an uninterrupted publication for five years until it was shut down in 1907.[32] The tremendous popularity of these journals was to make Liang the leading voice among Chinese intelligentsia during the early 1900's. From the forum of this journal, Liang com-

28. *LNCC,* I, 86–88.

29. Liang Ch'i-ch'ao, tr., *Chia-jen ch'i-yü* (The strange encounters of elegant females), in *YPSHC-CC,* ts'e 19, 88:1–220.

30. *LNCC,* I, 83–85.

31. *LNCC,* I, 148–150; 163–165.

32. Chang Ching-lu, *Chung-kuo chin-tai ch'u-pan shih-liao pu-pien* (Shanghai, 1957), p. 23; Tseng Hsü-pai, *Chung-kuo hsin-wen shih* (Taipei, 1966), pp. 203–206.

mented on current affairs and wrote political polemics against the Empress Dowager and her regime at Peking and also took upon himself the task of popular enlightenment by introducing new ideas from the West.

In addition to his journalistic activities, Liang was also concerned with education. Shortly after he had settled in Japan, a number of students who had previously studied with him in Hunan now managed to find their way to him. At first Liang accommodated them in his own living quarters and continued to tutor them in the same fashion as in the old days at the Shih-wu hsüeh-t'ang.[33] Later, however, these students were incorporated into the Kao-teng ta-t'ung hsüeh-hsiao (The Great Harmony High School) which he founded at Tokyo in 1899, again with the financial backing of Chinese merchants in Japan. This school was intended to provide some higher education for the younger generation of overseas Chinese. Liang served as headmaster.[34]

Amid these activities, Liang, even though in exile, never gave up hope of achieving reform by political action. Once in contact with the overseas Chinese communities, K'ang and Liang naturally thought of the possibility of tapping the human and financial resources of millions of overseas Chinese for their political purposes. In the early summer of 1899, K'ang Yu-wei, after being forced by the Japanese government to leave Japan as a result of pressure from the Ch'ing government, organized a Pao-huang hui (Protecting the Emperor Society) in Canada as the formal political organization for the reformist groups.[35] Liang naturally became an important member of the Pao-huang hui. Almost at the same time, Liang, along with eleven

33. *LNCC*, I, 90–93.
34. Ibid.; Feng Tzu-yu, I, 72–73.
35. *LNCC*, I, 88.

close friends in K'ang's group, formed a blood brotherhood within the Pao-huang hui.[36]

In undertaking political action, Liang was soon confronted with an agonizing political choice between reform and revolution, a dilemma which he shared with many other students at the time. It was a choice dictated by the fact that by the time the Pao-huang hui was organized among the overseas Chinese communities, Sun Yat-sen's revolutionary society, the Hsing-chung hui (Revive China Society), had long been active on the scene. It is true that up to the end of the 1890's the revolutionists' activities were largely confined to the overseas Chinese communities, treaty ports, and the secret societies in south China. However, as Chinese students went to Japan in increasing numbers in the years around 1900, the political potential of the new student group started to attract the attention of Sun Yat-sen who was now attempting to reorient his revolutionary strategy to win the support of these young intellectuals.[37] K'ang and Liang were naturally also eager to recruit Chinese students into their ranks and had to decide whether to look upon Sun Yat-sen's revolutionist group as friends or foes.

Before 1903 Liang in general seemed to be inclined toward friendship but lacked K'ang's approval. In fact K'ang had already shown himself cool toward the idea of befriending the revolutionists when some friends of Sun Yat-sen made attempts to contact him back in the years before he had gone into exile.[38] At the time K'ang

36. Ibid.
37. Harold Z. Schiffrin, *Sun Yat-sen and the Origins of the Chinese Revolution,* pp. 300–302, 306–309; see also his article, "The Enigma of Sun Yat-sen," in Mary C. Wright, ed., *China in Revolution: The First Phase, 1900–1913* (New Haven, 1968), pp. 419–474.
38. *LNCC,* I, 35–40; Feng Tzu-yu, I, 47–49; see also "Hsi-pao hsüan-i" (Selective translations from English newspapers), in *Shih-wu pao* (Chinese Progress; Shanghai), 15:12–13 (Dec. 14, 1896) and 19:14–15 (March 3,

and Liang fled to Japan in late 1898, Sun was also in Japan and immediately planned to approach them mainly through the mediation of their common Japanese friends. Sun did succeed in meeting Liang and some of K'ang's disciples. It seems to have been K'ang who stood in the way of what might have led to significant cooperation between the two groups.[39]

After K'ang left Japan in the early spring of 1899, contact between the two groups grew considerably. As a result the reformist group established a rapport with the revolutionist group. Very soon a merger of the two groups into a single party around the joint leadership of Sun Yat-sen and Liang was contemplated. But at this juncture, some members of the reformist group who disapproved of Liang's plan of coalescing with the revolutionaries divulged it to K'ang. K'ang, in a great fury, ordered Liang to leave Japan immediately for Hawaii to campaign for the cause of Pao-huang hui among the overseas Chinese there, obviously with the purpose of cutting off Liang's relationship with Sun Yat-sen.[40]

Liang's attempts at cooperation with Sun Yat-sen have been variously explained as an impulsive act of the moment, as political opportunism, or even as a Machiavellian maneuver. But a more logical explanation is to be found in the ambivalence inherent in his political outlook, an outlook formed before he went into exile in 1898. This ambivalence was in turn rooted in the ideological struc-

---

1897); see also his "Tung-pao hsüan-i" (Selective translations from Japanese newspapers), in *Shih-wu pao*, 21:22–24 (March 23, 1899). For the whole story, see Yen-p'ing Hao, "The Abortive Cooperation between Reformers and Revolutionaries," *Papers on China*, 15:93–95 (December 1961).

39. Ibid.

40. *LNCC*, I, 88–89; Feng Tzu-yu, II, 31–32.

ture of the reform movement itself. As suggested previously, the reform movement of the 1900's did not have a well-defined and homogeneous ideological basis. On the surface it seemed to be dominated by K'ang Yu-wei's reform ideology. But in fact this reform ideology concealed divergent political attitudes which ranged from gradualism to the political radicalism implied in T'an Ssu-t'ung's world view. Almost inevitably, out of this spectrum would develop an ambivalent attitude toward reform and revolution which was reflected not only in Liang's political outlook but also in that of some of his friends in the reformist group. There is thus no point in arguing whether in this period Liang's commitment was to reform or to revolution. Given the inherent ambivalence of his political outlook, his extremely sensitive and versatile mind, his temperamental penchant for change which he himself often admitted, each may very well represent one genuine aspect of his thinking.

Thus in Hunan in 1897, when the political circumstances were favorable, the radical side of the reform movement revealed itself. In the changed political situation of Peking in 1898, the gradualist aspect would then become the main concern of the reform movement. Now in exile in Japan, after the catastrophic failure of the reform movement made the incurable nature of the Ch'ing regime glaringly obvious, it was but natural for the inherent radical side of the reform movement to reassert itself. This radical aspect, being ideologically no different from the revolutionist movement as it existed then, naturally tended to merge with the revolutionist camp. It is mainly because of this tendency that for the Chinese intelligentsia the turn of the twentieth century marked a period of ideological turbulence during which the dividing line between the reformists and the revolutionists was not as sharply drawn as it came to be a few years later.[41]

Liang set sail for Hawaii toward the end of 1899. His visit to Hawaii was originally scheduled only as a short stopover on his way to the North American continent where he planned to campaign for the Pao-huang hui among the overseas Chinese there. But during Liang's sojourn in Hawaii, bubonic plague struck the island and a quarantine was imposed which now made nonwhite foreigners' travel to America very difficult. Liang was unexpectedly forced to stay in Hawaii for about half a year.[42]

Before his departure for Hawaii Liang had tended toward collaboration with Sun Yat-sen. When he went to Hawaii, he carried a letter of introduction from Sun Yat-sen, whose Hsing-chung hui had already developed a rather solid footing among the local Chinese populace. Sun's letter may have helped Liang to establish connections in the Chinese community, but we do not know to what extent. Liang himself was also a well-known figure among the overseas Chinese and this fact may also have helped him to become popular. Furthermore Liang, himself an outstanding Chinese literatus, joined the local San-ho hui (Triad Society), a very powerful secret society among the overseas Chinese. According to Liang, the majority of the Chinese in Hawaii belonged to this society. Before he became a member of the San-ho hui, very few local Chinese joined his own Pao-huang hui, despite the fact that he himself was very popular in the local community. After Liang joined the San-ho hui and was elected as its leader, many people became willing to sup-

41. Harold Z. Schiffrin, *Sun Yat-sen and the Origins of the Chinese Revolution*, pp. 255–282.
42. *LNCC*, I, 93, 111–112.

port the Pao-huang hui. Liang even claimed that being the leader of the local San-ho hui, he had all its members under his command.[43] Thus for him and for the Pao-huang hui the trip to Hawaii was apparently a great success.

Inevitably the expansion of Liang's Pao-huang hui was made at the expense of Sun Yat-sen's Hsing-chung hui. When Sun realized this, he sent an angry letter to Liang, charging that the latter betrayed an agreement of cooperation which they apparently had made before Liang went to Hawaii.[44] Liang's answer was typical of the wavering that had marked his political outlook all along. In a letter he wrote in the spring of 1900 to answer Sun's charge, Liang justified his political activities in Hawaii by maintaining that his present political approach was an eclectic one, necessitated by changing circumstances. He assured Sun that in principle he still advocated anti-Manchuism as a means of attaining the ideal of popular government. But the current political situation made it expedient to promote that ideal in the name of protecting the emperor (*ch'in-wang*). He was referring to the public furor stirred up then over the Empress Dowager's plan to force the abdication of the Kuang-hsü Emperor in favor of her favorite heir-apparent.

In Liang's view a popular uprising could be staged against the Ch'ing regime by capitalizing on this public furor and rallying people around the cause of protecting the emperor. After succeeding in protecting the emperor and getting rid of the Empress Dowager's regime, they could very easily realize the ideal of republicanism by electing the emperor president! So he urged Sun to be flexible, realistic, and to join forces with him, for their

43. Ibid., 89–90, 102.
44. Yen-p'ing Hao, p. 101.

cooperation would expedite the ultimate success of their common cause.[45] Apparently Liang's persuasion fell on a deaf ear, for there is no evidence of any further contact between them. Thus was ended for good the attempts at collaboration between revolutionists and reformists.

Liang's letter to Sun Yat-sen need not be explained as a mere rationalization, for at that time he and his friends were sincerely engaged in an effort to stage a popular uprising in the name of protecting the emperor. This revolt was the famous Hankow uprising of 1900.[46] The idea of an uprising against the Empress Dowager's regime was first conceived by T'ang Ts'ai-ch'ang, an enlightened Hunanese gentry-scholar and a fervent supporter of the Hunan reform movement in the years before 1898, as a way of avenging his closest friend, T'an Ssu-t'ung, who died a victim of the Empress Dowager's coup d'état of 1898.[47] He relied mainly on his old reformist friends in the K'ang-Liang group for support. In 1899 before Liang left for Hawaii T'ang went to Japan to confer with him about the plans for the uprising. Through Liang or through some other channel, T'ang was also in contact with Sun and his revolutionist group.[48] According to one source, T'ang in fact intended to cooperate with Sun and had even made plans to coordinate his insurrectionary activities in the area of the Yangtze Valley with those of Sun's group in the Kwangtung area.[49]

45. *LNCC*, I, 140–141.

46. Ibid., 99–138; see also E. Joan Smythe, "The Tzu-li Hui: Some Chinese and Their Rebellion," *Papers on China*, 12:51–67 (December 1958).

47. T'ang Ts'ai-chih, "T'ang Ts'ai-ch'ang ho Shih-wu hsüeh-t'ang," *Hunan li-shih tzu-liao*, 3:98–108.

48. Ibid.

49. Feng Tzu-yu, I, 74–75, 82–83, 85–86; see also T'ang Ts'ai-chih, p. 107.

This nonchalance toward the distinction between the reformists and the revolutionists is no surprise if one keeps in mind the confusion displayed by many reformists toward the problem of reform and revolution. T'ang's attitude was later further reflected in the manifesto he promulgated in setting up the Uprightness Society (Cheng-ch'i hui) — later renamed the Independence Society (Tzu-li hui) — as the conspiratorial front for the planned uprising. In this manifesto the central aim for the uprising was declared to be the protection and restoration of Kuang-hsü Emperor, but curiously enough, this manifesto also featured some anti-Manchu revolutionary statements.[50]

In spite of its ideological ambivalence and its alleged affiliations with the revolutionists, the Tzu-li hui was doubtless still primarily a reformist project, both in terms of its membership and financial resources. Almost the whole Pao-huang hui was mobilized to support the project. Liang played an important role, not only in soliciting funds for the uprising and seeking possible sympathy from some foreign governments but also in laying out long-term military and political strategy for the whole operation.[51] To Liang's profound disappointment, however, the whole project eventually fell through because of bungled preparations. The uprising was nipped in the bud by the Ch'ing government at Hankow.[52]

Thus Liang's political activities so far did not indicate that at that time he was committed to reform. In actuality, he did not make up his mind about the choice between reform and revolution until 1903 when his hitherto waver-

50. Feng Tzu-yu, I, 74; E. Joan Smythe, pp. 60–61.
51. For an understanding of the mobilization of the K'ang-Liang Reformist group in support of the Tzu-li Hui, see the correspondence between Liang and his friends in the year 1900, in *LNCC*, I, 99–134.
52. Ibid.

ing ideological outlook gradually hardened into a firm commitment to the cause of political reformism.[53] As the decade wore on, Liang doubtless became the most vocal leader among the reformist intelligentsia. K'ang, who had been forced to leave the country in 1899, had been touring around the world and could not be as influential as Liang, who was on the scene.[54] Furthermore, because of the voluminous writings which poured forth from his formidable pen since he left the country in 1898, Liang had now established himself as the most popular writer of the time, with a literary fame eclipsing even that of K'ang Yu-wei.

Liang's role as China's most popular writer of the first decade of the twentieth century cannot be measured merely in terms of his stature within the reformist group, but must also be appraised against the intellectual background of the rise of Chinese intelligentsia. The Chinese intelligentsia were divided into the contending camps of revolutionists and reformists; both were parts of the same social group, however, and they also had certain ideas and values in common, which transcended their apparent intellectual differences. Liang's widely read writings during the first decade of the 1900's must be credited with playing an important part in forging the basic outlook of the early Chinese intelligentsia.

It must be borne in mind that in the first decade of this century, Liang lived in Meiji Japan. The intellectual and socio-political ambience of Japan must have had some influence on the development of his thinking. What was the nature of this Japanese influence? More important, what was the relative weight of this influence in comparison with Chinese cultural tradition and the Western impact

53. For a detailed discussion of this problem see Chapter 8.
54. Jung-pang Lo, ed., *K'ang Yu-wei: A Biography and a Symposium* (Tucson, 1967), p. 179.

— the two forces which hitherto had molded the development of Liang's mind?

Japan had long been an object of interest to him, even before his exile in 1898. The reasons are not difficult to find. K'ang Yu-wei and Huang Tsun-hsien, two of his intellectual mentors, were fervent advocates of Japanese studies.[55] Important too in this regard was the surprising victory which Japan won in her war with China in 1895. Like many other Chinese intellectuals of that time, Liang felt humiliated but also intrigued by Japan's show of strength. When he went into exile in late 1898, Japan was no longer simply an object of intellectual interest; she became the ever present reality of Liang's immediate environment.[56]

There are several obvious ways in which Liang's presence in Japan could have influenced his intellectual outlook, for he had the opportunity to watch the social and political development of Meiji Japan at close range. Conceivably Japan might have appeared to him as a sort of social laboratory in which the value of Westernization and the modes of interplay between the indigenous tradition and Western impact could be directly observed. Furthermore, Japan preceded China by many decades in large-scale absorption of Western learning and had by the end of the nineteenth century amassed a large corpus of translations of Western literature which made available to Liang a Western vocabulary written in Chinese characters, a vocabulary that facilitated both his understanding and propagation of Western thought.

55. Richard C. Howard, "Japan's Role in the Reform Program of K'ang Yu-wei," in Jung-pang Lo, pp. 288–302.

56. For a discussion of Japanese influences on Liang's thought during his exile years, see Philip Chung-chih Huang, "A Confucian Liberal: Liang Ch'i-ch'ao in Action and Thought" (Ph.D. diss., University of Washington, 1966), chap. 4.

Aside from such imponderable influences of Meiji society as a whole, one might ask if there were any specific intellectual figure or school in Meiji Japan which had an appreciable impact on Liang's intellectual development. In his writings he often mentioned the Japanese authors whose works he had read. Among them such names as Fukuzawa Yukichi, Katō Hiroyuki, Tokutomi Sohō, Nakamura Masanao, and Yano Ryūkei stand out.[57] A detailed examination and full assessment of the influence of these Japanese thinkers on Liang is outside the scope of this book, but some general conclusions can be attempted. In order to assess their influence a distinction must be made between Liang's fluctuating practical concerns and instrumental values on the one hand and his basic moral and socio-political values on the other.

There is no question that Liang's contact with Japanese society as a whole as well as with its intellectual world was a factor in shaping some of his changing practical concerns. His biographies and novels written to propagate his moral and political ideals were, as he admitted, inspired by the Japanese "political novel" (*cheng-chih hsiao-shuo*) then in vogue.[58] The literary style which Liang used in many of his popular works was a characteristic mixture of classical and vernacular language, a distinctive style which might have been modeled on Tokutomi Rokan's style, as one Japanese scholar has suggested.[59] The fact that Liang clung to the idea of political revolution during the first few years after his arrival in Japan may have had some-

57. *Tzu-yu shu* (The book on liberty), in *YPSHC-CC*, ts'e 2, 2:8–9, 21, 28–39, 47, 49–57, 82–87, 126–129, 133–137; see also *Hsin-min shuo* (New citizen), in *YPSTC*, I, 114–115.

58. *Tzu-yu shu*, pp. 41–42.

59. Nakamura Tadayuki, "Chūgoku bungei ni oyoboseru Nihon bungei no eikyō," in *Taidai Bungaku* (Taihoku, Taiwan) vol. 8, nos. 2, 4, 5 (1942–1944), sec. 3, pp. 86–152.

thing to do with what Itō Hirobumi advocated as "destructivism" (*p'o-huai chu-i*).[60] His shifting views of the organizational structure of constitutional government may also have been influenced in varying degrees by such Japanese thinkers as Minobe Tatsukichi, Kakehi Katsuhiko, Onozuka Kiheiji, and Hozumi Yatsuka.[61] During Liang's exile in Japan, he was known to have become interested in problems of public finance; many of his ideas on this subject doubtless derive from Japanese sources.[62] In short, Liang's exposure to Japanese literature expanded his intellectual horizon, constantly shaping and reshaping his attitude toward many of his practical concerns.

But on the level of moral and societal values, Japanese influence on Liang is far from clear. If we focus on the influence stemming from Japanese tradition, three facts merit attention. To begin with, Japanese *bushidō* provided an important source of inspiration for Liang's advocacy of martial virtue.[63] It is not the only source, however, for his appreciation also stemmed from his reading of the history of ancient Sparta.[64] Moreover, in the history of Tokugawa and Meiji Japan, Liang had seen how the spread of Wang Yang-ming's moral philosophy and Zen Buddhism could contribute to the cultivation of activists and disciplined personalities.[65] Nevertheless, one must

60. *Tzu-yu shu,* pp. 25–26.
61. "K'ai-ming chuan-chih lun" (On enlightened despotism), in *YPSHC-WC,* ts'e 6, 17:13–83; "Tsa-ta mou-pao" (Miscellaneous answer to a certain newspaper), in *YPSHC-WC,* ts'e 6, 18:59–131.
62. Lin Chih-chün, "Hsü" (Preface to Collected works and essays from the Ice-drinker's Studio), ts'e 1, p. 1.
63. Liang Ch'i-ch'ao, *Chung-kuo chih wu-shih-tao* (Chinese bushidō), in *YPSTC,* VII, 1–100.
64. *Ssu-pa-ta hsiao-chih* (A brief history of Sparta), in *YPSHC-CC,* ts'e 4, 15:1–19.
65. "Lun tsung-chiao-chia yü che-hsüeh-chia chih ch'ang-tuan te-shih" (On the respective merits and demerits of religious leader and philosopher), in *YPSHC-WC,* ts'e 4, 9:45.

145

bear in mind that both trends of thought were nothing new for Liang, who had studied Lu-Wang moral philosophy and Zen Buddhism from early childhood.[66] Thus, on the level of moral and societal values traditional Japanese thought did not constitute a significant independent source of influence for Liang. It was largely an influence which served to coalesce with and reinforce certain elements of Western thought and Chinese tradition which already lay in the background of his thinking.

In addition to traditional Japanese thought, Liang imbibed a large amount of Western thought through Japanese translations. The problem is that translation of thought from one language to another cannot be free of distortion. As some linguists like Benjamin Whorf and Edward Sapir suggest, different languages embody different world views; hence the process of translation almost inevitably involves varying measures of distortion. Translation, according to this thesis, is necessarily interpretation. A question then immediately arises. Did the Japanese translation of Western literature which Liang had read involve such a degree of interpretation that Liang's understanding of the original Western ideal had been affected? This is a problem to which no definite answer can be given at this time. Social scientists and intellectual historians are not yet in a position to know exactly the complex relationship between language and thought; nor is any analytical literature on Japanese translations of Western thought available which could help us answer the problem in any definite way.

In their fervent and massive efforts to absorb Western culture, the Japanese resorted not only to translation but also to interpretation of Western ideas and ideals. It is

66. "San-shih tzu-shu" (An autobiograph of my last thirty years), in *YPSHC-WC,* ts'e 4, 11:16–17.

known that Liang had read many Japanese interpretations of Western ideals. Did the Japanese interpretation of Western thought exert an influence on Liang which is uniquely Japanese and hence must be distinguished from the influence of Western thought? Again the problem is insoluble at this stage of historical scholarship. There is as yet not enough analytical literature in the field of Japanese intellectual history to see whether those Japanese authors whose works Liang read had distorted in the process of their interpretation the original meaning of Western ideas and ideals.

To be sure, a preliminary examination of the thought of certain Japanese thinkers, such as Fukuzawa Yukichi, Katō Hiroyuki, Tokutomi Sohō, some of those writings Liang had read, leaves us with the impression that they tended to interpret Western social and moral ideals in a collectivistic vein because of their preoccupation with "enriching the state and strengthening the army" (*fukoku kyōhei*). The fact that many of Liang's writings also evinced a notable collectivistic strain might easily lead people to assume that Liang was influenced by Japanese thinkers in this regard. This is an unsound inference, however, since Liang's pre-exile works had already featured this collectivistic strain. This strain would thus be better accounted for by the similar national situation and nationalistic preoccupation which Chinese intellectuals generally shared with Japanese intellectuals at that time.

It is also true that the Japanese response to Western impact was sometimes conditioned by the need to preserve cultural identity. In this regard, again Liang's thought bore some similarities to that of many Japanese. But can we then draw the simple conclusion that Liang's thought in this respect was the result of Japanese influence? In short, Chinese and Japanese intellectuals were often confronted with more or less similar national situations and cultural challenges in modern times and hence would naturally share certain intellectual preoccupations and psychological needs in common. This very fact makes it difficult to impute influence one way or the other.

All the foregoing considerations suggest that while Japanese influence did help determine many of Liang Ch'i-ch'ao's practical concerns, it is, however, far from clear that it was as significant in determining his basic values and ideas. At the very least, on this level, the Japanese factor cannot compare with indigenous Chinese tradition and Western learning as an independent intellectual source.

6

The New Citizen

Public Morality and Private Morality

For Liang Ch'i-ch'ao exile to Japan in 1898 might have meant a profound personal misfortune for it denied him access to power or opportunity to implement his reformist ideal in the foreseeable future. Intellectually, however, exile was a godsend, for with political action temporarily impossible, Liang found the leisure to exert his intellectual talents. Furthermore, while living in Japan he could speak his mind free from the kind of restrictions and inconvenience which would certainly have been imposed on him in China. Finally, Japan provided him with an ideal environment where, having quickly learned to read Japanese, he could assimilate new thought and thus enrich his mind to a degree which would have been impossible in China.[1]

It is little wonder that the years in Japan found Liang at the height of his intellectual creativity. First in the *Ch'ing-i pao* and then in the *Hsin-min ts'ung-pao* he poured forth his new ideas and ideals. Profuse and powerful as his popular writings were, however, it was not until 1902 that he began to set forth his moral-political ideas in a comparatively systematic way in a widely read serial

1. About Liang's fervent interest in learning the Japanese language, see *LNCC*, I, 83–87.

titled *New Citizen,* the first part of which was published
in consecutive issues of the *Hsin-min ts'ung-pao* until he
went to America in the early spring of 1903. To understand Liang's socio-political thinking of the period from
1899 to 1903, it is necessary to focus on the first part of
Hsin-min shuo in an examination of his writings.

It is very significant that Liang used the word *hsin-min*
to name both his journal and his serial.[2] For *hsin-min* is
a central concept in the Confucian classic, *Great Learning.*
In the latter context the concept embodies the idea that
the core of Confucian statesmanship consisted in moral
education and renovation of people. This concept underlay Liang's socio-political thinking of the pre-exile years.
However, a complex of Western values had caused considerable erosion of the Confucian notion of statesmanship. Now in the new intellectual milieu of Meiji Japan,
the erosion had gone much deeper. The result was the
emergence of a set of new personality ideals and societal
values which Liang spelled out in his *Hsin-min shuo.* To
be sure, some Confucian elements inevitably remained in
the background. But more striking is the innovation in
Liang's reinterpretation of *hsin-min* as compared with this
same concept in *Great Learning.* Indeed the innovative aspect is so significant that the novel concept "new citizen"
is required to signify *hsin-min.*

Liang's innovation is first of all indicated in the emergence of the concept of *ch'ün* at the core of his concept

2. Liang's concept of *hsin-min* must be understood in two senses and
hence should be translated in two ways. When *hsin* is used as a verb,
hsin-min means and must be translated as "renovation of the people."
When *hsin* is used as an adjective meaning "new," *hsin-min* should be
translated as "new citizen." Both translations are used in this book de-
pending on the context in which it appears. *Hsin-min shuo* was a serial
which Liang published intermittently over two years (1902–1904). Its
first chapter appeared in the very first issue of *Hsin-min ts'ung-pao* (New
citizen journal); its last chapter appeared in the seventy-second issue.

of morality. It must be recalled that in the pre-exile years the Western induced transformation of Liang's political thinking was centered around this concept of grouping. Now this same concept was found to lie at the heart of his moral thinking as indicated in his definition of grouping as the central function of any moral system. It is the essence of morality, Liang argued, to strengthen group cohesion and to promote group interest.[3]

Liang placed morality into two categories. One was what he called public morality (*kung-te*), the other private morality (*ssu-te*). Public morality referred to those moral values which promote the cohesion of a group; private morality meant those moral values which function to achieve moral perfection of individual personality. It was of course public morality which was most indispensable for the cohesion of a group, but private morality was also very important for the obvious reason that the aggregate quality of a group as a whole ultimately depends upon the quality of the individual members of the group.[4] Thus in Liang's view, private morality was by no means only of individual concern; its primary value still lay in its serviceability to the collective interest of the group.

This collectivistic view of morality led Liang to a moral relativism which was doubtless a radical departure from the moral absolutism of Confucianism. As he pointed out, it is the invariable function of morality to serve the interest of the group, but the specific content of a moral system should always change with the time and the place. This is only natural because of the changing needs of a group. As an illustration of this moral relativism he cited certain facts of modern anthropology. He pointed out that among primitive people, some regarded women as public pos-

3. *Hsin-min shuo*, p. 76.
4. Ibid., pp. 12–13.

sessions, while others considered the institution of slavery to be perfectly moral. Modern philosophers should not casually dismiss these phenomena as immoral, Liang warned, because in view of the conditions of the times these values were suited to the interest of the specific group which espoused them.[5]

Involved in this moral relativism was an evolutionary view of morality which was of special concern for Liang. Moral values change in the course of time with the varying demands of group interests in different periods. But it was Liang's empirical observation that the development of morality had been uneven: public morality had generally been subject to more changes than private morality in the course of human history. For Liang his observation meant that in China there should be more development in the realm of public morality in response to historical changes.[6]

Liang's basic view of morality was then both collectivistic and evolutionary: collectivistic insofar as what he called the basic function of morality was concerned, evolutionary insofar as what he called the substantive moral rules were concerned. This collectivistic and evolutionary outlook had first dominated Liang's socio-political thinking; now it became dominant in his moral thought. In this connection, a critical question arose: with such new notions of morality, what should be the attitude toward the traditional moral system? Liang was, of course, very much aware of the long, rich development of moral thought in Chinese cultural tradition. Now all of a sudden it became apparent to him that this development was confined to the realm of private morality. So far as public morality was concerned, he found little development in the Chinese tradition.[7]

5. Ibid., pp. 14–15.
6. Ibid.
7. Ibid., p. 12.

With the new perspective which Liang gradually acquired in his years of exile, this unbalanced development of China's moral tradition can be seen at its clearest. Shortly after he arrived in Japan he read the rescript of the Japanese ministry of education on the contents of the ethics course offered in Japanese high schools. He was impressed by the comprehensiveness and variety of the subjects covered in that rescript, noting that Japanese ethics included subjects dealing with the individual, family, society, and state, even as far as to include such abstract topics as humanity and life in general.[8] In comparison, the traditional Chinese moral system was apparently too narrow with regard to the subject matter. This comparison had already stimulated Liang to conceive the idea of developing a new moral system for China. Now in 1902 when he wrote the *New Citizen* his knowledge of Western civilization had obviously increased considerably and his attention was naturally drawn to the even more striking contrast between Western and Chinese moral values.

The contrast would be patent, Liang argued, as soon as the five Confucian relationships were compared to Western ethics, which was divided into three categories: family, social, and state ethics.[9] Manifestly three Confucian relationships, namely, father and son, husband and wife, and elder brother and younger brother, corresponded to family ethics in the Western ethical system. One Confucian relationship, namely that between friends, fell into the category of Western social ethics. The remaining Confucian relationship between ruler and subject belonged to Western state ethics. This comparison made the deficiency of Chinese ethics immediately obvious.[10] In the first place, the Confucian relationship between friends occupied at

8. "Tung-chi yüeh-tan," pp. 85–86.
9. *Hsin-min shuo*, pp. 12–13.
10. Ibid.

best only one sub-category within the broad range of Western social ethics. Obviously it was impossible to confine one's social involvement just to friendship, for, as Liang said, even the most isolated individuals must have some other social involvements. From the standpoint of Western state ethics, the inadequacy of the Chinese moral system was even more evident. It was ridiculous to narrow down the political involvements of a citizen to the single ruler-subject relationship, and the very nature of the traditional ruler-subject relationship itself was objectionable.[11]

Judged by Western moral standards, Liang then argued, traditional Chinese morality was only well-developed in the realm of family ethics; in the realm of social ethics and state ethics, traditional morality proved to be woefully inadequate. What China needed most was public morality, or rather civic virtue, to balance the overemphasis of traditional Chinese ethics on private morality.[12] Liang thought it was his role to point out what these civic virtues were and thereby to formulate a new personality ideal for Chinese people to follow.

Nationalism and the Ideal of Citizenship

As we have seen, the central purpose of Liang's writings on moral renovation, which he started in the year 1902, was to develop what he called public virtue, at the core of which was still the concept of *ch'ün* which had already figured prominently in his pre-exile reformist writings. Indeed, almost immediately after Liang resumed his journalistic activities in Japan in 1898, he again posed the concept of *ch'ün* in his appeal to overseas Chinese

11. Ibid.
12. Ibid.

merchants to organize themselves into a cohesive community.[13] The important question is: what did Liang now mean by *ch'ün?* To begin with, as a further development of the corporate feeling of oneness, which was an important sense of the concept of grouping, it meant a capacity that a citizen of a modern state should have for sharing a strong sense of solidarity with his compatriots and for forming civic associations with them.[14] Inevitably *ch'ün* as a civic virtue in the above sense would involve as it did a strong revulsion not just against the inveterate and pervasive selfishness which Liang saw as a consequence of overemphasis on the ideal of self-cultivation in traditional culture; it was also directed against various forms of primordial attachment prevailing in traditional society which prevented China from developing into a really centralized state: "On the surface the government seems to be a centralized one. However, the country is actually divided into innumerable small units and groups on the basis of either territory or biological relatedness or occupation." [15] The prevalence of these divisive fundamental attachments sometimes even made Liang question whether China had stayed in the stage of tribal society without developing into a genuine state.

However aware Liang was of the fragmented nature of Chinese society and of the lack of civic solidarity in traditional culture, one does not find in his writings, as was evident in those of later generations of Chinese intelligentsia, a revulsion against the Chinese family system as a barrier to the civic cohesion of Chinese society. This is

13. "Shang-hui i" (On commercial association), in *YPSHC-WC*, ts'e 2, 4:1–7.
14. *Hsin-min shuo*, p. 76.
15. "Kuo-chia ssu-hsiang pien-ch'ien i-t'ung lu" (On the development of ideas on state and their differences and similarities), in *YPSHC-WC*, ts'e 3, 6:17–18.

clear in Liang's attitude toward the core of the traditional family system — the value of filial piety. Instead of repudiating filial piety as a cultural hindrance for developing new political loyalty, Liang tended to take it for granted; indeed, he sometimes seems to have thought that filial piety could serve as a basis for forming new group identifications and political loyalty.[16] But this should not be too surprising if one bears in mind the fact that Liang lived in late Meiji Japan when filial piety was seen as a very useful buttress for nationalism.

Ch'ün, understood as the civic virtue of sharing a sense of solidarity with fellow compatriots, does not in itself indicate the kind of political community to which it refers. One must recall the ambivalent nature of the concept of *ch'ün* in Liang's pre-exile writings where it referred at once to both the national community and the world community. The crucial question to be answered now is: did Liang's concept of *ch'ün* retain that ambivalence or did it become a full-fledged concept of nation-state?

There is no question that when Liang wrote *Hsin-min shuo* in 1902, *ch'ün* already meant for him unequivocally the idea of a nation-state. But the transition from an ambivalent concept of *ch'ün* to the clear and distinct idea of a national community had been a gradual one. For although the idea of the nation-state figured prominently in Liang's writings very soon after his arrival in Japan, he did not immediatly relinquish K'ang Yu-wei's formula of "three ages" and still looked forward to the emergence of a universal moral community in the future Age of Universal Peace.[17] But as early as 1901, Liang had already explicitly criticized the ideal of such a universal community

16. *Hsin-min shuo,* p. 14.
17. *Tzu-yu shu,* p. 8.

as impractical.[18] By the time he wrote the *New Citizen* he vehemently attacked the concept as a hindrance to the development of China as a state. In Liang's view, the ideals of internationalism, great harmony, and universal love, though morally sublime, were antithetical to the value of competitiveness which Liang now learned was so essential to the progress of human society. In this way *t'ien-hsia* was rejected and *kuo-chia* was exalted as the ultimate focus of loyalty. Liang said it would be a sign of barbarism for human loyalty both to stop short of and to go beyond this focus. In this way, the nation-state became for Liang the "terminal community." [19]

Liang's unqualified commitment to the ideal of a nation-state was accompanied and buttressed by a new view of world order dominated by social Darwinism. In general, two levels must be distinguished in considering the traditional Chinese world order as conceived by a Confucian gentry-scholar. On the philosophical level the Chinese view of world order was dominated by a sort of utopian ideal of a universal moral community in which the whole world, as Wang Yang-ming said, exists as one family. But on the political and also popular level, it was dominated by a Sinocentric image in which China was conceived to be the center of the world surrounded by an indeterminate number of satellite states of different rank. Whatever the discrepancy between these two levels, they shared one common element, namely, the ideal of harmony; in the former case, universal harmony, in the latter, hierarchical harmony.

In the course of the nineteenth century, however, the Sinocentric view of world order was gradually destroyed

18. "Nan-hai K'ang-hsien-sheng chuan," pp. 66, 83, 86.
19. *Hsin-min shuo*, pp. 17–22.

by the expansion of Western nations into East Asia. As for the view of universal harmony, since it was ensconced in Confucianism mainly as an ultimate philosophical ideal and hence was necessarily less bound up with political reality than the Sinocentric world order, it remained more or less intact. One of the interesting features of late Ch'ing thought is a discernible tendency on the part of some Chinese scholars to resort to the philosophical view of universal harmony in trying to come to terms with the new world reality created by the Western expansion. In fact, K'ang Yu-wei's ideal of universal harmony and T'an Ssu-t'ung's world view of *jen* were a notable part of this tendency. Thus by the time Liang became an important figure on the intellectual scene in the late nineteenth century, it was not the Sinocentric world view, which had long since been smashed by Western expansion, but the moral view of universal harmony, which had prevented him from accepting the nation-state as the "terminal community."

We have already seen how he gradually came to reject the notion of universal harmony and became committed to the ideal of the nation-state after he went to Japan. But the significance of the formulation of the ideal of the new citizen in 1902 is not confined to the emergence of a full-fledged notion of a nation-state; it also signified a new view of world order which imparted some meaning and coherence to a political reality which the Chinese people had long known but with which they had never come to terms.

This new world order as conceived by Liang was the opposite of the traditional view. To begin with, he envisaged a world composed of a great number of races and nations. Liang noted that the whole of mankind was divided into five races of different colors, namely, the black, the red, the brown, the yellow, and the white. In the course of human history, these races naturally developed in contact with each other. But instead of living together in harmony, they had continuously engaged in fierce struggles for racial survival.[20] For Liang these intergroup struggles were nothing to be condemned; they were inexorable facts of human history dictated by the natural condition of the world. The result of these struggles was that human races could be divided into two principal varieties: namely, what he called the historical races (*yu li-shih ti jen-chung*) and the unhistorical races (*fei li-shih ti jen-chung*). The former category referred to those races that formed cohesive groups and hence developed capacities to play an important role in human history, the latter to those who did not form cohesive groups and who were often subjugated by others. Among the human races, only the white and yellow could be called historical, while all the rest belonged to the category of unhistorical.[21]

The historical races, Liang then emphasized, could be further divided into two categories: namely, the world-historical (*yu shih-chieh-shih ti*) and the non-world-historical (*fei shih-chieh-shih ti*). The former designation referred to the races who had the capacity to expand outside the territory of their origin and to have a world-wide impact by promoting human progress; the latter obviously referred to those who could not play such a role in human history. Measured by this standard, it was the white people who alone deserved the name of world-historical. But Liang quickly noted that not all white people deserved the designation; for the white people consisted of three sub-races: the Hamitic, the Semitic, and the Aryan.[22]

20. "Hsin shih-hsüeh" (New historiography), in *YPSHC-WC,* ts'e 4, 9:11–12.
21. Ibid.
22. Ibid., pp. 15–16.

While Liang admitted that the Hamitic and Semitic people had contributed to ancient European civilization, modern European civilization was, in his view, the sole creation of the Aryans. Historically the Aryans had been comprised of four peoples: Latins, Celts, Teutons, and Slavs, and Liang saw modern European history as dominated by rivalries among these four peoples. Out of their intense struggles it was the Teutons, especially the Germans and the Anglo-Saxons, who had emerged as the most powerful peoples in recent European history. Judging from the trend of world politics around the turn of the twentieth century, Liang made the further observation that the strongest power was doubtless the Anglo-Saxon people.[23] Look at the map of the world today, he said, and you will find that Anglo-Saxon people have occupied more than one fourth of the total land of the earth, that they have ruled over more than one fourth of the total world population, that their spheres of influence are daily expanding, and furthermore, that English has become the most widely used language in the world.[24] Thus Liang concluded: "In view of these facts, we should know who is the best nation in the world. Compare the five races of different colors and there is no question that the white race is the best. Compare the different peoples within the white race and there is no question that the Teutons are the best. Compare the different nations that are composed of Teutonic peoples and there is no question that the Anglo-Saxon is the best. This is no snobbish nonsense. It results from the inescapable working of the law of natural evolution." [25] In contrast to the traditional image of world order, Liang's image was that of a world in which inter-

23. Ibid., pp. 14, 17–20; *Hsin-min shuo*, pp. 7–11, 7, 11.
24. *Hsin-min shuo*, pp. 8–9.
25. Ibid.

group conflicts were inherent and resulted in a tendency toward domination by the Teutonic nations.

Liang then considered how those Anglo-Saxon and Germanic nations became so strong that they could dominate the world. Unquestionably the emergence of nationalism in modern Europe was an important factor. But more relevant to the shaping of the present world order was the transformation of nationalism into what Liang called national imperialism (*min-tsu ti-kuo chu-i*), which took place in the late nineteenth century.[26] Although the encroachment of foreign powers on China had been his primary concern, Liang had not dealt with the problem of imperialism in more than a superficial way until he went into exile in Japan. In 1899, he wrote a long essay titled "A Note of Warning on Dismemberment." [27] In this essay, although he did not employ the term "imperialism," his analysis and the distinction he made between what he called "visible dismemberment" and "invisible dismemberment," implied a rather sophisticated understanding of modern imperialism. By "visible dismemberment" Liang meant territorial conquest; by "invisible dismemberment" he meant cession of rights, especially economic rights such as those for railway buildings, internal navigation, and so forth. "Invisible dismemberment," which in Liang's view was more disastrous in its consequences than visible dismemberment, clearly implied economic imperialism.[28]

The idea of economic imperialism became increasingly prominent in the writings he published in the next few years. A careful examination of the foreign policies of

26. *Hsin-min shuo*, pp. 3–4; "Lun min-tsu ching-cheng chih ta-shih" (On the general trend of national competition), in *YPSHC-WC*, ts'e 4, 10:10–11.

27. "Kua-fen wei-yen" (A note of warning on dismemberment), in *YPSHC-WC*, ts'e 2, 4:19–43.

28. Ibid., pp. 30–33, 36–37.

Western industrial powers in the nineteenth century convinced Liang more and more that modern imperialism was
primarily economic in nature. The impetus to tremendous
Western expansion across the world, he observed, stemmed
basically from the phenomenal economic development that
had taken place in the West since the eighteenth century.
Such phenomenal industrial and commercial growth resulted in economic overproduction in the West which had
to find an outlet in new markets outside Europe. The
European powers in the beginning made North America
and Australia their first outlets, then turned to South
America and Africa as the main targets for economic
expansion. As these outlets dwindled, the center for Western economic encroachment and imperialist struggles gradually switched to Asia. Liang knew well enough that Asia
had long been subjected to Western economic exploitation
and colonial expansion. But in the first stage India had
been the central target. Now in the second stage, as Liang
observed with utmost apprehension, imperialistic expan-
sionism seemed directed toward China.[29] Although imperialism appeared in various forms, in Liang's view the
most basic and formidable form was economic. Herein lay
the basic cause of the most dreadful "invisible dismemberment." [30]

Closely related to its economic orientation was the
popular basis of Western imperialism. When a modern
Western state expanded, Liang observed, expansion was
not brought about merely through manipulation on the
part of a ruler or a ruling minority; it was often the result

29. "Lun chin-shih kuo-min ching-cheng chih ta-shih chi Chung-kuo
chih ch'ien-t'u" (On the general trend of competition between the
citizenry of modern nations and China's future), in *YPSHC-WC*, ts'e 2,
4:56–67; see also "Lun min-tsu ching-cheng chih ta-shih," pp. 10–35.
30. Ibid., pp. 26–27.

of the collective effort of the whole citizenry of the nation. It was tied to the political ambition of the ruler as well as the economic interest of the people at large. In other words, Liang looked upon modern imperialistic expansion as an aggregate effect of the growing strength, predominantly economic, of every individual member of the nation.

In this sense, modern imperialism was very different from the imperialism of ancient times.[31] "The present-day international competitions among European and American countries are not like the imperialistic aggrandizements launched by Ch'in Shih-huang-ti or Alexander the Great or Chinggis Khan or Napoleon, who were driven by their ambitions to take great pleasure in military adventures. It is [also] not like [that of] those tyrants of the states in the age of feudal disunity who resorted to military adventures because of personal grudges or interests of the moment. The motivating force [of modern international competition] stems from the citizenry's struggle for survival which is irrepressible according to the laws of natural selection and survival of the fittest. Therefore the current international competitions are not something which only concerns the state, they concern the entire population. In the present-day international struggles in which the whole citizenry participate [and compete] for their very lives and properties, people are united as if they have one mind. The international competitions of the past which were the concerns of the rulers and their ministers would subside after a period. But the current international struggle will last forever because it is constantly a matter of concern for the life and property of the people. How dangerous this is! How will we, who

31. *Hsin-min shuo,* pp. 4–5.

bear the brunt of this international struggle, stave it off?" [32]

There was no other way to thwart this ever-expanding imperialism, Liang said, except to develop Chinese nationalism. Just as the invading Western imperialism was popularly based, so must Chinese nationalism be. Only the collective effort of a whole nation could possibly stem the expansion impelled by the assembled strength of a foreign nation. In order to gather the collective strength of the total national community, its members must be made to see that they had a stake in its existence and growth and hence be willing to participate in its public life. In Liang's view, this popular character of nationalism could be seen most clearly in the concept of citizenry (*kuo-min*), which separated a modern state very sharply from the traditional type of state (*kuo-chia*).[33] As the character *chia* (family) in the term *kuo-chia* suggests, the traditional state was conceived essentially as a family writ large, implying that it was regarded as the private property of one dynastic family. But according to the modern concept of citizenry, the state was strictly the public property of the people who compose the state. "The state is an aggregation of the people as a whole. If it is the people of a state who govern, legislate, and plan for the interest of the whole state and stave off the troubles which might afflict the state, the people then cannot be bullied and the state cannot be overthrown. This means citizenry." [34]

For Liang the very concept of modern citizenry implied popular sovereignty. The citizenry were no longer subjects as they were under a traditional monarchy; they were

32. "Lun chin-shih kuo-min ching-cheng chih ta-shih chi Chung-kuo chih ch'ien-t'u," p. 59.

33. *Hsin-min shuo*, pp. 4–5; "Lun chin-shih kuo-min ching-cheng chih ta-shih chi Chung-kuo chih ch'ien-t'u," pp. 56–57.

34. Ibid., p. 56.

the locus of sovereignty in the state. Unlike the traditional ruler whose mandate to rule was thought to stem from the will of heaven, the ruler of a modern state must derive his authority from the consent of the people.[35] To be sure, as Liang noted, in the modern Western state there was still a distinction between the ruler and the ruled. But the important point was that the people were the ruler and the ruled at the same time. A modern citizen not only had obligations to fulfill vis-à-vis his government, he also had political rights to make his opinions and preferences count in the formation of that government and its policies.[36]

In Liang's mind, popular sovereignty entailed political participation. In contrast to the traditional state where people were passive, the citizenry of a modern state participated actively in political life. Seen in this light, the national community was a community of the will and purpose of its composing members, and the state was no more than an organizational instrument of such a national community. In this manner the idea of the nation-state involved the concept of citizenship, and nationalism became inseparable from democratization.[37] Liang was doubtless influenced by a very popular trend of political thought in late nineteenth-century Europe, which conceived democracy and nationalism as if they were the opposite sides of the same coin. This natural combination was made even more plausible by the fact that England, which had commanded Liang's admiration as the most powerful nation in the world, had combined them in perfect harmony.

In summation, Liang Ch'i-ch'ao's concept of national-

35. "Kuo-chia ssu-hsiang pien-ch'ien i-t'ung lun," pp. 15–18.
36. Ibid., p. 16.
37. *Hsin-min shuo*, pp. 16–23.

ism included the following characteristic features: it was a reaction against a loosely knit and inert society in which people did not have civic sentiment and a corporate feeling of oneness essential to the formation of a unified national community; it meant an unqualified commitment to the nation-state as the terminal political community; it implied the democratization of a nation-state; it originated primarily as a response to foreign imperialism. This anti-imperialistic orientation of Liang's nationalism needs to be emphasized, for it is exactly this feature which, in the long-term historical perspective, put Liang in the mainstream of Chinese nationalism in its incipient stage.

As a clearly conceived ideology and a recognizable political movement Chinese nationalism crystallized only in the late 1890's and the early 1900's.[38] But just at this critical formative stage, it split into two currents. One, represented mainly by Liang, regarded Chinese nationalism as primarily an effort to meet the challenge of foreign imperialism. The other, represented by Sun Yat-sen and his revolutionist group, viewed Chinese nationalism as primarily anti-Manchu in orientation. To be sure, imperialism was also an important theme in the writings of some of the burgeoning revolutionary intelligentsia, for example, Tsou Jung, Ch'en T'ien-hua, and Yang Shou-jen.[39] But these revolutionists began writing about imperialism around 1902 and 1903, at least two or three years later than the first publication of Liang's view of

38. See Paul A. Cohen, "Wang T'ao's Perspective on a Changing World," in Albert Feuerwerker, ed., *Approaches to Modern Chinese History* (Berkeley, 1967), pp. 133–162. See also Cohen, "Wang T'ao and Incipient Chinese Nationalism," *Journal of Asian Studies*, 26.4:559–574 (August 1967).

39. *Hsin-hai ko-ming wu-shih chou-nien chi-nien lun-wen chi* (Peking, 1962), I, 259–277, and II, 375–393. See also Yang Tu-sheng, "Hsin Hu-nan," in *Hsin-hai ko-ming ch'ien shih-nien chien shih-lun hsüan-chi* (Hong Kong, 1962), vol. I, 2:612–648.

imperialism in the *Ch'ing-i pao*. Furthermore, it must be noted that although these new revolutionary intelligentsia had been concerned with the problem of imperialism for a number of years, because of their increasing contact with Sun Yat-sen, which culminated in their cooperation in founding the revolutionary organization, the T'ung-meng hui, in 1905, they tended to shift their attention from anti-imperialism to anti-Manchuism. While Liang, in the period from 1898 to 1903, had sometimes toyed with the idea of anti-Manchuism, it remained a secondary and evanescent theme at best.[40]

Viewed in this historical perspective, there is no question that Liang stood in the mainstream of Chinese nationalism, not only for the obvious reason that the main impetus to the birth and growth of Chinese nationalism after all stemmed from foreign imperialism, but also on the ground that only an anti-imperialist orientation could provide Chinese nationalism with a flexible position to withstand what Clifford Geertz called "integrative revolution," which often accompanied the emergence of nationalism in developing nations.[41] China was a multi-ethnic state; in such a state, nationalism might very likely bring in its wake, as it did later, ethnic separation, which, along with other centrifugal tendencies, fed by various forms of primordial loyalties, was in danger of tearing China apart as a modern state. Anti-Manchuism was certainly a form of this ethnic separatism, which may have served as a politically expedient battle cry for the moment but certainly ran counter to the long-term goal of Chinese nationalism.

40. See Liang's letter of 1902 to K'ang Yu-wei in *LNCC*, I, 157–159.
41. See Clifford Geertz, "The Integrative Revolution," in Clifford Geertz, ed., *Old Societies and New States* (New York, 1963), pp. 105–157. See also Harold Z. Schiffrin, "The Enigma of Sun Yat-sen," pp. 454–457.

Struggle and Progress

The second set of public virtues which Liang recommended as part of his ideal of the new citizen may be regarded as growing out of the ideal of dynamism (*tung*), which was at the center of his personality ideal in the years preceding his exile. Increasing contact with Western thought after his exile to Japan made it possible for him to articulate what was once an amorphous ideal.

Liang's Social Darwinist world view inevitably entailed his acceptance of the idea that struggle was an inexorable fact of nature and human condition. Indeed, it was not only inevitable but also desirable, for, according to Liang, it accounted for the progress of Western nations. By the same token, the root of China's stagnation could also be traced to the comparative lack of struggle and the long-standing tradition of cultural bias against it in her history.[42] Sometimes Liang even went so far as to view the differences between the historical developments of China and the West solely in terms of the concept of struggle. In a comparison of the different historical developments of China and Europe, he maintained that ancient China down through the Chou dynasty ran parallel to the historical development of the West, that is, from the age of kinship and tribalism to the age of feudalism. In the feudal age of the Chou dynasty, China was divided into different states constantly warring and competing with each other. This very fact of competitive struggle among the different states, just as in the West, explained the cultural efflorescence in the late Chou.

42. "Lun Chung-kuo yü Ou-chou kuo-t'i i-t'ung" (On the differences between the form of state of China and those of European countries), in *YPSHC-WC,* ts'e 2, 4:63–65.

At this point the similarities between the historical developments of Europe and China stopped and thereafter each pursued a different historical path. Two differences, in Liang's view, distinguished the post-Roman historical development of Europe from the post-Chou development of China. One difference was that while post-Roman history had been characterized by multi-state competition, post-Chou China had developed into a unified empire. The other difference was that European societies in the post-Roman period had been divided into classes, while the post-Chou society of China had remained a classless one throughout. On the surface, the fact that China had been a unified and classless society seemed to be a blessing for the Chinese people. But in actuality, Liang emphasized, the blessing was a misfortune in disguise. For, as shown clearly in the historical development of European societies both the multi-state situation and societies based on class were conducive to competition which proved to be a powerful catalyst to progress. By the same token, the classless and unified society of China must have stifled competition and hence should be held responsible for her present debility.[43]

Clearly, then, Liang had turned aside from the traditionally prized value of harmony and moderation and had accepted the value of competitiveness. But his acceptance was by no means an unproblematic one. Liang's basic preoccupation was with *ch'ün*, with collective power and group cohesion. Given such a collectivistic preoccupation, what really interested him about Social Darwinism was the world image it projected of human groups locked in a life-and-death struggle for survival; the kind of Social Darwinism which Liang could understand and appreciate was

43. Ibid., pp. 62–67.

not what Hofstadter termed "Darwinian individualism" but what he called "Darwinian collectivism." [44] In Liang's own terms, the kind of competitive struggle which he was ultimately concerned about was what he would call "external competition" (*wai-ching*), which meant international competition, rather than "internal competition" (*nei-ching*), which meant competition within a nation.[45]

To be sure, when Liang was writing the first part of his *New Citizen* the distinction between "internal competition" and "external competition" may not yet have been in the forefront of his mind; Liang seemed to have an unbounded confidence in the concept of competitive struggle as a value of universal validity. But one suspects that at this stage Liang's confidence was based on an unstated assumption that competitive struggle between individuals within a group would strengthen the individual and thus ultimately promote the collective strength of the group. Liang seems to have taken for granted the idea that a group's capacity for engaging in "external competition" somehow depended on the cohesion and strength which grew automatically out of "internal competition." In the end, then, "internal competition" was viewed as no more than an instrument to cope with what he regarded as an ineluctable feature of the external world and human condition. Thus built into Liang's view of competitive struggle was an element of ambiguity which later could cause him to change his evaluation of this concept when he became aware of its possible incompatibility with his central concern, the cohesion and growth of a nation.

Liang's acceptance of the Darwinian value of competitive struggle was inseparable from his faith in another

44. See Richard Hofstadter, *Social Darwinism in American Thought* (Philadelphia, 1945), pp. 174–176.

45. "Erh-shih shih-chi chih chü-ling t'o-la-ssu" (The monster of twentieth-century-trust), in *YPSHC-WC*, ts'e 5, 14:33–35.

modern Western value — progress. In fact in some sense Liang accepted the value of competitive struggle primarily because of his belief that the latter was an important condition for progress. Thus, unlike his acceptance of the value of competitive struggle, which was ambiguous and contingent upon its instrumentality, Liang's commitment to the value of progress was ultimate and unqualified.

His interest in the Western concept of progress must be traced to the years prior to his exile. During that period progress had already become a captivating ideal for him, mainly through the influence of K'ang Yu-wei and Yen Fu. Indeed, in the form of K'ang Yu-wei's formula of "three ages," it had become an important basis of Liang's reformist ideology. After he went to Japan, as a result of contact with Western thought the cryptic formula of "three ages" gradually lost its hold on him. The idea of progressive change, however, remained dominant in his mind. He replaced the New Text School's idea of progress with a view of history based on the modern secular idea of evolution, noting that there were two kinds of change in the world, namely cyclical and evolutionary.[46]

Evolutionary change meant an unending and uninterrupted progress in a definite direction; it was, however, confined to the human and organic world whereas cyclical change applied to the rest of the kingdom of nature. This kind of evolutionary change Liang also called historical change. But historical change, Liang noted, was not necessarily linear. Rather it was primarily a spiral change; for historical change often took the form of one long step forward followed by a short step backward; the main direction of change was still toward progress. Without this distinction one might mistakenly identify spiral change

46. "Hsin shih-hsüeh," pp. 7–8.

with cyclical change.[47] Mencius had remarked that human history was no more than a series of recurrences of order and disorder. "This remark of Mencius," Liang explained, "is due to his misleading reading of spiral change as circular in form. He had not taken a broad look at the general trend of human history in the previous thousand years and discerned its real direction. He only saw the progression and retrogression, the ebb and flow which took place in a short period and mistook them as the reality of history." [48]

The basic reference point for the concept of human progress, Liang noted, was always the group rather than the individual. In terms of native ability and intelligence an individual modern man was not necessarily superior to an individual ancient man. It was modern society which was definitely an improvement over ancient society. As far as biological evolution was concerned, man was the terminal point for animal evolution and the adult was the terminal point as far as the biological growth of the human individual was concerned. Any further evolution that human beings made had then to take place on the group level. Therefore, for Liang the dominant fact about human beings, as evidenced in the experience of human history, was their capacity for social evolution.[49]

To drive home the collectivistic point of reference for the concept of progress Liang very soon became fascinated by the thought of a Social Darwinist thinker, Benjamin Kidd, whose ideas became popular in the Anglo-Saxon intellectual world for a time around the turn of the twentieth century.[50] Liang seemed to find in Kidd's social

47. Ibid.
48. Ibid., p. 8.
49. Ibid., p. 9.
50. "Chin-hua-lun ko-ming-che Hsieh-te chih hsüeh-shuo" (The theory of Benjamin Kidd who made a revolutionary change of the evolutionary

thought an effective antidote to the widely promoted individualistic interpretation of the Darwinian ideas of adaptation and struggle. To begin with, Liang noted, Kidd denounced the natural disposition of human beings to pursue their individual interest as "egoistic," "anti-social," and "anti-evolutionary." [51] The purpose of a living organism's struggle should not be its self-interest but mainly to secure collective survival for its species in the future. As Liang understood it, Kidd's idea of social progress meant essentially that "the individual must be sacrificed for the society and the present must be sacrificed for the future." [52] By way of Kidd's social doctrine, Liang arrived at a radically collectivistic notion of social progress.

Given such a cult of social progress every means should be found to curb the natural disposition to pursue one's own interest. Liang took great interest in Kidd's suggestion that religion was very useful in combatting man's inveterate addiction to self-interest and thus in promoting social progress, since religion always enjoined men to sacrifice the individual's present interest and to look forward to the larger collective interest in the future.[53] But what most fascinated Liang was Kidd's collectivistic and utilitarian concept of death. Liang noted that death was a universal problem that was most puzzling and frightening to every human being. However outstanding and heroic a person was, his attitudes could hardly be unaffected by his view of the meaning of death. Thus the meaning people attached to death inevitably had great bearing on society. With such social significance, the meaning of death becomes a focal problem for all the

theories), in *YPSHC-WC*, ts'e 5, 12:80. For a summary of Kidd's social thought see Richard Hofstadter, pp. 98–101.

51. "Chin-hua-lun ko-ming-che Hsieh-te," pp. 79–80.
52. Ibid., pp. 79–81.
53. Ibid., p. 80.

major religions in the world. But the trouble with the notions of death in various world religions, according to Kidd, was that they all tended to see the meaning of death from an other-worldly viewpoint. Kidd approached the meaning of death in a scientific way and discussed it from a this-worldly point of view. For this reason, Liang believed that Kidd made a great intellectual contribution, where most world religions failed, by discovering the functional value of death in relation to social progress.[54]

Death, Liang noted, had invariably been viewed with terror and anguish everywhere. But what was often overlooked was the positive meaning which Kidd discovered in the phenomenon of death: death was an indispensable condition for social progress. The reasons are typically Darwinian. When the external environment was in the process of drastic changes, society needed frequent adaptations in order to meet external change. Death had the function of increasing and accelerating change by cutting short old lives and thus yielding room for new generations. This change of generations enabled people to take on new habits and characters which were more adapted to the changing environment and would contribute to social evolution. If it were not for death effecting a change of generation, old attitudes and habits would tend to persist and slow changes would result. For the human species this would mean a lack of adaptability to the environment and failure in the struggle for survival.[55]

This view of death from the standpoint of social evolution seemed to be reinforced by an observation Kidd made of lower species: the continuous existence of these species as a whole involved no individual deaths. The simpler organisms, he noted, were a mere assemblage of single

54. Ibid., pp. 82–83.
55. Ibid., p. 81.

cells. They reproduced themselves by splitting and multiplying these cells. In this way an infinite number of new cells might be reproduced from the original cells while these original cells need not die away. Hence these lower organisms may be regarded as having "infinite life." In contrast, organisms high on the evolutionary scale had finite life in the sense that they had a limited life expectancy. In other words, an individual organism of a higher species might very well live for a shorter time than an individual member of the lower species. But the higher species might last longer by means of evolution.[56]

Among those higher species whose individual members had finite life, competition inevitably developed. Victory would go to those who had faster changes of generation and consequently more adaptability to the environment. Noting this observation by Kidd, Liang could not help but sing praises to death: "So death is the mother of progress and a great event in human life. By virtue of death everyone can make himself profitable to his race, by virtue of death the existing race can make itself profitable to the future race. How great is the use of death!" [57]

Underlying this notion of death was not only a radical collectivism but also what Liang called futurism (*wei-lai chu-i*).[58] Kidd emphasized that it was not just the collective interest of the species as a whole that mattered; what really mattered was the collective interest of the future. Indeed the orientation to the future was one outstanding characteristic which distinguished the higher from the lower species. As an illustration of this observation, Liang pointed to the fact that the higher species, notably human beings, in general devoted a much greater amount of time

56. Ibid., pp. 81–82.
57. Ibid., p. 82.
58. Ibid., p. 85.

and effort to rearing their offspring than did the lower species. As a corollary of this and other examples, Liang concluded that the harder a species worked for the future, the higher its position on the evolutionary scale. Similarly, the harder a human group worked for the future, the higher its position was.[59]

Through this sort of collectivistic futurism found in Kidd's thought Liang finally arrived at an intellectual stance which was sharply critical of liberal democratism in the West. According to Kidd, the dominant trend of modern Western thought was "populism" (*p'ing-min chu-i*), the essence of which was no more than the idea that government is set up to serve the people. But regrettably this "populism" tended to be exclusively oriented to the people's interest in the present, to the neglect of the future. This lack of orientation toward the future seemed to be especially prominent in classical British liberalism, which was based on the moral theory of utilitarianism. British liberalism may then be regarded as an extreme development of the "ideology of the present" (*hsien-tsai chu-i*).[60] It is interesting that for this "ideology of the present" Liang singled out as the principal representatives not only John Stuart Mill but also Herbert Spencer. Spencer, Liang conceded, developed a doctrine of social evolution, but because he paid too much attention to the present to grasp the important truth that the present was bound to pass away and what counted was always the future, his thought could not be called genuine futurism. Implicit in this criticism of Herbert Spencer was a repudiation of what Hofstadter called "Darwinian individualism." [61]

According to Kidd, the "ideology of the present" sat-

59. Ibid., p. 84.
60. Ibid., pp. 84–85.
61. Ibid., p. 85; Richard Hofstadter, pp. 174–176.

urated English liberal thought as well as German thought in the late nineteenth century. The dominant intellectual trends at that time in Germany were Marxian socialism and Nietzschean individualism. Although both were intellectually respectable doctrines, they were too much oriented to the present and lacked a sense of the future. Kidd concluded, in Liang's words, "The nineteenth century is the age of populism and the age of ideology of the present. However, since the doctrine of biological evolution has daily developed, the intellectual world is bound to undergo a change. The ridiculousness of such ideals is of course patent. In essence, they did not grasp the important truth that the present is actually the price of the future. If there is only the present, then there is not the slightest meaning and value. Only for the future does the present take on meaning and value." [62] Behind such an impassioned and unmitigated commitment to futurism undoubtedly lay a deification of social progress.

Activism and Voluntarism

Another outgrowth of Liang's previous concern with dynamism is found in the ideal of activism which he recommended as an essential virtue of the new citizen. Implied in the ideal of activism was another ideal, that of voluntarism. This ideal was epitomized in the concept of effort (*li*), which Liang regarded as the antithesis of fatalism (*ming*).[63] Although the opposition of *li* and *ming* did not receive elaborate formulation until a few years later, it lay at the core of Liang's ideal of activism and ran through much of his writing on the ideal of the new citizen.[64] For an understanding of Liang's ideal of activism

62. Ibid., pp. 85–86.
63. See the poem Liang composed in 1901, *LNCC,* I, 147.
64. Liang later elaborated his idea of effort versus fatalism first in his

it is necessary first to elucidate his voluntarism as embodied in his contrast of effort and fate.

Liang's fervent advocacy of voluntarism stemmed basically from his observation that fatalism was endemic in
traditional Chinese consciousness. The main source of this
fatalism was, in his view, Taoism, which he had already
excoriated in his pre-exile writings as characterized by
passivity and resignation.[65] But this life view, Liang now
stressed, was also shared by Confucianism in its later vul-
garized form, even though he still believed that Confucianism in its pristine form encouraged a philosophy of
activism. Underlying this corrupted view was a deep-seated
belief in fatalism, the basis of which could be found in
Confucius' idea of fate. Of course, Liang admitted, in
Confucianism there was no unified and definite interpretation of the broad idea of fate. Some Confucians had a
qualified belief in fate in the sense that man need only
do his best while letting fate work out the consequences.
Other Confucians were disposed to an unqualified belief
in fate in the sense that man should do nothing and give
himself up completely to the mercy of fate. But it was
apparent that both shared a belief that the ultimate outcome of human events was determined by fate. The woeful
consequence was that fatalism had long saturated the
Chinese national consciousness and created in the Chinese
people an indifference to the fortune of their country.[66]

Of course Liang also knew that the Buddhist concept
of karma, at least on the popular level, had been interpreted by many to mean fatalism. But Liang saw this

---

philosophy of Mo-tzu, which he published in 1904, and in a long article
published in 1910. See *LNCC*, I, 201; and "Kuo-chia yün-ming lun" (On
the national fate), in *YPSHC-WC*, ts'e 8, 22:94–103.

65. *Hsin-min shuo*, p. 29.

66. Ibid., p. 29; see also *Tzu-Mo-tzu hsüeh-shuo* (Mo-tzu's doctrines),
in *YPSHC-CC*, ts'e 10, 37:12–14.

fatalistic interpretation of karma as a gross misunderstanding of Buddhism. Karma, according to a strictly Buddhist interpretation, in fact had connotations that ran counter to the concept of fatalism.[67]

To be sure, Liang did not deny that the notion of karma was predicated on a law of causal determinism. But this law involved no belief in fatalism. Stated simply, the law of karma meant that moral thinking and good deeds resulted in good character but that immoral thinking and evil deeds resulted in bad character. By cultivating bad character one would remain hopelessly tied to the "wheel of life," full of sorrow and suffering; by cultivating good character one was working toward his ultimate release from that woeful wheel.[68]

Stated in this way the law of karma clearly implied that every man was the sole molder of his life and master of his destiny. One's present life conditions were completely determined by his past deeds and thoughts; one's present actions and thoughts were the complete causes of his life conditions in the future. Thus for Liang the law of karma was the very antithesis of fatalism; its causal determinism paradoxically could serve as the very basis of a voluntaristic life view. As Liang said, "Buddhism teaches belief in effort without fate; even if it says there is fate, the fate is purely something which can be shaped and swayed by the human effort itself." [69]

Like the Buddhist notion of karma the Darwinian concepts of natural selection and survival of the fittest might also be interpreted to mean a kind of determinism that would lend support to the traditional idea of fate. Since these concepts now constituted for him a sort of basic

67. Ibid., p. 17.
68. Ibid.
69. Ibid., p. 17; see also "Kuo-chia yün-ming lun," pp. 97–98.

frame of reference for understanding the external world and human life, it was very important for Liang's assertion of the potency of human effort to purge these Darwinian concepts of any implications of fatalism. However powerful the concept of nature was as a governing agent for the evolution of the world in the Darwinian framework, living creatures were not viewed as completely passive. It was still within the power of these creatures to become adapted to the conditions of nature and to live on in this world. Modern works on natural evolution, Liang noted, could provide many examples of survival through successful adaptation and extinction through failure to adapt. For Liang Darwinism could not simply be identified with naturalistic determinism.[70]

Darwinism, Liang further argued, might mean naturalistic determinism for sub-human living creatures, but certainly not for human beings. Human beings were distinguished by their unique endowment of a spiritual mind. Fate might govern the rest of nature but had no control over men, the spiritual being whose autonomy brooked no interference from outside. Hence Liang argued: "I think that effort is opposed to fate. Wherever effort can be applied, there is no room for the existence of fate. Fate is something which can only lurk in places left outside the dominance of effort. Therefore fatalism can apply to the natural world but not to spiritual beings . . . Therefore the term fate is decidedly not what we as human beings are supposed to use."[71]

Of course, Liang admitted, one might still argue for the dominance of fate in the human world by pointing to innumerable instances where rewards do not correspond to effort. But, he warned, the apparent disparity between

70. *Tzu-Mo-tzu hsüeh-shuo*, pp. 14–15.
71. Ibid., p. 15.

effort and reward in individual cases should not be too readily ascribed to interference by fate. For if we broaden our perspective and look at society as a whole, we may find that the incongruity between effort and reward is very likely at bottom a consequence of the inadequate collective effort of the total society. For example, the premature death of Yen Hui, who was traditionally deemed a moral paragon and Confucius' favorite disciple, was often adduced as a classical illustration of the disparity between effort and reward as a result of the blind dictates of fate. But, Liang argued, Yen Hui's premature death may very well also be ascribed to the lack of medical facilities and inadequate knowledge of the means of preserving health. In other words, in a society where medical facilities and health services were well developed through human effort, Yen Hui's premature death could perhaps have been prevented. A look at the increase in life expectation in modern European history certainly pointed to such a possibility. In seventeenth-century Europe, Liang noted, the average life expectancy was thirteen years; in eighteenth-century Europe it increased to twenty. "It is then obvious that long life and premature death are doubtless not controlled by fate but by human effort. As for poverty or wealth and the high or low status [of individual persons], whether they are fair or unfair, hinges upon whether the collective effort of the total society is applied appropriately or inappropriately." [72]

In short, in Liang's view the incongruity between human effort and social reward was more often than not the consequence of inappropriate institutional arrangements, which were after all created by men and hence could be changed by human effort. But unfortunately these man-made institutional arrangements were often looked upon

72. Ibid., pp. 15–16.

as the inexorable dictates of fate and hence were unalterable by human effort. In a society, for instance, men who were born in a certain caste generally tended to think that their status was predetermined by fate. It was, however, conceivable that through human effort the caste system could be abolished. Look at the Western experience, Liang said. In the Anglo-Saxon aristocratic society of several centuries ago, a man of humble origin could hardly aspire to become a prime minister as Disraeli did in nineteenth-century England, or to become president as Lincoln did in nineteenth-century America. For Liang, then, the Western historical experience clearly bore out his belief that human effort could prevail over fate.[73]

So far, one vital question has been left unanswered: if Liang had such confidence in the triumph of human effort over fate, what did he really mean by the concept of effort? As Liang himself admitted, there was no lack of belief in the potency of human effort in Chinese cultural tradition. Especially in what he called genuine Confucianism, which essentially enjoined an attitude of involvement in the world, the belief in the efficacy of effort is in fact prominent. Thus in pitting effort against fate Liang might very well have been thinking of the Confucian tradition.[74] But in this connection the fact that he drew mainly upon Western experiences to illustrate his belief in the power of human effort is significant, for it suggests that Liang's faith in human effort was primarily Western-inspired. This suggestion is amply borne out by an investigation of his two concepts, namely, perseverance (*i-li*) and what he called the adventurous and enterprising spirit (*mao-hsien chin-ch'ü chih ching-shen*), which he recom-

73. Ibid., pp. 16–17.
74. For a critical discussion of the development of the idea of *ming* in traditional Chinese thought, see T'ang Chün-i, *Chung-kuo che-hsüeh yüan-lun* (Hong Kong, 1966), pp. 500–612.

mended as essential attributes of the new citizen he envisaged. On close analysis both concepts reveal a concept of effort which is much closer to the modern Western notion of "rational mastery over the world" than to the Confucian ideal of "rational adjustment to the world." [75]

In Confucian moral thought, which put a high premium on character discipline, perseverance was doubtless a prominent virtue. However, it must be noted that in the framework of Confucianism the virtue of perseverance refers more to a sustained effort to improve moral character for the purpose of realizing Confucian moral ideals than to an unremitting effort to master the outside world for the sake of attaining practical goals. In other words, the Confucian virtue of perseverance means primarily a determined effort to fulfill an inner moral imperative. But what Liang called perseverance referred primarily to a determined will and relentless effort to conquer the outside world and attain the envisioned goal. Implicit in this effort is often an exuberant confidence in the eventual mastery of the world by human effort. This is evident in the following observation Liang made about the need for and efficacy of perseverance. "Human effort has been constantly battling against the course of nature, engaged in a process of struggle. The course of nature has often been at odds with the expectations of human beings. So its resistance to human effort is very great and intense. However, the admirable tendency of human beings to progress will never rest content with the status quo. So the whole life of a man is just like sailing against the currents in a river for several decades without being able to rest for one day. This is not just the situation with one person. The whole nation and even the whole world are all daily plodding on in this way . . . In this world throughout history

75. *Hsin-min shuo,* pp. 23–31, 96–104.

there has been a tremendous variety of cases of success or failure. However, the reason for these cases of success or failure can be summed up in the proposition that those who have perseverance succeed and those who do not fail." [76]

This confidence in the capacity of determined and sustained effort to overcome environmental difficulties and attain goals is also reflected in the kind of Western historical figures whom Liang regarded as models of the virtue of perseverance: Moses, who underwent countless hardships and reverses with unbelievable fortitude and finally brought the Israelites out of slavery in Egypt and back to the Promised Land; Christopher Columbus, who pursued his life-long goal of overseas exploration with indefatigable spirit; inventors who tried with immense patience to achieve scientific innovations and entrepreneurs who persevered in undertaking risky business endeavors; statesmen, like Disraeli and Garibaldi, who struggled for their political ideals with unrelenting drive. [77] The glowing terms and the exciting tone with which Liang depicted these historical figures and their exploits clearly conveyed his deeply felt belief: with sustained effort, any difficulty can be overcome and anything can be done.

This persevering effort to conquer and accomplish, Liang further pointed out, was not just characteristic of Western individuals; it also distinguished some Western nations. He pointed to England and Russia as examples of the minority of nations who were capable of persevering effort for national expansion. But unfortunately China did not belong to this minority. On the whole, the single-minded, unremitting perseverance required for great

76. Ibid., p. 96.
77. Ibid., pp. 97–101.

achievement seemed to be particularly wanting in the Chinese national character.[78]

An even more striking characteristic of modern European people, Liang discovered, was what he called "the enterprising and adventurous spirit." In his view, there was no more important value than this spirit for the Chinese people to learn from modern Western civilization. "There is more than one factor which explains the superior strength of European nations in comparison with Chinese people. However, almost the most important among these factors is the resourcefulness of European people in their enterprising and adventurous spirit."[79] Liang seems to have felt that this spirit was the motivational well-spring of modern European dynamism, however diverse the forms it might take.[80] In short, modern European history seemed to be crowded with enterprising and adventurous souls; and this momentous fact more than anything else explained the tremendous European expansion in the modern world. "Today the Aryan people have planted colonies everywhere on the earth and become the masters of the whole world. How do they achieve this? The answer is that they have an adventurous and enterprising spirit." [81]

The passion with which Liang described the prevalence of this adventurous and enterprising spirit made his commitment to the modern Western value of mastery over the world beyond doubt. Liang believed it would be possible to identify the four components which made up this vital spirit even thought it was difficult to find a single Chinese

78. Ibid., pp. 99–103.
79. Ibid., p. 23.
80. Ibid., pp. 23–25.
81. *Chang Po-wang Pan Ting-yüan ho-chuan* (A joint biography of Chang Ch'ien and Pan Ch'ao), in *YPSHC-CC,* ts'e 3, 5:15.

185

concept as its equivalent. The first, Liang noted, was hope. Human beings lived in two realms: the realm of action and the realm of the ideal, or the realm of the present and the realm of the future. A spiritual striving for the realization of an ideal in the future meant hope, which, he emphasized, lay at the basis of the progress of civilization. "The reason for the existence of human beings and the emergence of human civilization is nothing but the sense of the future." [82] Futurism was an indispensable component of the adventurous and enterprising spirit.

The second component was zeal. Human beings have an immense and flexible capacity for achievement and this capacity is proportional to the zeal they have. A single-minded person with zeal could frequently generate an amount of capacity one would not expect to find under normal circumstances. This zeal was best exemplified in the fervor with which the Protestants fought the Catholic Church in the sixteenth and seventeenth centuries; in the popular enthusiasm for the nationalist and democratic revolutions which swept Europe in the nineteenth century; also in the romantic love between man and woman who would sacrifice everything, even their lives, to defy interference from families and public opinion. Such single-minded and burning zeal, once aroused, could drive men to work wonders.[83]

But one must not simply identify the adventurous and enterprising spirit with mere fond hope or blind emotional drive, for Liang hastened to add that the third component of the adventurous and enterprising spirit was what he called wisdom. He meant that hope and zeal cannot stand alone but must be guided by wisdom or intellectual vision. Without the guidance of wisdom one

82. *Hsin-min shuo*, pp. 25–26.
83. Ibid., pp. 26–27.

would become enslaved by religious leaders, ancient sages, customs, power, and authority, and even one's own whims and desires. Under so many intellectual shackles, how could one develop an adventurous and enterprising spirit?[84]

Finally we come to the last component of the adventurous spirit, namely, courage. Liang explained the nature of courage by recounting an anecdote about the famous English admiral, Nelson. He once went to wander alone in the mountains when he was five years old. During his wanderings, a storm broke out, and when night fell he did not return home. Thereupon his family sent people to look for him. They finally found him sitting alone in a shanty on the top of a mountain. Later his grandmother scolded him for his eccentric behavior and asked him why even such a terrifying phenomenon as the storm could not make him go home, Nelson answered: "Fear? I never saw fear, I do not know what it is!" For Liang another vivid illustration of the quality of courage was Napoleon's remark that the word "difficulty" can only be found in a fool's dictionary and the French people have no use for the word "unable." In Liang's view, these men should serve as paragons of courage for the new citizen of China.[85]

Hope, zeal, wisdom, and courage formed the vital components of Western cultural dynamism. Eventually Liang found no better way to sum up the whole complex of qualities than to quote a popular Western song:[86]

> Never look behind, boys,
> When you're on the way;
> Time enough for that, boys,
> On some future day.

84. Ibid., pp. 27–28.
85. Ibid., pp. 28–29.
86. Ibid., pp. 29–31.

Though the way be long, boys,
    Face it with a will;
Never stop to look behind,
    When climbing up a hill.

First be sure you're right, boys,
    Then with courage strong,
Strap your pack upon your back;
    And tramp, tramp along.

When you're near the top, boys,
    Of the rugged way,
Do not think your work is done,
    But climb, climb away.

Success is at the top, boys,
    Waiting there until,
Patient, plodding, plucky boys,
    Have mounted up the hill.

It is significant that in trying to sum up the adventurous spirit Liang had to point to historical figures in the West and even to quote a Western song. Liang had difficulty in describing this spirit in Chinese terms. It is interesting that the only concept in the Chinese cultural tradition which Liang found equivalent to the adventurous spirit was the Mencian concept of "great morale" (*hao-jan chih-ch'i*). The latter concept in the context of Mencian thought was meant to refer to an irrepressible courage which stemmed basically from one's moral confidence. Specifically, the distinctive characteristic of this Mencian concept was its moral orientation.

The adventurous spirit, on the other hand, had a motivational source in what was often called Faustian-Prometheanism. As such, it was a quality, raw, compelling, powerful, but not necessarily moral; in fact, it was more often than not morally neutral and, as amply shown in modern European history, could be harnessed for a variety of purposes. In equating the Mencian great morale with the adventurous spirit, Liang obviously left out the distinctively moral quality of that original Mencian concept. To begin with, one finds the moral reference conspicuously lacking in the four components which Liang claimed made up the adventurous spirit. Furthermore, the kind of courage he saw in the personalities of Nelson and Napoleon and which he emphasized as essential ingredients of such a spirit was exactly that raw courage criticized in the *Mencius* as lacking in moral direction and hence to be distinguished from the moral courage which was believed to lie at the core of the Mencian great morale.[87] Liang's disregard of the moral orientation of the original Mencian concept, whether conscious or unconscious, may thus be seen as a subtle yet unmistakable indication of the increasing erosion of Confucian moralism due to the penetration of Western cultural dynamism ever since the late nineteenth century.

Rights and Liberties

Liang had already accepted and become committed to such Western democratic ideals as popular rights (*min-ch'üan*), popular sovereignty (*min-chu*), and legislative assembly (*i-yüan*) in his pre-exile years. A critical distinction must be made between the concept of democracy and that of liberalism. The acceptance of democracy does not necessarily mean commitment to liberalism. For one may espouse democracy from a collectivistic standpoint as many

87. Ibid., p. 25. For an understanding of the difference between the morally directed courage prized in Chinese cultural tradition and Western courage as part of the syndrome of Faustian-Prometheanism, see Hsü Fu-kuan, "Meng-tzu chih-yen yang-ch'i chang shih-shih" (A tentative interpretation of Mencius' concept of *chih-yen* and *yang-ch'i*), in Hsü Fu-kuan, *Chung-kuo ssu-hsiang-shih lun-chi*, pp. 142–154.

did, whereas the core of Western liberalism first and foremost consists in a commitment to individualism and to its institutional embodiment, civil rights and liberties.[88] We have then to pose the question: did Liang's advocacy of democratic ideals also mean his commitment to Western liberalism?

On the surface the answer seems to be affirmative. Almost from the very beginning his writings of the exile years were replete with such liberal concepts as *ch'üan-li* (rights) and *tzu-yu* (liberties). In fact, these liberal concepts occupied an important place among the public virtues which he recommended in his *New Citizen*.[89] In introducing these liberal values, Liang, however, ventured into a realm where he was ill-equipped to chart a clear and precise course for his readers. In the first place, because these liberal values were lacking in Chinese cultural tradition there was little in his intellectual background to prepare him for an adequate understanding of them. Furthermore, there is the even more important fact that when Liang recommended these liberal values as a part of the public virtues his central preoccupation was with the collectivistic concept of *ch'ün,* which would almost inevitably have prevented him from seeing certain essential dimensions of these liberal values. Thus it is little wonder that in the *New Citizen* he eventually formulated ideals which, in the last analysis, one would hesitate to call liberal.

Liang's exile in Japan almost immediately exposed him to a flood of literature on Western liberal ideals. Typically, Liang's initial responses were very enthusiastic but added up to an eclecticism which a more consistent intellectual stance would not have allowed. It is interesting

88. J. L. Talmon, *The Origins of Totalitarian Democracy* (London, 1955), pp. 1–3; see also Guido De Ruggiero, *The History of European Liberalism* (Boston, 1959), pp. 50–66, 370–380.

89. *Tzu-yu shu,* pp. 21–24, 40–41.

that in discussing liberal ideals he drew upon the writings of John Stuart Mill and Rousseau without being aware of the significant differences which separate the English and French concepts of liberty.[90] Furthermore, there is the inexplicable fact that his tendency to a Social Darwinist world view did not prevent him from a profession of admiration for the classical liberal doctrines of natural rights and social contract which in theory could not fit into a Darwinian framework.[91]

Liang had already come to a vague appreciation of English liberalism when in 1899, inspired by John Stuart Mill's thought on liberty, he named a collection of his notes *The Book on Liberty (Tzu-yu shu)*.[92] But he did not state his position clearly until 1902 in his famous essay, "On the Relationship between Government and People" ("Lun cheng-fu yü jen-min chih ch'üan-hsien"), where he accepted the classical liberal concept of government as a night watchman. Yet strangely enough in the same essay he also upheld the collectivistic notion that over and above government and the people there exists the state, which must be regarded as having an independent personality of its own and as the locus of the highest sovereignty of the country.[93] This simultaneous acceptance of the night watchman theory of government and the theory of an independent state meant that Liang never grasped clearly the core of British liberalism — guarantism, that is, that

90. "Lu-so hsüeh-an" (A study of Jean Jacques Rousseau's thought), in *YPSHC-WC*, ts'e 3, 6:97–110; "Lun cheng-fu yü jen-min chih ch'üan-hsien" (On the limitations of government's authority with regard to people), in *YPSHC-WC*, ts'e 4, 10:3–4. For the distinction between the French and the English conceptions of liberty, see F. A. Hayek, *The Constitution of Liberty* (Chicago, 1960), pp. 54–70.

91. "Kuo-chia ssu-hsiang pien-ch'ien i-t'ung lun," p. 19; see also *Tzu-yu shu*, pp. 12–13; "Lu-so hsüeh-an," pp. 97–110.

92. *Tzu-yu shu*, p. 1.

93. "Lun cheng-fu yü jen-min chih ch'üan-hsien," p. 1.

a state is established first of all for the protection of civil liberties and the rights of the individual citizen.

At this time the most eloquent exponent of Western liberalism in Liang's mind was doubtless Rousseau, whose concepts of popular sovereignty, social contract, and general will often cropped up in his writings during the first few years of his exile.[94] Unlike Sun Yat-sen, who often found in Rousseau's thought a justification for the exaltation of the state, Liang regarded Rousseau's democratic doctrines as the most effective antidote not only to traditional despotism but also to the slavish mentality of the Chinese people. That Rousseau's thought appealed to Liang was quite understandable in view of the latter's intellectual mood at that time. For what then dominated his thought was the mindlessness and abysmal lethargy of the Chinese people revealed in the disastrous failure of the reform movement in 1898. In Rousseau's thrilling doctrines Liang seemed to find some kind of spiritual medicine which could help the Chinese people shake off the incubus of a servile character and rejuvenate themselves.

In a letter written to K'ang Yu-wei in 1900, Liang urged him to recognize the need of the Chinese national character for Rousseau's ideal of liberty. "Today we see the catastrophic culmination of the corruption and degeneration that have afflicted China in the past few thousand years. The prime source of this corruption and decay must be traced to the slavish character [of the Chinese people]. And this so-called liberty is what is needed to make people conscious of their own character and thus to enable them to shake free from control by others. This illness [of slavishness] cannot possibly be cured without taking the medicine of liberty." [95] In this passionate search for a cure

94. *Tzu-yu shu*, p. 44; "Lu-so hsüeh-an," pp. 97–110.
95. *LNCC*, I, 125.

for the lethargy of Chinese people, Liang was apparently more interested in the emotional appeal of Rousseau's liberal ideals than in the fine texture of its intellectual content.

As Liang's understanding of Western thought deepened with his increasing contact with Western literature, his preoccupation with group cohesion and national unification soon led him to feel the danger of the doctrine of natural rights and eventually to recoil from this brand of liberal thought. Thus in 1901 Liang warned that the idea of natural rights might have the dangerous consequences of promoting an anarchist outlook and thereby disrupt order and stability.[96] In 1902 Liang wrote a moving biography of Madame Roland, whom he depicted as the leading spirit of the French Revolution. In this portrait Madame Roland was dramatized as a tragic heroine who fought zealously for the ideal of liberty but ultimately died a victim of the destuctive forces unleashed by thaɩ ideal. Liang's portrayal of Madame Roland's sacrifice at the altar of liberty conveyed clearly his disenchantment with Rousseau's ideals of liberty and nautral rights.[97] After 1902 he seldom mentioned them.

Among all the different contexts in which Liang understood the concepts of liberty and rights, it was the Social Darwinist concept of might-as-right (*ch'iang-ch'üan*), as expounded in the writings of Katō Hiroyuki, which had the most persistent appeal for him. At the heart of this concept lies the tendency to reify rights or freedom as some sort of force or power. While this reification is certainly an egregious travesty on the moral and legal concepts of freedom or rights as understood in the mainstream of Western

96. "Kuo-chia ssu-hsiang pien-ch'ien i-t'ung lun," p. 19.
97. *Lo-lan fu-jen chuan* (A biography of Madame Roland), in *YPSHC-CC*, ts'e 4, 12:1–14.

liberal tradition, it is nevertheless a natural outgrowth of Liang's Social Darwinist outlook and his ideal of a dynamic and assertive personality. In Liang's mind, then, the concept of rights was inseparably linked with the concept of struggle. As long as struggle was an ineluctable part of human condition, rights or freedom were absolutely essential to the existence and dignity of human life.[98]

This inseparability of rights and struggle is nowhere more clearly reflected than in his emphatic reference in his *New Citizen* to Rudolf von Jhering's idea that the ideal of rights is predicated on the concept of struggle. Interpreting Jhering, Liang stated that although the end of human rights was peace, fighting was an indispensable means to that end. As long as human rights have to struggle with the forces of wrong and evil, which are always a part of human life, fighting is indispensable. Liang quoted Jhering's words, "Concretely speaking, the life of rights is a struggle." [99] Liang further referred to Jhering's allusion to the ancient Greek image of justice holding scales in the left hand and a sword in the right. The sword without the scale would be brutal; the scales without the sword would make the enforcement of rights ineffective.[100] The image implied that rights and struggle should be part and parcel of an assertive and dynamic personality.

But what Liang was ultimately concerned with was not individual rights but the collective rights of the human group, or more specifically, of China as a nation. Thus his appreciation of rights as an essential element of personality derived basically from his conviction that a vigorous citizenry would constitute a strong and independent state. So what started out to be a stirring defense of individual

98. *Tzu-yu shu,* pp. 23–24, 29–31.
99. *Hsin-min shuo,* p. 32.
100. Ibid.

rights in his *New Citizen* wound up on a strongly collectivistic note. "The combination of fractions of rights
will make up the right of a totality. All the individual
senses of right will add up to a collective sense of rights of
the whole nation. Thus cultivation of the sense of national
right must start with the individual." [101] "The citizenry
is an assemblage of individual citizens. The national right
is the collection of individual rights . . . The strong
citizenry then make up a strong state; the weak citizenry
make up a weak state; . . . the citizenry in possession of
rights makes up a state with national right." [102] "The state
is like a tree. The sense of right is like the root of the tree.
If the root of the tree is destroyed, however long and
strong the trunk of the tree becomes and however luxuri-
ant the flowers and foliage of the tree grow, the tree will
wither and die. In a storm it will be destroyed even sooner.
A citizenry without a sense of right, when confronted with
foreign incursion, is like a withered tree in a storm. I see
that among the millions of people on earth, with the exception of the black barbarians in India, Africa, and
Southeast Asia, no other people's sense of rights is as weak
as that of the people of our own country." [103]

Thus in Liang's view the Western liberal idea of rights
was no mere academic concern; the Chinese people's lack
of a sense of rights lay at the root of China's weakness as
a nation. But why did the Chinese fail to have a sense of
rights? Liang put the blame on China's cultural tradition,
which encouraged a meek philosophy of life. Chinese sages,
Liang emphasized, always enjoined an attitude of tolerance
and meekness; they always urged people to refrain from
avenging wrong and to reciprocate insults with good will.

101. Ibid., p. 36.
102. Ibid., p. 39.
103. Ibid., pp. 34–40.

This longstanding cultivation of a meek philosophy had produced an inveterate spirit of resignation and submissiveness, which made the Chinese people unable to stand up to enemies and to take strong actions against their aggression.[104]

It must be remembered that Liang had repudiated this attitude of meekness and resignation as a fatal weakness of the Chinese character prior to his exile. But at that time he did not put the blame on the whole Chinese cultural tradition; only Taoism was singled out as the root of the illness. Instead of Taoism, Liang now put his finger on the central Confucian ideal of *jen* as the major source of Chinese meekness. The distinction between *jen* and *i* (righteousness), he argued, could be seen as a major index of the difference between Chinese and Western civilization; Chinese civilization put a premium on *jen*, while Western civilization gave high value to *i*. The moral value of *i* signified an injunction to assert one's self-interest, neither doing harm to other people, nor brooking insults and aggression from them. *Jen*, on the other hand, carried within itself a tendency to overemphasize the importance of securing harmonious relationships with others to the neglect of one's own rightful sphere of action and interest. The moral ideal of *jen*, he said, may serve mankind in the remote future world of great harmony, but in China's present circumstances it tended to breed in the Chinese people a habit of reliance on the good will of others and thereby to undermine the Chinese people's self-assertion.[105]

The same, Liang continued, could be said of benevolent paternalism (*jen-cheng*), which had been an important political ideal in China for thousands of years. It too

104. Ibid., p. 35.
105. Ibid., pp. 35–36.

tended to nourish a passive reliance on guidance and control from above and inevitably had the deleterious consequence of paralyzing the Chinese people's will to resist autocratic power. In short, both the moral ideal of *jen* and the political ideal of *jen-cheng* were seen as inimical to the spirit of self-assertiveness central to the ideal of rights. The new citizen, whom Liang envisaged as the agent for the future revitalization of China, should therefore turn his back on the traditional ideal of *jen* and cultivate the ideal of *i*, in which Liang saw an embryonic sense of rights.[106]

This attack on the moral ideal of *jen* needs particular emphasis. For, as we have seen, *jen* was a central ideal in Neo-Confucianism, which had played a focal role in the thought of both K'ang Yu-wei and T'an Ssu-t'ung and hence bulked large in Liang's intellectual background. It is interesting that in one of K'ang Yu-wei's early works, he also contrasted the two Confucian virtues of *i* and *jen*. He identified the former with a tendency toward moral egoism and authoritarianism while equating *jen* with the tendency to egalitarianism and altruism.[107] Hence K'ang saw in *jen* a key to moral solidarity and in *i* a block to it. Now Liang reversed this contrast. But this reversal must not be taken to mean a change of value from collectivism to individualism. To be sure it implied an acceptance of the Western ideals of enlightened self-interest and assertive personality. However, these Western ideals were accepted not as intrinsic values but as secondary values instrumental to the attainment of the collective power of the state. Thus Liang's attack on *jen* in the interest of the Western liberal ideal of right must be understood, paradoxically enough, as a shift from the moral value of solidarity and harmony

106. Ibid.
107. Richard C. Howard, p. 309.

to the political value of national cohesion and power.

Liang did not have unified and consistent notions of Western liberal ideals. For example, in the *New Citizen* there was another section devoted to the explication of the concept of liberty in which he used a formulation very different from his formulation of rights.[108] But divergent as his understanding of these two Western liberal ideals were, they were all manifestations of his concern with the problem of *ch'ün*. To begin with, Liang maintained that in the light of the growth of liberalism in the West, the idea of liberty could be understood in four senses: political liberty, religious liberty, national liberty, economic liberty. The concept of political liberty, however, could be further separated into three aspects: the liberty maintained by the common people against the aristocracy; the liberty maintained by the citizenry as a whole against the government; the liberty maintained by the people in the colony against their mother country.

Thus, in the last analysis, there were altogether six problems involved in the concept of liberty: first, whether the common people had achieved equal rights and no one was privileged; second, whether the whole citizenry who had reached the qualified age could participate in the process of political decision; third, whether the people in the colony could establish their own government and enjoy their rights as they previously had when they were the citizenry of the mother country; fourth, whether the people had attained the liberty of believing in the religious creed of their own choosing without interference from the government; fifth, whether a nation had obtained the liberty of establishing a sovereign and independent government without encroachment and interference from other countries; sixth, whether the laborer, either working

108. *Hsin-min shuo,* p. 40.

for landlords or capitalists, had risen above the status of slave and was free from oppression.[109]

Liang emphasized that not all six problems of liberty were relevant for China. In the first place, the problem of equality had no significance for China because, in Liang's view, an aristocracy had been abolished far back in the time of the Warring States and class distinctions had long since disappeared in China. Since China possessed no colony, the problem of the self-government of a colony was naturally meaningless for her. Religious freedom should constitute no problem either, because China was not a religious country and hence had not been beset by any religious conflicts throughout her whole history. As to economic freedom, the problem of labor might emerge in the future, but in view of China's present economic backwardness, it had no immediate urgency. As Liang analyzed the situation, only two problems of freedom concerned China: namely, the problem of political participation (ts'an-cheng) by the people, and the problem of building up a nation-state. In others words, at the present stage, China needed to be concerned only with what he called national freedom and political freedom. Furthermore, Liang emphasized that the two problems were basically the same; the solution of one meant the solution of the other.[110]

His concepts of freedom can best be analyzed in the framework Carl J. Friedrich suggested in a study on freedom. According to Friedrich, freedom consists of two dimensions: freedom of independence and freedom of participation. He explained these two dimensions as follows: "When and to the extent that human beings, either individually or collectively, act politically — that is, opine, prefer, decide questions of policy — without the inter-

109. Ibid., pp. 40–41.
110. Ibid., p. 44.

ference of other human beings, they shall be called free . . . If such action is primarily taken in the perspective of being able to do what one pleases in a private sphere, we shall speak of freedom of independence, if primarily in the perspective of participating in group action, of freedom of participating." The freedom of independence, in Friedrich's analysis, may refer to two situations: either to the independence of the individual from social and communal bonds or to the independence of one group from another.[111]

In Friedrich's terms, Liang's two concepts of freedom can then be identified as freedom of national independence and freedom of political participation. Viewed in this light, it is not too difficult to see why Liang thought of these two freedoms as practically identical. On the one hand, without national freedom, freedom of participation would be out of the question under foreign subjugation. On the other, without freedom of participation, the people would in no way contribute to national strength, which, if feeble, would inevitably jeopardize national freedom. Thus in Liang's mind, just as nationalism was inseparable from democratization, the freedom of participation and the freedom of national independence were essentially two sides of the same coin.

Apparently, in his concept of freedom there was little place, if any, for the freedom of individual independence. Liang's notion of constitutional government serves as a good illustration of this point. Almost from the very beginning of his contact with Western thought, Liang was fascinated by Western constitutionalism, especially as an effective antidote to traditional despotism. For him a constitutionalist government was preeminently a limited gov-

111. Carl J. Friedrich, *Man and His Government, An Empirical Theory of Politics* (New York, 1963), pp. 253–255

ernment which boiled down to two essential ingredients: a promulgation of a written constitution and the primacy of the legislative organ in the constitutional government. In other words, what interested Liang mainly in Western constitutionalism was the idea that a government should be set up and operate according to a promulgated constitution in which a popularly elected legislature played the leading role.[112]

Liang's interest in this Western phenomenon ultimately derived from his belief that constitutional government was a system which could ensure the political participation of the majority of the people. It must be noted in this connection that the mainstream of Western constitutionalism is primarily concerned with what is often called guarantism, or a system of legally guaranteed civil liberties[113] and only secondarily with specific ways of organizing government. In Liang's mind the reverse seemed to be true: constitutionalism became primarily concerned with the problem of structuring the government in a way to ensure popular political participation and was only very tangentially, if at all, concerned with the problem of guaranteeing civil liberties.

The reason for this different emphasis in Liang's understanding of constitutionalism must be found in his collectivistic concern with *ch'ün*. His ultimate concern was the formation of a cohesive and strong nation-state and he believed that political participation could contribute to the latter end. Though he was not unaware of that dimension of freedom understood in the sense of individual in-

112. "Li hsien-fa i" (On setting up a constitution), in *YPSHC-WC*, ts'e 2, 5:1–6; "Lun li-fa-ch'üan" (On the legislative power), in *YPSHC-WC*, ts'e 4, 9:101–107.
113. Giovanni Sartori, "Constitutionalism: A Preliminary Discussion," *American Political Science Review*, 56.4:853–864 (December 1962); see also Sartori, *Democratic Theory* (Detroit, 1962), pp. 17–26, 353–374.

dependence he was, however, so occupied by his concern with national independence that he tended to see any measure of individual freedom as potentially injurious to his cherished end of collective freedom. This is perhaps why he did not see individual independence as an essential dimension of the ideal of freedom. It is perhaps also for this reason that at one point in his *New Citizen* he went so far as to deliberately repudiate individual freedom in the interest of collective freedom: "Freedom means freedom of the group, not individual freedom. In the age of barbarism, individual freedom prevails and no collective freedom develops. In the civilized age, the freedom of the group develops while individual freedom decreases." [114] This attitude led Liang to view Western constitutionalism more as an institutional means to secure popular participation than as an institutional means to guarantee civil liberties.

It may be suggested here that Liang's conception of freedom was very typical of many people in the developing countries, who were likewise preoccupied with the freedom of national independence and the freedom of participation but were prone to sacrifice the latter to the former when conditions called for it. However popular they might be, such concepts of freedom were foreign to the mainstream of modern liberal thought, which had freedom of independence from public control as its core.[115] Rather, these ideas were similar to what are understood as ancient liberties in classical Greek political thought.

It must be remembered that when the ancient Greeks discussed freedom they were thinking mainly in terms of political participation in the decisions of public affairs in

114. *Hsin-min shuo,* pp. 44–45.
115. Carl J. Friedrich, p. 355.

their communities. The ancient Greeks who actively participated in the political life of the *polis* knew little of freedom in the sense of individual independence; they had no notions of civic liberties and it is well-known that the private life of the citizen of a *polis* was anything but free from public interference. Equally significant in this connection is the fact that the Greeks' enthusiasm for freedom of participation was combined with a fierce love for the freedom of independence for each particular *polis*. As with Liang, the Greeks also considered the freedom of group independence primary; they generally felt that when group independence was threatened, individual freedom must be suspended.[116] In view of these similarities between Liang's concept of freedom and that of the ancient Greeks, it is by no means accidental that during these years Liang was a fervent admirer of the political life of the ancient Greeks. Indeed Liang seemed to see no distinction between the freedom of ancient Athens and modern English freedom; he treated them alike as the primary specimens of Western freedom.[117] Obviously the dimension of individual independence which is so central to the modern English idea of freedom and is also what distinguishes that freedom from ancient liberties was overlooked in this indiscriminate identification.

In spite of his insensitivity to the freedom of individual independence, Liang occasionally referred to individual freedom in his *New Citizen*. The reason may be found in Liang's concept of the individual self, which made it possible for him to make sense of individual freedom within a collectivistic framework. Doubtless because of his Neo-

116. Ibid.; see also Giovanni Sartori, *Democratic Theory*, pp. 250–266.
117. *Ssu-pa-ta hsiao-chih* (A brief history of Sparta) and *Ya-tien hsiao-chih* (A brief history of Athens), in *YPSHC-CC*, ts'e 4, 15:1–19, and 16:1–8.

Confucian and Buddhist intellectual background, Liang believed that an individual man had a dual self: the bodily self and the spiritual self. The real self was not the body, but the spirit. Freedom was acquired, he emphasized, when the spiritual self had dominance over the bodily self. Thus one would be less unfortunate when the bodily self was in chains than when the spiritual self was enslaved by others. But the worst misfortune was when one became a slave to oneself.

By this self-enslavement Liang actually meant that one's spiritual self lost autonomy and fell prey to one's inner inadequacies, either intellectual or emotional. According to him, there were four kinds of spiritual bondage to which the Chinese were vulnerable. The first was enslavement by ancient sages; the second was enslavement by fashions and conventions; the third was enslavement by the environment; the last was the almost ubiquitous human slavement by passions and desires. Real freedom was achieved only by freeing oneself from such spiritual bonds. Understood in this sense, freedom meant for Liang self-mastery, an idea strongly reminiscent of Confucian self-cultivation. Liang added, "Self-mastery means self-conquest and self-conquest means strength. With self-conquest and strength, how free one is!" [118]

By now it should have become evident that understood in the sense of self-mastery, individual freedom not only need not contradict but also could form a natural complement to collective freedom within a Social Darwinist framework. For if the nation as a social organism was no more than the sum total of the whole citizenry, the rationalization of the individual citizen's personality would naturally contribute to national strength and consequently also to national freedom. In this context it is then hardly

118. *Hsin-min shuo,* pp. 46–50.

surprising that Liang remarked that "collective freedom is an accumulation of individual freedom." [119]

This concept of self-mastery also forms an important component in another ideal of Liang's, namely *tzu-chih*. In his writing the word *tzu-chih* had three connotations. It meant either individual self-mastery, self-government, or national self-rule. Quite expectedly all these three connotations were closely interdependent. People who could achieve mastery of their personalities were qualified to organize self-governing communities, and national communities where people with disciplined personalities practiced self-government would brook no foreign control or interference.[120] Self-mastery, then, was regarded by Liang as a prime condition for the realization of popular participation and of national self-rule. Ultimately it was still in a collectivistic framework that self-mastery gained significance for Liang.

The foregoing analysis shows that instead of having consistent and unified meanings, these two liberal ideals of rights and freedom have four different meanings. Two salient facts emerge from my analysis of these four meanings. The first is that freedom in the sense of individual independence was conspicuously lacking, an oversight by no means accidental. Liang's basic preoccupation with the concern of collective freedom almost inescapably prevented him from seeing that dimension of freedom which Isaiah Berlin called negative freedom.[121] The second salient fact closely related to the first was that the four senses in which Liang understood freedom, however different from each other, all more or less revolved around his collectivistic preoccupation with *ch'ün*. Thus basically he

119. Ibid., pp. 46–47.
120. Ibid., pp. 50–54.
121. Isaiah Berlin, *Two Concepts of Liberty* (Oxford, 1958).

came to terms with Western liberal ideals within a collectivistic framework. While he had doubtless become committed to the ideal of democracy, he did not seem to have grasped, let alone become committed to, the spirit of Western liberalism.

Social Utility and Economic Growth

Finally we must turn to discuss the last group of public virtues which Liang prescribed in his *New Citizen,* namely, social utility and economic growth. These values were of course not entirely new to Liang. In his pre-exile years he might not have known the names of Thomas Hobbes and Jeremy Bentham; he might not have become aware of all the intellectual subtleties involved in such concepts as profit, utility, and wealth. But as far as the basic values were concerned, Liang had doubtless already accepted them as legitimate and desirable concerns for human beings. Did he have anything new, then, to add to what he already had said about these Western values?

To begin with, because of his increasing contact with Western thought during his stay in Japan, Liang no doubt developed a firmer grasp of the meaning and implications of Western utilitarian values. Meanwhile, he began to develop a more balanced appraisal of Chinese cultural tradition. He no longer laid all the blame at the door of Taoism, as he formerly had, for the failure of Chinese tradition to recognize these values; now he openly took Confucianism to task. Mencius and Tung Chung-shu, he maintained, were all wrong in repudiating the values of profit and utility; they were too idealistic to be practical. The search for profit was inherent in human nature; to disregard it would be unrealistic.[122] To rectify such an

122. "Sheng-chi-hsüeh hsüeh-shuo yen-ko hsiao-shih" (A brief history of the development of economic theories), in *YPSHC-WC,* ts'e 5, 12:4–5.

attitude, China should learn from the West, especially from the utilitarian thought of Thomas Hobbes and Jeremy Bentham.[123]

Almost from the very beginning, however, Liang's acceptance of Western utilitarian values was not without misgivings. He soon became aware of the difficulty the idea of self-interest posed to his central collectivistic concern, namely, the possible contradiction between self-interest and public interest. We now know from Élie Halévy's classical analysis of philosophical radicalism that this was also an acute problem for Bentham, who found the solution not in Adam Smith's theory of natural identification of interest but in Helvetius' concept of the artificial identification of interest.[124] But for Liang, who apparently assumed that Bentham had solved the whole problem of conflict between public and private interest by assuming their natural identification, an acute problem arose in the face of the grim fact that this natural identification was empirically unfounded.

In this context Liang said: "According to Bentham, the best motives of human beings consist in self-interest; but he also often talked about the ideal of the great happiness of the greatest number of people. That is because he thinks that public profit and private profit often accord with each other, they are identical, not divergent. But the actual situation is often not what he expects. Public interest and private interest not only cannot coincide with each other, they also clash with each other in nine out of ten cases. If this is in fact so, then the principle that it is always

123. "Ho-pu-shih hsüeh-an" (A study of Hobbes's thought), in *YPSHC-WC*, ts'e 3, 6:89–95; see also "Lo-li chu-i t'ai-tou Pien-hsin chih hsüeh-shuo" (The doctrine of Bentham, the master of utilitarianism), in *YPSHC-WC*, ts'e 5, 13:30–47.

124. Élie Halévy, *The Growth of Philosophical Radicalism* (London, 1928), pp. 17–20.

human nature to seek happiness and utility cannot serve as the criterion of morality. This is really a problem of life and death for the whole Benthamite doctrine." [125] From Liang's collectivistic standpoint, if some means could not be found to prove the basic harmony of private interest and public interest within the framework of Benthamite doctrine, the whole Benthamite utilitarianism would then be untenable.

Eventually Liang's belief in the Benthamite doctrine was saved by Katō Hiroyuki's defense of utilitarianism. According to Liang, Katō maintained that man's egoistic nature could provide the basis for altruistic activities. For it was often the case that men found that cooperation with others would ultimately redound to his own self-interest. Furthermore, man often had an intrinsic need to love others; love for others was basically an extension of self-love in the sense that it satisfied his own needs to love. All these considerations meant that man's egoism need not clash with the collective interest of the society and in fact could provide a viable foundation for the latter.[126]

Ingenious as Katō's theoretical defense of Benthamite utilitarian doctrine might be, Liang still could not throw off all his reservations about Benthamite utilitarianism. What worried him was whether the general public could really have an enlightened self-interest which, Katō believed, would make people altruistic and thus contribute to public interest. In a country like China where most people were uneducated, Liang seemed to feel that he had plenty of reasons for doubt. He observed that it was far more likely that people without the required education and intelligence would distort Benthamite doctrine to rationalize their hedonistic egoism.[127] For this reason his

125. "Lo-li chu-i t'ai-tou Pien-hsin chih hsüeh-shuo," pp. 37–38.
126. Ibid., pp. 38–39.
127. Ibid., p. 39.

enthusiasm for Western utilitarian values always contained a strain of skepticism which made him reluctant to recommend them unreservedly for popular consumption.

By now it should be clear that what made Liang balk at Benthamite utilitarianism was its susceptibility to individualistic interpretation. He had no objection to the ideals of profit and utility as long as their points of reference were collectivistic. Liang's collectivistic view of utilitarian values was reflected in the profound interest he later developed in Mo-tzu's ideal of public interest, noting that in Mohism the ideal of love was often found linked with the concept of profit. How could these two values harmonize with each other if Mo-tzu did not have in mind the interest of the society as a whole? This devotion to public interest, in Liang's view, lay at the basis of Mo-tzu's admirable ascetic activism.[128] He admitted that Mo-tzu sometimes had talked about self-interest, but only for the purpose of getting the ideal of public interest accepted by people in general who would have normally tended to ignore it. Thus self-interest had only instrumental value for Mo-tzu whose ultimate commitment was doubtless to the value of public interest. It is precisely for the centrality of public interest in Mo-tzu's thought that Liang called Mohism "perfect utilitarianism." [129]

For Liang, then, utilitarianism, rightly understood, meant devotion to public interest. He urged this sense of public interest as an imperative to the new citizen of China. In this world of free-for-all and tooth-and-claw struggle, every nation must fight for the expansion of its own collective interest. The people who only knew moral righteousness and disregarded the vital importance of collective interest were bound to lose and go under.[130]

128. *Tzu-Mo-tzu hsüeh-shuo*, pp. 18–19.
129. Ibid.; see also *YPSTC*, III, p. 31.
130. "Sheng-chi-hsüeh hsüeh-shuo yen-ko hsiao-shih," pp. 2–5.

It is in this context that Liang introduced what he considered an all-important distinction between two kinds of citizen, productive (*sheng-li*) and non-productive (*fen-li*). Apparently Liang borrowed the idea from Adam Smith's famous distinction between productive labor and non-productive labor. Seizing on this distinction with an obsessive interest, Liang now tried to formulate the idea of contribution to national interest as a civic virtue for the new citizen of China. Central to civic virtue was an imperative which commanded every citizen to keep uppermost in mind the fact that the national fortune of any country hinged upon the respective proportions of its productive and non-productive citizens. A high proportion of productive citizenry in relation to non-productive citizenry would constitute a strong country; a reverse ratio would constitute a weak country.[131]

What did Liang really mean by a productive or non-productive type of citizen? More specifically, in what sense did he understand contribution to national interest? The answers to these questions turn on Liang's notion of public profit or social utility. A close scrutiny of his writing on these values shows that in his use of the terms they were often understood in both a broad and a narrow sense.

In its broad sense, profit meant for Liang a sort of general social utility. Under this general notion any type of work or activity which could be shown to contribute to social progress or national development in one way or another would be accepted as profitable. Later Liang was led by this notion of social utility to criticize Mo-tzu's utilitarianism as too narrow, noting that Mo-tzu's view was confined to "visible, physical, and direct" matters, while "invisible, spiritual, and indirect" concerns were often regarded as inconsequential or even deleterious. Cer-

131. *Hsin-min shuo,* pp. 95–96.

tain cultural concerns, such as rites and music which Mo-tzu particularly dismissed as devoid of utility, could in fact be of great use to society indirectly. Such a restricted view of utility seemed to Liang hardly adequate for promoting social progress.[132]

Liang's broad notion of profit or utility was most clearly evidenced in his classification of what he regarded as productive types of people, productive types of human strength, and productive kinds of work. To start with, Liang said, there were two types of people productive of profit: first, the kind of people who were direct producers of profit, like peasants and artisans; second, the kind of people who were indirectly productive of profit, like businessmen, soldiers, statesmen, educators, and so on. Furthermore, in terms of human labor there were also two kinds productive of profit: physical and mental; the latter could be further divided into two varieties: intellectual and moral. Finally there were six categories of productive work: first, discoveries and inventions; second, extractive labor; third, the processing of raw materials; fourth, manufacturing; fifth, communication and transportation. After enumerating these five categories of technological and economic labor, Liang finally called attention to a kind of work which, though not directly productive of profit, was nevertheless indirectly also productive of social utility. The work done by administrators, soldiers, modern professional men like medical doctors and teachers, and such artists as literary writers fell into this category.[133] The implications of this classification of productive labor are momentous. Liang's deep commitment to social utility as a modern value made him recognize many types of work which had no place in the traditional scheme of

132. *Tzu-Mo-tzu hsüeh-shuo,* pp. 20–24.
133. *Hsin-min shuo,* pp. 83–84.

values. There is no question that Liang had made the transition from the Confucian restricted concept of vocation to the modern notion of occupational contribution to society.

Aside from such a broad notion of utility, Liang also had a narrow concept which meant economic utility. Out of this concept eventually grew a crude yet unmistakable notion of economic growth, the core of which could still be found in the well-known statement from the Confucian classic, *Great Learning:* "There is a great *tao* for the production of wealth. Let the producers be many and consumers few. Let there be activity in the production and economy in the expenditure. Then the wealth will be always sufficient." In Liang's view, this central tenet of traditional economic thought could also serve as a guiding principle for modern economic thinking.[134]

The reason for Liang's view must be sought in his acceptance of Adam Smith's labor theory of value. Under Smith's influence, Liang was naturally disposed to see labor, more than land and capital, as the basic source of wealth. By the same token, he was fascinated by Smith's concept of productive and non-productive labor. Here he found a simple explanation of the way to accumulate national wealth, which was also very similar to the traditional economic principle embodied in the *Great Learning.* "Broadly speaking, then, the rise or decline of a country hinges solely upon whether a return can be made on the investment of its total capital and labor or not. It is those who can get a return on investment and create a profit out of capital who are called producers in the *Great Learning;* economists would credit them with productive labor. Those who cannot get a return on investment waste capital and lose interest. It is they who are called consumers in

134. Ibid., pp. 80–81.

the *Great Learning*. Their labor the economists would regard as non-productive." [135] In Liang's view, both Confucian economic thought and modern economic thinking agreed on the principle of encouraging production and discouraging consumption.

In identifying the Confucian economic principle with Adam Smith's view of economy, however, Liang had in fact turned away in a very significant sense from orthodox Confucian economic thought and had gone far in the direction of accepting the modern idea of economic growth. It must be noted that the central orientation of orthodox Confucian economic thinking was toward the maintenance of a stable subsistence economy. In this context, the principle of encouraging production and discouraging consumption was reduced almost to an exclusive emphasis on discouraging consumption either by means of limiting inner desires or of curbing outer expenditure. Liang's interpretation of this principle, however, put preponderant emphasis on the production of wealth. To be sure, at this time he also spoke of the necessity for practicing thrift and curbing consumption, but he now conceived them to be ways to save and accumulate capital. There were two uses for total annual national income; one part was used for consumption and the other for the saving of capital. The more expenditure for consumption was cut down the more capital could be saved for accumulation and investment.[136]

Because of the mechanism of continuous investment and reinvestment, sustained capital accumulation over an extended period could result in tremendous wealth for the nation. The key to the question whether a country took

135. Ibid., p. 83; see also "Sheng-chi-hsüeh hsüeh-shuo yen-ko hsiao-shih," p. 30.
136. *Hsin-min shuo*, pp. 82–83.

the road of economic growth or stagnation lay in the simple factor of surplus profit. Liang tried to spell out the momentous implications of governing a country's economic investment by the concept of surplus profit. A country with a given amount of capital, he noted, would increase its economic output annually by a factor of four if it continued to plow back its surplus profit for reinvestment. In four years, the proportion of output of similarly endowed countries which did and did not invest their surplus profit would be 64 to 1 respectively.[137] He was apparently enthralled by the striking difference this simple concept made in the end.

Such then are the civic virtues Liang developed as essential attributes of his personality ideal for the new citizen. The significance of this personality ideal can hardly be overstressed for this was the first time in Chinese history the ideal of citizenship had been formulated. We have traced the processes by which Liang's citizen ideal was gradually developed out of the Confucian personality ideal of sage-statesman. In order to bring his ideal of the new citizen into sharper focus, it is necessary to compare it, first to the Confucian personality ideal of sage-statesman and then to the Western ideal of democratic citizen.

To begin with, the points of reference for the Confucian personality ideal and Liang's ideal of new citizen are different. The Confucian personality ideal was applicable only to *chün-tzu,* the moral elite of a society. Liang's ideal of citizenship was meant for every member of the political community. The individual member of the political community had seldom been the focus of attention in Confucian political culture. The emphasis fell

137. Ibid., pp. 81–82.

rather on the moral elite on the assumption that they alone were the principal actors in politics.

Did the Confucian personality ideal share with Liang's ideal citizen the concept of political participation? The answer cannot be an unequivocal yes. While it is true that both the Confucian *chün-tzu* and the new citizen had the obligation to participate in the political life of the community, each participated in a different way inasmuch as the political framework for participation was dissimilar in each case. In the case of the new citizen, political participation took the form of exercising the franchise; in the case of the Confucian *chün-tzu*, it took the form of bureaucratic service or informal local leadership. Moreover, it is often overlooked that although citizenship, according to Liang, opened political participation to every member of the community, the Confucian personality ideal implied an exclusion of the majority of the members of the community from political participation. In other words, the other side of the coin of the Confucian personality ideal was the existence of subjects who politically had no rights and were obliged to follow the leadership of their moral superiors. In this way the Confucian personality ideal was basically elitist while Liang's ideal of citizenship was essentially egalitarian.

The difference between the Confucian personality ideal and Liang's ideal of the new citizen can also be seen in the different concepts of loyalty involved. The ultimate loyalty of a citizen was unequivocally due to the corporate entity of state or citizenry. The ultimate loyalty expected of a Confucian *chün-tzu* was not clearly defined. It is never clearly prescribed, for instance, whether a Confucian *chün-tzu's* ultimate loyalty should go to the state or the family should there be a conflict between the two; nor was it unequivocably stated whether he should be ultimately loyal to the ruler or to Confucian moral ideals, or as was often said, to the *chün-t'ung* (imperial way) or to the *tao-t'ung* (way of the *tao*).

The commitment to render service or to make a contribution to the state and society is of course built into both the Confucian personality ideal and Liang's ideal of new citizen. But they differed significantly in their respective notions of how that service could best be rendered. For a Confucian *chün-tzu,* there was only one way to fulfill his commitment, namely, through public office. With Liang's broad concept of social utility different ways were conceived by which a citizen could render his services to the state and society. In other words, in Liang's personality ideal of citizenship the modern ideas of professional specialization and occupational contribution were given at least implicit cultural sanction.

Last, but by no means least, one found in Liang's personality ideal of the new citizen a striking note of civic activism which was very similar to that peculiar ideal of Machiavellian Italy, *virtu*. As defined by C. J. Friedrich, "*virtu* is the kind of excellence needed in the citizen of a republic and in the ruler and leader as well." It "involves manliness which means courage and prowess, but also self-discipline and steadfastness. *Virtu* means a willingness to fight, but also a willingness to sacrifice oneself for the *patria*. It means a determination to succeed but also a recognition of the civic obligations to serve." [138] If one remembers Liang's passionate paean to the ideals of struggle and futurism, to the adventurous and enterprising spirit, and to the paramountcy of national interest in his

138. C. J. Friedrich, *Constitutional Reason of State* (Providence, 1957), p. 18.

New Citizen, the parallel between them and the qualities of *virtu* is patent.

Yet *virtu* represented a complex of qualities that were certainly lacking in the Confucian tradition. To begin with, it ran counter to the Confucian premium on the values of moderation and harmony. More important, whereas a distinctive characteristic of the Confucian personality ideal was decidedly its moral orientation, *virtu* was non-moral in character. According to Friedrich Meinecke, *virtu* "might include moral qualities, but primarily it is to designate something dynamical, something put by nature into men, heroism and the strength to accomplish great political and military deeds, but particularly to found and maintain flourishing states." In fact it is distinctively a personality ideal concomitant to the emergence of modern state. Thus, as Meinecke further defined it, it is "by no means unregulated force of nature, it is force transformed into rational and purposive conduct, *virtu ordinata.*" [139] Inasmuch as the modern idea of state was something new to the Confucian political tradition, *virtu* was something new to Confucian moral tradition.

A comparison of the new citizen with the modern Western ideal of the democratic citizen is of interest. Admittedly, Western democratic citizenship itself is a very complex concept, whose meaning is by no means well-defined. But by and large it seems safe to say that modern democratic citizenship is shaped by three cultural traditions in Western heritage: the Greek, the Hebraic, and the Christian-Roman.[140] Each of these three traditions contributes an important component to the formation of

139. Ibid., pp. 121–122. See also Friedrich Meinecke, *Machiavellism,* tr. Douglas Scott (New Haven, 1957), pp. 31–38.

140. H. Mark Roelofs, *The Tension of Citizenship: Private Man and Public Duty* (New York, 1967), pp. 31–154.

modern citizenship: from the Greek, the idea of participation; from the Hebraic, the idea of service; and from the Christian-Roman, the idea of individual privacy. If the three ideas are taken together, Western citizenship implies a duality, the public and the private selves. A citizen is committed to participation in and service to the community, but he is also entitled to an inviolable sphere of privacy guarded by the institution of civil freedom and rights. The Western citizen is then held to be both a public person and a private person, to be both in and yet also outside of society. Obviously a tension between the public and the private selves is built into the duality of Western citizenship but the important point is that the tension is, in fact, essential to, instead of being injurious to, the institution of modern democratic citizenship.[141]

Yet such a tension between the public and the private selves is conspicuously lacking in Liang's formulation of citizenship. The central note that emerges from this formulation is that of collectivism; the public self of the new citizen has almost completely overshadowed its private self. Admittedly, in his delineation of citizenship, Liang sometimes had a tendency to identify the Western ideal of individual freedom with the concept of self-mastery or character discipline. In fact, as we shall see later, when Liang undertook to formulate his particular notion of the private self, the concept of character discipline became its core. But his notion of the private self understood in the sense of self-mastery was primarily conceived in the interest of the citizen's fulfillment of public obligations and hence must be distinguished from that of the private self involved in Western democratic citizenship. The latter means essentially that every individual person has a private vocation in the sense that the good to be achieved

141. Ibid., pp. 155–161.

by its pursuit is to be measured in personal terms and not by reference to any public consequences that may result.[142] Seen in this light, Liang's concept of citizenship is much closer to the ancient Greek citizenship where collectivistic orientation was central than to the modern democratic citizenship where individualism constitutes an essential component.

142. Ibid., pp. 31–154.

Reform versus Revolution: Liang's Attitudes toward Politics and Tradition

Given Liang Ch'i-ch'ao's extensive innovations of value, one question is inevitable at this time: was he a revolutionary, or a reformist? For Liang himself, this question was by no means merely an academic one, for the burgeoning Chinese intelligentsia was then dividing into two camps: revolutionists and reformists. Liang, a central figure among them, had to choose a side. The choice he made and hence the image he projected was an ambivalent one. This impression was further compounded by the casual and confusing way in which Liang and his contemporary intellectuals used the words "revolution" and "reform." In consequence the question whether Liang was a reformist or a revolutionary cannot be answered without a prior semantic clarification.

The problem of reform versus revolution, at least with regard to Liang, actually involves two separate problems. First, it involves his attitude toward the existing political order in China; second, it involves his attitude toward China's cultural tradition. Since his attitude toward the one bears no necessary relation to the other, these two problems must be treated separately.

Liang's complex attitude toward the problem of reform

or revolution in his first two years of exile in Japan was reflected in his willingness to work simultaneously with both the revolutionaries and the reformists. This can be explained by the fact that the reform movement with which Liang was originally associated was not ideologically homogeneous but included a spectrum in which both the idea of reform from above and the idea of antidynastic revolution were represented. Although after the debacle of the Hankow uprising in 1900 Liang had stopped trying to work with the revolutionaries, he had by no means made up his mind about the problem of reform versus revolution. In terms of broad societal goals and personality ideals, he was quite certain what he wanted for China in the future. But he was still wavering in regard to what political approach he should adopt to realize these goals.

This wavering was reflected in his writing. In one important essay where he explicitly dealt with the problem of reform versus revolution, he began by arguing that reform was no effective remedy to China's ills, that only revolution could be. But he emphasized that by the English word "revolution" he really meant "transformation of the citizenry" (*kuo-min pien-ko*) rather than "dynastic overthrow" (*wang-ch'ao ko-ming*).[1] In China people often confused "revolution" with "dynastic overthrow" when, in fact, revolution as Liang understood it, need not necessarily involve "dynastic overthrow," as shown clearly in the case of Meiji Japan.[2] In short, if Liang did not come out explicitly against the idea of "the violent overthrow" of the Manchu regime he at least seemed to have intended to minimize its significance. This same reluctance to endorse the idea of violent anti-Manchu revolution was suggested in his popular portrayal of Madame Roland's role

1. "Shih-ko" (On revolution), in *YPSHC-WC*, ts'e 4, 9:40–44.
2. Ibid., pp. 42–43.

in the French Revolution. In this work revolution is described as a deluge breaking up the dam and eventually sweeping away both the evil and the good.[3]

However, Liang tended elsewhere to recognize the need for the violent overturn of the political status quo. At one place in his *New Citizen* he emphasized the need for all kinds of destruction at the present stage of China's development, including the destruction of the existing political order, as a necessary step to social progress.[4] His willingness to see the existing Manchu government violently torn down was made more evident in a letter to K'ang Yu-wei, in which he told K'ang that he and some of K'ang's other students all thought anti-Manchu revolution was necessary.[5]

What all these contradictory statements added up to was a perplexing indecisiveness. This tone underlay his widely read biographical sketches of Mazzini, Garibaldi, and Cavour where he upheld all three as paragons of nationalistic patriotism regardless of the fact that the first two were revolutionaries whereas the latter was a reformist.[6] The clearest indication of Liang's uncertainty lay in a long serial *Hsin Chung-kuo wei-lai chi* (The future of new China), which he published in 1902 in his newly founded literary journal *Hsin hsiao-shuo*.[7] The serial began with a celebration of the fiftieth anniversary of China as a constitutional republic. During the ceremony an old scholar was invited to make a speech recounting his memory of a significant debate between the founding father of the republic, Huang K'o-ch'iang, and a friend of his, Li Ch'üping. The debate took place at a time when both were

3. *YPSTC*, IX, 1–24.
4. *YPSTC*, I, 100–114.
5. *LNCC*, I, 157–159.
6. *YPSTC*, IX, 1–102.
7. *YPSTC*, XIII, 1–99; *LNCC*, I, 172–173.

still patriotic young scholars and were just about to launch their careers dedicated to rejuvenating China as a strong and independent country.[8]

The crux of the debate was the problem of which political approach they should adopt to achieve their long-cherished goal. Li took a revolutionary stance, maintaining that China could only be saved by way of the violent overthrow of the existing political order and the immediate establishment of popular rule.[9] Huang was opposed to Li's revolutionary stance on two grounds: first, that a violent overthrow of an existing political order in which the imperialist powers already had so much vested interest might lead to the latter's military intervention; second, that China had no tradition of popular rule and Chinese people had not yet developed the capacity for self-government. Following the revolutionary approach, China would inevitably reap what modern France did after the French Revolution, namely, political instability. In Huang's view, the modern democratic ideals of liberty and equality could only be realized in China on the basis of unity and order; and there was no better way to attain democratic ideals while maintaining political unity and order than a gradual reform from above.[10]

Balanced and logical as Huang's gradualist approach might sound, in the end he could not show his opponent how a benighted despotic regime could be counted on to undertake all the necessary reforms.[11] Since both protagonists are imaginary figures in Liang's fiction, the debate between them may be conceived as the debate within Liang himself. That it ends on an inconclusive note implies that Liang had not yet made up his mind about the

8. *YPSTC*, XIII, 4–30.
9. *YPSTC*, XIII, 30–68.
10. *YPSTC*, XIII, 30–68.
11. Ibid., pp. 67–69.

problem of reform versus revolution. As this fictional work suggests, Liang could conceive of China's long-term goal as that of a constitutional republic; yet he was not sure what political approach he should pursue to achieve that goal. His characteristic dilemma would not be clearly resolved until after 1903.

The second question involved in the problem of reform versus revolution was: did Liang take a revolutionary stance toward China's cultural tradition? He had claimed in the *New Citizen* that by spelling out civic virtues he was aiming at a moral revolution (*tao-te ko-ming*).[12] Did this mean then that Liang in this period had turned completely away from Chinese moral tradition? Did Liang mean by "moral revolution" the same thing the iconoclasts of the later May Fourth period did? And can we simply say with Joseph R. Levenson that during this period Liang had become intellectually alienated from tradition and saw all human values as coming from the West? [13]

In trying to answer these questions, one must guard against the rhetorical tendency Liang's writings sometimes betrayed. What he called moral revolution in fact meant neither wholesale acceptance of Western moral values nor complete rejection of traditional moral values. For as Liang explained, the concept of *hsin* as used in the phrase *hsin-min* should be understood in two senses: on the one hand it meant the refining of the best one already had; on the other, it meant making up for what one lacked by borrowing from outside.[14] Thus what Liang claimed to be a moral revolution, on close investigation, was really

12. *Hsin-min shuo*, p. 15.
13. J. R. Levenson, *Liang Ch'i-ch'ao and the Mind of Modern China*, pp. 84–87, 92–101.
14. *Hsin-min shuo*, p. 5.

no more than a selective synthesis of traditional and Western cultural values.

Since our previous examination of Liang's formulation of civic virtues revealed a massive penetration of Western values in his thinking, one would tend to regard his claim to have undertaken a selective synthesis of traditional and Western values as a bit too pretentious; it may well be rationalization to compensate for wounded cultural pride. Pretentious and contrived as Liang's claim may sound, one should not thereby be led to overlook the kernel of truth concealed in it. During this period Liang never went so far as to attack the Confucian moral system *in toto;* this fact is rooted in the basic dichotomy Liang made between public and private morality. Only a combination of the two made a complete moral system. It is true that during this period Liang was mainly occupied with the introduction of the idea of public morality from Western civilization into Chinese consciousness; and perhaps because of this fact, he seldom expressed himself at length on the problem of private morality. The distinction between public and private morality, however, still underlay Liang's attitude toward Western moral values; a careful investigation of his letters and other scattered writings indicates that on many important concerns of private morality his commitment to tradition was unquestionable.

First of all, for all his criticism of the Confucian moral tradition, he never went so far as to question many Confucian precepts on personal conduct and personal relationships. More important, he still took for granted Confucian family ethics, which centered on the moral value of filial piety. As for his concerns with character discipline, the little available evidence still shows the predominant influence of Buddhism and Confucianism. This influence is seen in his scattered works on the problem of "cultivation of mind," which was already a prominent concern in his pre-exile writing. With "cultivation of mind," Liang noted, one would achieve spiritual autonomy vis-à-vis the disturbances of the outside world, which he considered an essential basis for any moral or political action.[15]

To illustrate the meaning of this traditional concern, Liang drew upon a well-known story in the literature of Zen Buddhism. According to this story, two Zen monks argued about a flag swirling in the wind. One monk argued that this phenomenon meant in fact only that the wind was blowing while the other disagreed by maintaining only that the flag was swirling. When they argued back and forth without being able to reach any conclusion, the famous sixth patriarch of Zen Buddhism solved the problem by asserting that it was neither the wind blowing nor the flag swirling, but that the human mind was changing. In Liang's view this story served to point up the primacy of mind in determining human conduct; any person who once saw this truth and acted on it would be free from any disturbances of mind from outside and would thus become an outstanding individual.[16]

His deep commitment to the Confucian-Buddhist approach to character discipline is perhaps most clearly seen in the letters he wrote to K'ang Yu-wei and his friends in 1900. It was in this year that the reformist group suffered the debacle of the Hankow uprising, on which Liang had pinned so much hope and to which he had devoted so much effort. Because both he and his friends thought that he himself had to bear much of the blame for this unhappy incident, he was under tremendous emotional stress. As an aid to self-criticism and self-discipline he turned to the

15. *Tzu-yu shu*, p. 15, 45–46, 75–77; see also *Hsin-min shuo*, pp. 48–50, 51–53.
16. "Wei-hsin" (Idealism), in *Tzu-yu shu*, pp. 45–46.

collection of Tseng Kuo-fan's family letters, which in his view contained a mine of precepts on such concerns. As he reported in his letters to friends, he followed Tseng Kuo-fan's model, keeping a diary during this period for daily examination and criticism of his own thoughts and behavior. He conducted his self-examination and self-criticism using five precepts as guides. The first was to use his mind to control worldly desires and distractions for self-mastery (*k'o-chi*), the second was to ensure the sincerity of his will (*ch'eng-i*), the third was to stress the primacy of attitudinal seriousness (*chu-ching*), the fourth was to inure himself to hard work (*hsi-lao*), and the final precept was to cultivate a habit of endurance (*yu-heng*).[17] These precepts he derived from such Confucian literature on character discipline as Wang Yang-ming's writings and Tseng Kuo-fan's family letters. Can one say that Liang had no commitment to Chinese cultural heritage on these matters?

Meanwhile, in regard to many moral values, Liang had, however, accepted without reservation the superiority of Western culture and had become very critical of Chinese cultural tradition. In fact, Liang's attack on the deficiency of the Chinese cultural tradition with respect to public morality carried the ominous implication that he was questioning the usefulness of Chinese moral tradition for the modern citizen. He may have believed, as he often claimed, that the blame for the failures of Chinese moral tradition could not be put entirely on Confucianism, but he could not dissociate Confucianism completely from the failures of the Chinese cultural tradition.

It should be recalled in this connection that, like K'ang Yu-wei, Liang had previously been a zealous advocate of the "propagation of the Confucian faith." Even after he

17. See Liang's letters to K'ang Yu-wei in *LNCC*, I, 119–121, 122–123.

went into exile in Japan he continued at first to champion Confucianism as the national creed. Now, in view of the fact that he had fervently embraced a host of Western values and thereby become critical of Chinese cultural tradition in many respects, one may ask whether he still advocated the need to propagate Confucianism as the national creed.

Liang gave the answer in an article published in 1902.[18] In it he openly relinquished his previous espousal of Confucianism as the national creed and disengaged himself from the campaign to exalt it, which K'ang Yu-wei and some of his followers were still zealously promoting in many overseas Chinese communities at that time.[19] But it is curious to see that Liang did this, as he claimed, not because he lost confidence in Confucian moral values but mainly because of pragmatic considerations about the utility of religion in general for a modern state and society. To begin with, the dogmatism of religious doctrines would inevitably place a straitjacket on the development and spread of knowledge, which was so essential for the development of modern society. Furthermore the propagation of religion was often a cause of animosity and dissension among people and sometimes even resulted in disastrous religious wars, as in the European experience. China's foreign relations had already been strained by antimissionary riots in the past. The campaign to propagate Confucianism would only further exacerbate the situation and thus might well jeopardize China's national security.[20]

18. "Pao-chiao fei so-i tsun K'ung lun" (The preservation of faith is not the way to exalt Confucius), in *YPSHC-WC*, ts'e 4, 9:50–59.

19. As revealed in Liang's letters to K'ang Yu-wei, K'ang and his followers spent great sums of money to celebrate Confucius' birthday every year in Yokohama and to build temples for the cult of Confucius in Singapore. See *LNCC*, I, 152.

20. "Pao-chiao fei so-i tsun K'ung lun," pp. 51–52, 54–58; see also Liang's letter to K'ang Yu-wei in *LNCC*, I, 152–153.

Finally the trend in the West pointed to the decline of Christianity and the growing secularization as reflected in the rise of science and in the tendency toward the separation of religion and politics. If Christianity as a religious force was already shrinking in the West, what was the point of promoting Confucianism to counter it? [21]

Thus, on the surface the publication of this article did not seem to imply a lack of belief in Confucianism on Liang's part. In fact he still claimed that he found much to commend in Confucianism as an ethical system. However one cannot but suspect that Liang did not speak his mind candidly, in view of his critical attitude toward some important values of Confucianism and, in fact, an investigation of some of his personal correspondence at this time reinforces this suspicion. In a letter written to K'ang Yu-wei arguing against Kang's exaltation of Confucianism he said: "In the opinion of your disciple [Liang himself], there is nothing more urgent than to change the Chinese mind by introducing new theories. However, in the beginning there is bound to be some destruction. There is much in Confucianism which does not fit the new world. In case one continues to advocate its preservation, that would only mean working against one's own intentions." [22] Further on in this letter Liang even hinted that he intended to cooperate with some of K'ang's other disciples in writing a large book devoted to exposing and rectifying the flaws and foibles found in Confucianism. This profound dissatisfaction with Confucianism can also be in-

21. "Pao-chiao fei so-i tsun K'ung lun," pp. 53–55; see also Liang's letter to K'ang in *LNCC*, I, 152–153.
22. *LNCC*, I, 152; Liang's opposition to K'ang's idea of promoting Confucianism as the public faith was probably influenced by Huang Tsun-hsien, with whom he often exchanged correspondence during this period. See Huang Tsun-hsien's letter to Liang in Ch'ien Chung-lien, *Huang Kung-tu hsien-sheng nien-p'u*, in Huang Tsun-hsien, *Jen-ching-lu shih-ts'ao chien-chu* (Shanghai, 1957), pp. 66–67.

ferred from the fact that Huang Tsun-hsien, a respected friend of Liang's ever since the days of the *Shih-wu pao,* wrote a letter at this time advising against Liang's criticism of Confucianism. Huang's advice was evidently based on some criticism of Confucianism which Liang had made privately.[23] One can only surmise that it was perhaps Liang's cultural pride which prevented him from coming out openly in criticism of Confucianism.

Liang's critical stance toward Confucianism was soon evident in his search for a new public faith. Aware as he was of some disadvantages in promoting a religious belief, he was also conscious of the important functions a public faith could perform for a modern society and a modern citizen. About nine months after the appearance of the article intended to disengage him from the campaign to promote Confucianism as the national creed, he produced another article reconsidering the advantages of religion. Whereas differences in religious faith could mean dissension or wars for a society, the propagation of a shared faith might also bring about a unified mind and thus contribute to social solidarity. Furthermore, religion might also exert morally edifying and restraining influences on human behavior.[24]

But for Liang as a dedicated activist the motivational value of religion for moral and political action was more significant. Philosophical wisdom might help men understand things better; for action, however, religion was far more important. To begin with, Liang noted, religion could be an unfailing source of hope. Although men live in the present, they always look forward to the future. Hope is what goads men on to undertake all kinds of

23. *LNCC,* I, 153, 161; see also Huang Tsun-hsien, p. 69.
24. "Lun tsung-chiao-chia yü che-hsüeh-chia chih ch'ang-tuan te-shih," in *YPSHC-WC,* ts'e 4, 9:44–50.

projects. But when men hope, there is always the risk of being disappointed and becoming disheartened. With religious belief in the existence of the soul and the other world, men can never lose hope, never become disheartened, but remain always dedicated to their work. Furthermore, religious faith can make men transcend those worldly entanglements and distractions which might prevent them from being resolute in their commitment to the salvation of the world. Finally religious belief in the existence of the soul and after-life can help men overcome the fear of death and thus become a fountainhead of courageous spirit. Unimpeded by worldly entanglements and the fear of death, human action naturally becomes resolute, dynamic, and forceful.[25] With these considerations, Liang seems to have penetrated the relationship between religious faith and the non-rational source of human motivations and actions.

These considerations were based on his keen observation of historical characters. Almost all the outstanding achievers of the past have been motivated by religious zeal. Consider, he said, such heroic figures in Western history as Oliver Cromwell, Joan of Arc, William Penn, George Washington, Abraham Lincoln, Mazzini, Cavour, and Gladstone. Their lives were all examples of the motivational power of religious faith. Some of these historical figures may have had no formal religious faith but all the admirable character strength displayed in their social and moral actions doubtless sprang from religious sentiments. Such examples were not lacking either in the histories of China and Japan. Liang called attention to the fact that Zen Buddhism was a source of strength to many extraordinary men in modern Japan, especially Saigō Takamori. More examples were K'ang Yu-wei and T'an

25. "Kuo-tu shih-tai lun" (On the age of transition), in *YPSHC-WC*, ts'e 3, 6:27–32.

Ssu-t'ung, whose reformist zeal, in Liang's view, derived a great deal from their faith in Mahayana Buddhism.[26] All these historical examples pointed to religion as a motivational well-spring for exceptional actions and outstanding achievements.

It seems obvious that what Liang prized in religion was not any specific religious faith or doctrine but the motivational function of religious faith. No wonder then that Liang also appreciated profoundly those idealistic philosophies which could be functionally equivalent to and hence substitutes for religion in motivating great achievements. Russian nihilists, for example, were mostly atheists, but they were generally resolute and courageous in action. The reason, Liang noted, was their religious faith in Hegelian philosophy. The idealistic philosophy of Wang Yang-ming could also be seen in this light. Its invigorating and elevating effects were clearly shown in the high morale of Chinese scholars in the late Ming. Liang even considered Wang Yang-ming's idealistic philosophy an important force behind the Meiji Restoration.[27] In sum, a religious faith could promote social solidarity, generate political commitment, and motivate courageous action.

Liang now found such a religious faith in Buddhism. Ever since he studied with K'ang Yu-wei at Canton, Mahayana Buddhism had been an important part of his education. Buddhism had not only been help for spiritual direction and character; its Bodhisattva ideal also furnished a source of cultural motivation for socio-political action. Now he went so far as to claim that the new socio-political order which he envisioned in his *New Citizen* could find a cultural sanction in Buddhism.[28]

26. "Lun tsung-chiao-chia yü che-hsüeh-chia chih ch'ang-tuan te-shih," pp. 45–49.
27. Ibid., p. 45.
28. Ibid., pp. 45–46.

In the first place, Liang pointed out, in contrast to other religions which often induced religious faith by playing upon human superstition, Buddhism called for the generation of faith through philosophical enlightenment. Nothing could illustrate this more clearly than a prime tenet of Mahayana Buddhism which enjoined the attainment of Buddhahood through the cultivation of compassion and enlightenment (*pei-chih shuang-hsiu*). This spiritual enlightenment must not be mistaken for a dogmatic belief in the existence of Buddha. The claim to believe in Buddha without really understanding his teaching was regarded in Buddhism as a more serious sin than blasphemy; the fact that one dared to blaspheme the Buddha proved that one still had a skeptical mind, which, if once enlightened, might well turn into a genuine faith. For forty-nine years Buddha had tried to expound his doctrines by all kinds of philosophical arguments because he wanted to make people attain genuine religious faith through the gradual accumulation of wisdom. In Liang's view, then, the Buddhist emphasis on the attainment of faith through intellectual enlightenment seemed to resolve the dilemma that resulted from the alleged incompatibility between intellectual enlightenment and the dogmatism of religious faith.[29]

Liang's second reason for commending Buddhism was that Buddhism, more than other religions in the world, sought universal perfection, not just individual perfection, as its ultimate goal. This characteristic feature of Buddhism was clearly manifested in the distinction in Mahayana Buddhism between the ideal of Bodhisattva and that of Arhat-Buddha. The latter referred to those buddhas

29. "Lun Fu-chiao yü ch'ün-chih chih kuan-hsi" (On the relationship between Buddhism and social order), in *YPSHC-WC*, ts'e 4, 10:45-52; see also D. T. Huntington, "The Religious Writings of Liang Chi-tsao," *Chinese Recorder and Missionary Journal*, 38.9:470-474 (September 1907).

who were concerned only with their own individual salvation without caring for the salvation of others. But the ideal of Arhat was held in great contempt by Buddha who, according to the Mahayana tradition, had sworn not to teach the truth to Arhats and had asserted that Arhats could never become buddhas; only those who seek buddhahood via Bodhisattva could succeed.[30]

What was the ideal of Bodhisattva? In Liang's mind, it was inseparably related to that of universal salvation in the framework of Buddhism. A Bodhisattva was one who cared for the sufferings of the world and vowed to save others before saving himself. For an aspirant to buddhahood it was naturally his highest aspiration to become a buddha. For the sake of saving others the Bodhisattva was even willing to sacrifice his highest aspiration. Nothing could better illustrate how highly the ideal of universal salvation was prized in Mahayana Buddhism. What really concerned Liang, however, was the likelihood that the same spirit of selfless devotion to the welfare of others, which the ideal of Bodhisattva inspired, could be harnessed to foster patriotic sentiments and a sense of social responsibility.[31]

This spirit was already implied in the distinction between Bodhisattva and Arhat that Buddhism was not a simple world-abnegating religion. Contrary to what most Sung Neo-Confucianists maintained, the attitude of quiescence and world-abnegation was directly at odds with the central spirit of Mahayana Buddhism. Buddha had said one should neither abhor the cycle of life and death nor should one love nirvana; both hell and heaven were all pure land. In fact, Liang emphasized, Buddhism featured a strong this-worldly activism which was expressed at its

30. "Lun Fu-chiao yü ch'ün-chih chih kuan-hsi," p. 46.
31. Ibid., pp. 46–47.

clearest in Buddha's reply to his disciple's question as to who should descend into hell to save people: "Buddha should descend into hell; not only descend into hell but also stay constantly in hell, not just constantly stay in hell but also always enjoy hell, not only always enjoy hell, but also to make hell perfect and dignified." With Bodhisattva's zeal to venture into hell and to make it over into a dignified habitat, Liang believed, a good number of dedicated souls could save not only a country but even the whole world.[32]

A further strength of Buddhism could be found in its belief in the limitless life of the soul as against its limited physical existence. If men were obsessed with the idea that their lives could not last longer than the short span of a few decades, they would be constantly haunted by the fear of death and thereby very likely become selfish and morally degenerate. But if men knew that there was an after-life for the soul, they would become free from the fear of death. Once transcending this basic fear, men could dedicate their lives to the realization of great ideals. T'an Ssu-t'ung's life served as a good example. The reason why T'an could fearlessly die a martyr for his cause, Liang pointed out, was that he believed in an after-life for the soul and was hence invulnerable to the fear of death and the attractions of worldly pleasures. Where did T'an derive his belief in the life of the soul? From Buddhism, Liang said; in his view, T'an's *Jen-hsüeh* was nothing more than a practical application of Buddhist ideals.[33]

Another commendable feature of Buddhism, according to Liang, was its teaching of the basic equality of all sentient beings with regard to their potential for becoming Buddha. Unlike other religions, which invariably enjoin

32. Ibid., p. 47.
33. Ibid., pp. 47–48.

all men to bow before a supreme deity, Buddhism upheld the belief that the Buddha-nature exists in the mind of every human being. In other words, in Buddhism there was no unbridgeable gap between Buddha and ordinary human beings, as there was in other religions which tended to place a gap between men and deity. In terms of the basic capacity for attaining buddhahood, all men were equal and no discrimination should be made between them.[34]

Finally, Liang also saw a distinguishing feature of Buddhism in its belief that nothing but one's own efforts could help one attain salvation. Almost all other religions, he pointed out, rely on some outside force for salvation. In this respect, Mahayana Buddhism is different from and hence, in his view, superior to other religions. Curiously enough, Liang maintained that in Hinayana Buddhism one could still find the idea of reliance on an outside force for salvation. But such an idea could not be found in Mahayana Buddhism where salvation was conceived completely as the result of one's own effort. Nowhere else could this emphasis on self-reliance be seen more clearly than in the Buddhist law of karma. Liang emphasized the ineluctable cause-and-effect relationship between one's moral deeds and one's fortune and found in the moral determinism implied in the law of karma a buttress for his ideal of voluntarism and activism.[35] In short, Liang seemed to see at the heart of Mahayana Buddhism the kind of activism which he recommended in his *New Citizen*.

For Liang, then, Buddhism was not only a source of spiritual direction but likewise an important cultural basis for socio-political development. Such an unqualified de-

34. Ibid., pp. 48–49.
35. Ibid., pp. 49–51.

piction of Buddhism as worldly activism is patently an exaggeration. Furthermore it must be noted that in Mahayana Buddhism the ideal of Bodhisattva as a suffering savior is central, while the ideal of self-reliance, which is focal in Theravada Buddhism, is much toned down. Yet Liang stressed both ideals as central to Mahayana Buddhism. In his depiction of Buddhism Liang seemed to be more concerned with finding cultural sanction for the new civic values he espoused than with an objective presentation of Buddhist doctrines.

In short, Liang was no radical cultural revolutionist as he sometimes seems to have been during this period. Just as Chinese cultural tradition looked complex and varied to him, his attitudes toward it were also complex and varied, sometimes determined by genuine intellectual commitment, sometimes dictated by didactic considerations, and sometimes perhaps also unconsciously influenced by his need to preserve cultural identity.

The New Citizen and Statism

In the early spring of 1903, Liang Ch'i-ch'ao temporarily put aside his editorial work at the *New Citizen* journal and visited North America. With this visit began a clear trend in Liang's thinking toward statism (*kuo-chia chu-i*), which, in the last analysis, represented not so much a new departure as an extreme development of some basic tendencies already latent in his thought. This trend toward statism became increasingly apparent and shaped his political attitude toward many important problems in the next few years.

Liang had planned a trip to America for quite a few years, but not until 1903 could he go. He set sail at Yokohama in February and landed at Vancouver. During the next seven months he traveled over the continent. Because Liang's primary objective was to see the United States, he spent most of his time touring that country and sightseeing in its important cities.[1]

Although he had been writing about Western democracies for many years, this was the first time he had set foot in a major Western democratic country and saw the workings of democracy at first hand. In view of Liang's enthusiasm for democracy one would expect his travel in the United States to have reinforced such enthusiasm. Yet

1. *LNCC*, I, 174–192.

the copious notes he wrote about his travel point to an attitude far from sanguine.[2] In fact, one detects in his observations of democracy a distinct note of misgiving, which
foreshadowed his harsh criticism of democracy after his return from America.

Liang's doubts about democracy are partly a tribute to
his critical ability in discerning certain seamy aspects of
contemporary American political life. To begin with, he
found to his regret that, for some reasons, men of first-
rate caliber as a rule tended to shun political life with the
result that many American presidents in the nineteenth
century were mediocre and lackluster personalities.[3] Liang
also considered the spoils system an ugly degeneration of
political life; and in his opinion this system had still not
been effectively remedied by the civil service system established in the late nineteenth century. Liang also noted
with great distaste the frequency of elections, especially
at the city level, as a tremendous source of waste and corruption. In observing popular elections at first hand, Liang
seemed to be occasionally besieged by the doubt whether
a democratic system, which was often oriented to courting
popular acclaim rather than to real problems, was any
better than an autocratic system. Of course, what Liang
criticized was more often than not some unique feature
of American political life or the defects of what he often
called republicanism, both of which did not necessarily reflect any shortcomings of democracy itself. And for all his
reservations, Liang still recognized the remarkable growth
of the United States as a country and gave credit to its
democratic system.[4] Yet he left the United States with the
impression that democracy as a working political system
was far from the ideal he had once thought it to be.

2. *YPSTC*, XII, 1–236.
3. Ibid., pp. 100–106.
4. Ibid., pp. 226–232.

Even such a system, Liang found, had to have unique conditions for its birth and growth. To begin with, he discovered that American liberalism had developed slowly on a foundation which had been laid before the American Revolution and was deeply rooted in the local liberal institutions of colonial days. He said the American Republic was like a towering mansion made up of many small buildings which had existed long before the mansion was built. The reasons for the magnificence and durability of this mansion must be sought in these small component buildings. Similarly, the secret of success of American democracy must be found in the political institutions of states, towns, and counties, which had been gradually fashioned since the sixteenth century. In short, the lesson he derived from studying the American Revolution was that democracy could only be built from the bottom up on a foundation of local institutions over a long period of time. The same reasons explained the brittleness of liberal institutions in both France and Latin America where democracy did not evolve out of a long tradition but was born of an act of revolution.[5]

Even the initial growth of such a democracy, Liang further noted, was not achieved without considerable coercion. Though American liberalism was rooted in local liberal institutions, the creative welding of these fragmented institutions into a democratic state owed much to deliberate planning on the part of a few great statesmen. What was more significant was the long-term trend of American political development, which, in Liang's view, seemed to be marked by an increase in the power of the central government. Liang was apparently influenced in this judgment by his first-hand observation of the presidency of Theodore Roosevelt, whose speeches and politi-

5. Ibid., pp. 213–216.

cal postures seemed to have a persistent appeal to him during his tour in America. On the basis of his observation of contemporary politics, Liang predicted that, along with imperialism, centralization would be a future trend in the politics of the twentieth century. As this trend toward centralization gathered momentum, the trend toward liberalism, Liang believed, would be overshadowed.[6]

The last stop on Liang's visit to the North American continent was San Francisco, where he stayed for a month to see the largest overseas Chinese community in America.[7] This close contact with the overseas Chinese seemed to reinforce his mounting doubts of democracy, especially with regard to its viability as a political system for China. This impression was largely a result of his probe of those voluntary associations formed in the community. He admired the comprehensive and progressive provisions found in the constitutional regulations of some of these associations, but he found to his dismay that almost all these associations had a variety of weaknesses that characteristically reflected certain defects of the Chinese national character.

To begin with, Liang discovered that deeply ingrained in the minds of such overseas Chinese was the inveterate familism, which, just as in China, was largely responsible for the inability of the overseas Chinese community to develop into a civic society. Aside from familism, Liang saw in these overseas Chinese strong basic sentiments which he called "village mentality" (ts'un-lo ssu-hsiang). By "village mentality" he referred broadly to those attachments which grew out of long residence in a specific region, be it village or city or province. In view of the fact that these local sentiments were also the building blocks of

6. Ibid., pp. 219–220.
7. Ibid., pp. 168–203.

the American Republic, Liang did not see this "village mentality" as completely negative. But if overdeveloped, as it was in China, it would stand in the way of the growth of nationalism.[8]

Side by side with these basic sentiments and particularistic ties, Liang further observed, was the Chinese inability to rise above their frivolous selfishness to higher ideals, and the Chinese incapacity for self-rule. Hence behind the impressive facade of the constitutional regulations of many of their public associations apathy toward public affairs was often found. What was more depressing was that an outwardly representative institution often turned out to be under the autocratic control of a few powerful local figures; or more often it was reduced to a government by the mob under the sway of many unruly young men in the locality. In fact Liang regarded this government by the mob as a typical pattern characterizing the working of almost all the voluntary associations which cropped up among the Chinese, both at home and overseas. Combined with elections which were invariably marred by all kinds of disputes, this pattern of representative meetings made a mockery of the democratic claim of these public associations.[9]

Liang became most pessimistic about the prospect of developing democracy in China when he reflected upon the fact that the overseas Chinese community at San Francisco, with a population of no more than thirty thousand people, had six newspapers, and doubtless was the most advanced community of Chinese people. Of course, he commented, there were a few outstanding people in China. But "while it is possible to rely on a few among millions to practice [governmental] interventionism for augmenting national

8. Ibid., pp. 194–195.
9. Ibid., pp. 196–198.

power it is impossible to infer from a few exemplary figures among a million the feasibility of liberty." [10] He even went so far as to regard any premature and rash attempt at setting up a democratic system in China as doomed. Thus he concluded his travels in America with an urgent appeal to the Chinese people to refrain from reading Rousseau's theories or from following Washington's example before submitting to the iron discipline of great statesmen like Kuan-tzu and Shang Yang or Lycurgus and Cromwell.[11]

Liang's misgivings about democracy and his preference for political authoritarianism must not be seen merely as a sudden change of mind in consequence of his observation of a democratic system at work in the United States and especially in overseas Chinese communities. The strongly centralized and authoritarian tendencies of the Meiji oligarchy, accompanied by the remarkable growth of Meiji Japan as a nation, could not fail to impress Liang. Because he had lived in Japan around the turn of this century, it is almost inevitable that he would be swayed by the general tendency among Japanese intellectuals to turn away from the liberal stance of Anglo-Saxon political thought to the authoritarian emphasis of nineteenth-century German statism. All these factors now became prominent in Liang's thinking because of his first-hand observation of what he called Western imperialism.

That Liang should see in American life such a haunting image of imperialism is not surprising because the intellectual atmosphere was then dominated by imperialistic ambitions and Anglo-Saxon racism, which found an eloquent and dramatic preacher in Theodore Roosevelt. Inevitably during his tour Liang's attention was drawn to

10. Ibid., p. 198.
11. Ibid., pp. 198–199.

the Rough Rider's jingoistic speeches and his aggressive postures in the international arena. During his short visit to Washington, he managed to arrange a brief interview with Roosevelt. In Liang's notes he also gave copious reports on Roosevelt's program for naval expansion and the latter's imperialistic interpretation of the Monroe Doctrine. Beneath the awe and enthusiasm shown in Liang's report one can sense a gripping fear that China might become the victim of these programs and doctrines some day.[12]

Liang also knew that imperialistic fever in America was no mere accidental product of the propaganda of a few public figures. During his tour through the major urban centers of America, its skyrocketing financial and industrial power could hardly escape his attention. In fact in his travel notes we find an unfailing interest in American industrialism and big business prosperity.[13] When he visited New York he managed to have a five-minute talk with J. P. Morgan, about whom he later wrote in glowing terms in his notes, calling him the "Napoleon of the business world." [14] In Liang's mind imperialism was inevitably linked with American industrial and financial expansion.

Liang found an institutional tie between fast-growing industrialism and imperialism in the emergence of the sprawling business organization — the trust. When he was first confronted with this gigantic organization during his visit to New York, he was overawed, straining his vocabulary to give a detailed description of it in his notes, which were sprinkled with statistics and tables. Liang called the trust a "giant monster" whose power would dominate the

12. Ibid., pp. 91–97, 117–125.
13. Ibid., pp. 25–26, 26–43.
14. Ibid., pp. 67–70.

world of the twentieth century and was far beyond the reaches of Alexander and Napoleon.[15] Indeed, his mind was so occupied by this new concept that after he went back to Japan he continued to study the problem and eventually published a long article in his *New Citizen,* titled "The Monster of the Twentieth Century — the Trust." In this article, the trust was subjected to extensive analysis.

Liang's appraisal was by no means a completely negative one. In fact an undertone of marvel and awe was often detected. Yet for all his admiration, a note of alarm was sounded almost from the very beginning. The giant monster would soon stride across the Pacific, and China would be its easy prey.[16] Such a tooth-and-claw image of economic imperialism was in fact nothing new in Liang's world view, which had long since taken Darwinian collectivism as its premise. Now a first-hand observation of economic imperialism at its source brought out sharply an implicit outcome of Darwinian collectivism which drove Liang to an anti-liberal political stance.[17]

Competition as the mechanism to propel social progress, Liang argued, usually took two forms whose utility changed with time. Sometimes "internal competition" was at a premium. To drive home his point he again resorted to the Darwinian metaphor of the "total" (*t'o-tu*) and the "unit" (*yao-ni*). Because a "total" was no more than an aggregation of "units," it was obvious that only strong units made a strong total. How to make an individual unit strong? Let the individual units, he said, compete with each other and this internal competition would eventually do the

15. Ibid., pp. 26–41.
16. *YPSHC-WC,* ts'e 5, 14:61.
17. Ibid., pp. 33–34.

trick. It was precisely in fostering competition and individual strength that the value of individualism and liberalism lay.[18]

But at other times, "external competition" took precedence over "internal competition." For when internal competition was promoted to a certain degree beyond which the group interest would be impaired, it was necessary to shift the emphasis to the need for coercion and integration within a group. Otherwise the group would lose its capacity for engaging in competition with others, and foreign subjugation would then ensue. The value of authoritarianism and interventionism then lay in strengthening the integration of a group and thus fostering the capacity of the group for engaging in "external competition." For Liang this logic had been well illustrated in the historical trend of the modern world since the eighteenth century. As he noted, for some time after the middle of the eighteenth century, individualism and liberalism had been the ruling forces in the world. In the late nineteenth century, however, the trend was toward an emphasis on the augmentation of government power in reaction to a previous emphasis on individualism and liberalism. Liang saw this change clearly in the growing influence of imperialism and socialism, which, while different in many respects, shared the common tendency to augment governmental power.[19]

Given these implications of Darwinian collectivism, it is no surprise to find Liang, soon after his return from America, enthusiastically embracing the political theories of German statism and assaulting what in his eyes was Western liberalism par excellence — Rousseau's political ideals, without, of course, being aware of the strong strain

18. Ibid.
19. Ibid., p. 34.

of collectivism in Rousseau's thinking. Liang's rambling arguments against Rousseau revolved around one central idea: Rousseau's liberal thought, however splendid otherwise, was not suited to the purpose of China's state-building. To begin with, Liang took sharp exception to Rousseau's view that a citizen could join or leave his state at will. It was possible to organize a corporation in this way, he countered, but it was not possible to set up a state on such a precarious basis.[20] By the same token, Rousseau's concept of universal consensus as the basis of social contract was untenable, for it was self-evident that no law could meet the approval of all concerned. In Liang's view it was similarly preposterous to claim equal status for all the people in a country, since leadership and hierarchical authority were implicit in the process of erecting a state.

Liang seemed to feel that at the basis of these misleading conceptions of the origin and nature of the state was Rousseau's failure to draw a basic distinction between citizenry and society. Whereas society was no more than a constantly changing association of private individuals, a citizenry was a fixed and unchanging whole which must have a much more endurable foundation than was provided in Rousseau's doctrine of social contract. This was especially true for China at her present stage. Whatever one might say about the value of Rousseau's liberalism for European countries, which had long established their unities, what China most needed was organic unity and effective order; freedom and equality were all secondary needs. In Liang's own words, China was yet to make the transition from "tribal people" (*pu-min*) to citizenry (*kuo-min*); Rousseau's thought was decidedly unsuited to the

20. "Cheng-chih-hsüeh ta-chia Po-lun-chih-li chih hsüeh-shuo," (The theory of the great political scientist Bluntchli), in *YPSHC-WC*, ts'e 5, 13:67–68.

all-important task of welding tribal peoples into a citizenry.[21]

Where, then, was the political doctrine which could serve the purpose of achieving organic unity and effective order and thus help the Chinese people make the transition? Liang now found the answer in the thought of a German thinker — Johann Kaspar Bluntschli's statism.[22] The attractions of Bluntschli's theory of statism for Liang are obvious. To begin with, Bluntschli's refutation of republicanism seemed to confirm all the doubts which Liang had formed about democracy as a result of his visit to America. To be sure, Liang pointed out, Bluntschli was by no means oblivious to certain advantages of republicanism, which had the virtue of shielding many people against the abuse of state power. But regrettably such a system had to grow in a special soil, as clearly indicated in the growth of the United States. This lesson is corroborated in the adverse experience of modern France. The French republic, according to Bluntschli, had had a very hazardous career in the nineteenth century because the French people in general had very unstable characters and the establishment of the republic was not preceded by a tradition of self-government. Liang naturally welcomed all these arguments made by Bluntschli as a happy support of his previous observations.[23]

But Liang further stated that for Bluntschli the disadvantages of republicanism were not confined to the requirement of special conditions for its establishment. Even after it was established, the system was often marred by other disadvantages manifested in nineteenth-century America, such as an incapacity for certain qualitative im-

21. Ibid., pp. 27–29.
22. Ibid., p. 67.
23. Ibid., pp. 77–79.

provements of cultural life, a reluctance for democratic reasons to establish a standing army and the consequent impairment of national strength, and a tendency to discriminate against people of the lower class in spite of its pronounced commitment to the ideal of egalitarianism.[24] But what most intrigued Liang was Bluntschli's observation that a republican system, being frequently subject to the sway of a capricious popular will, was often unable to provide a stable foundation for the state.

Liang went beyond Bluntschli's thought to draw further upon Gustav Bornhak's theory of the state to accentuate the inadequacy of republicanism as a political system. Bornhak first of all noted that a society invariably consisted of all kinds of social groups, whose divergent interests made their conflicts with each other inevitable. The function of the state was to rise above the conflicting interests of these social groups and to reconcile them. In a monarchy the monarch who stood above the social groups in the country would easily perform this function of state. But in a republic, the people were both the ruling and the ruled, so that there would be no higher authority standing above the people and regulating all the conflicts between social groups. For this reason, in a republic, social conflicts often developed into revolutions which made political stability difficult to maintain. One could readily see the validity of this observation by observing those republics in South America where political order was frequently disrupted by the outbreak of revolutions.

Hence in Bornhak's view, as in Liang's, the stable growth of a republic was a historical rarity which often could only be found in small countries which had strong religious unity, ethnic homogeneity, and social solidarity. Even the United States was no exception, for the secret of

24. Ibid., pp. 79–81.

the successful growth of the United States as a republic, as Liang never tired of pointing out, must be sought in the states in colonial times which were no different from small-sized republican countries.[25]

What most impressed Liang was Bornhak's concrete illustrations of all the destructive consequences which would flow from the attempt to establish a republic by revolution. Bornhak began by noting that a republican revolution would often mean shifting power to the people, who were invariably divided into different social groups. Since the historical rights and privileges possessed by these groups had been disrupted and the sacredness of government had been undermined, a political order was almost impossible to maintain. Violent social conflict would then inevitably ensue. In the beginning the most powerful were often those people of the lower class who were without property and who were also most eager to spread the cause of revolution. But eventually it was often the class of the rich and the privileged who emerged triumphant from social conflicts. These persons, being most concerned with the protection of their vested interests, would naturally try all means to restore order and stability in the society. Inevitably they would be led to attempt the reestablishment of the old monarchy. But since the legitimacy of that monarchy was by now already deeply discredited, it would be very difficult to reestablish it. Even if reestablished, the new monarchy would be too weak to tackle all the troubles which plagued the society. The result was often the rise of a popular strong man to replace the old weak monarchy with a democratic dictatorship. This pattern of historical development was evident in the examples of ancient Rome and modern France.[26]

25. Ibid., pp. 81–82.
26. Ibid., pp. 82–84.

What made this democratic dictatorship so frightening to Liang was that under this kind of political system one could have neither freedom nor stability. The democratic dictatorship usually commenced with the rise of an outstanding political figure who became a dictator with the support of the army. Having achieved power, the dictator also knew that naked power could not justify itself. He would then seek to establish his legitimacy through a plebiscite. Capitalizing on the people's thirst for stability and order and their disillusionment with freedom, the dictator, with all his power, could easily have his leadership legitimized by the plebiscite, whether as a president or as a monarch. He might also adorn his rule with such democratic institutions as a constitution and national assembly and claim that his government was held accountable to the people. But all these adornments could not conceal the fact that his power was essentially autocratic. The dictator could not be made responsible for his actions except by way of revolution.[27]

In sum, Bornhak's arguments appeared to have convinced Liang that in a country where the required conditions were lacking, the attempt to set up a republican form of government almost invariably resulted in an irresponsible dictatorship, as illustrated in the experience of republicanism in France and in those small republics in Latin America since the early nineteenth century.[28] For Liang these arguments were by no means of mere theoretical interest; they helped make up his mind about a problem of highest practical import. Ever since he had gone into exile in Japan where he had come into contact with Sun Yat-sen and other revolutionists, he had been confronted with the possibility of establishing a republic in China by

27. Ibid., pp. 84–85.
28. Ibid., pp. 80, 85.

means of revolution. Although practically speaking he stood opposed to the camp of revolutionists, his thoughts often evinced an ambivalence toward the idea. Now his trip to America and his intellectual contact with German statism resolved his doubts and hardened his position. He became a confident and firm opponent of revolutionary republicanism, which was rapidly gaining support among the Chinese intelligentsia at the time.

Democracy, Liang said, generally took two forms: republicanism and constitutional monarchism. If he followed Bluntschli and Bornhak in repudiating republicanism, what was his attitude toward constitutional monarchism? Liang's stance on this issue was by no means as clear-cut as his position on republicanism. His fervent exposition and recommendation in 1903 of Bluntschli's statism apparently implied his acceptance of the latter's ideal of limited constitutional monarchy as the most suitable form of government for China. But later in 1905 Liang published another long article boldly extolling the virtues of enlightened despotism and arguing against constitutional monarchism as untimely for China in her present situation. Liang's espousal of enlightened despotism was not a stable one either; for soon he was to engage in campaigning for the constitutionalist movement when it was launched in 1906.

Liang's ambiguous attitudes toward constitutional monarchism and his occasional flirtations with political absolutism were by no means adventitious, as is clear from his refutation of constitutional monarchism in his long article, "On Enlightened Despotism." [29] In this article Liang again sounded a note of pessimism which had already permeated his observations of American democracy: constitutional monarchism presupposed certain conditions

29. "K'ai-ming chuan-chih lun," in *YPSHC-WC,* ts'e 6, 17:13–83.

which did not exist in China in her present stage. In the first place the operation of a constitutional government was a very delicate and complicated task which required a certain level of education on the part of the people who administered it. Without sufficient education and political experience the Chinese people were inadequate to the task.

Furthermore, according to Liang, the working of a constitutional government also required certain institutional conditions like a census, extensive transportation facilities, the codification of law and the establishment of law courts, and the like, which were patently lacking in China. In the face of these difficulties and inadequacies, a premature attempt to set up a constitutional government could only result in discrediting it.[30] Although these are the explicit reasons Liang gave for refuting constitutional monarchism, a deeper reason was implicit in his arguments for favoring enlightened absolutism over constitutional monarchism. Liang had emphasized the distinction between "external competition" and "internal competition" and now enlarged upon it at the beginning of his discussion of enlightened despotism.[31]

Apparently his first-hand observation of imperialist expansion, fueled by the inexorable power of modern industrialism, had made the external competition of China his most burning concern. Liang's contact with the exposition by Bluntschli and Bornhak on the inherent difficulties involved in national integration as well as his observation of the divisive tendencies which prevented internal solidarity in China placed the problem of "internal competition" in a different light. Previously, Liang said, misled by the theory of natural harmony developed by the Chinese Taoist and some Western thinkers, he had simply assumed

30. Ibid., pp. 77–83.
31. Ibid., pp. 14–15.

that internal competition would result in natural harmony. Now he found that this assumption was untenable and that, given the universal conflict for survival, solidarity and order within a state were difficult to attain. This was especially true of China in view of her present perilous position in the grip of imperialist aggression. Thus, for the sake of external competition, internal competition must be curbed and regulated. Instead of internal competition "internal order" became foremost; domination imposed by the public authority in the interest of order was to be the supreme consideration. It is in this context that Liang said: "Domination is sacred." [32]

Liang placed the emphasis upon the central role of domination in the political order almost inevitably at the cost of liberal values. The institutionalization of domination necessarily entailed the differentiation of the whole society into the ruling and the ruled or the coercing and the coerced. This meant that inequality and hierarchy were elements built into social organization. Furthermore, the phenomena of inequality which ensued from what Liang called "coercive organization" need not be particularly deplored. It was a matter of nature that human beings were unequal in strength and ability. Without publicly organized domination, the weak would still be inescapably coerced and buffeted by the strong. Thus, while publicly organized domination would certainly induce inequality and circumscribe freedom, the cost involved would still be much less than that which would ensue if natural inequality were allowed to run its own course.[33]

The organized domination that Liang regarded as a necessity inherent in the political order could be manifested either in the form of "barbarian absolutism" (*yeh-*

32. Ibid.
33. Ibid., pp. 15–16.

man chuan-chih) or in that of "enlightened absolutism" (*k'ai-ming chuan-chih*). What were the criteria, then, that governed the two forms of organized domination? "Barbarian absolutism" was defined by Liang as that form of organized domination centered on the self-interest of the individual ruler and typified by Louis XIV's remark "*L'état c'est moi.*" On the other hand, enlightened absolutism was defined as that form of domination centered on the "interest of the objects of domination" and exemplified in Frederick the Great's observation, "Der König ist der erste Diener des Staats." [34]

In Liang's view enlightened absolutism had not only been a recurrent phenomenon in world history; it also had a long and respectable intellectual history and could be found in the ancient Chinese Legalist philosophers as well as in such modern European political thinkers as Machiavelli, Bodin, and Hobbes.[35] Such thinkers he would have excoriated relentlessly a few years earlier. Now he searched their writings for prescriptions for the political order of China.

An examination of Liang's interest in the thought of these men, however, suggests that his central concern was not with "enlightened absolutism" per se, but with a much broader underlying problem namely, "reason of state." It is well known that in the Western tradition of political thought, at least since Machiavelli, there has existed an intellectual trend, manifested most notably in the writings of Bodin, Hobbes, Richelieu, Colbert, and Hegel, whose paramount concern has been the rational conduct of government to ensure the survival and security of the state irrespective of its moral and ideological consequences.[36]

34. Ibid., pp. 21–23.
35. Ibid., pp. 23–34.
36. C. J. Friedrich, *Constitutional Reason of State*, pp. 1–128.

Specifically "reason of state" consists in the justification of such rational conduct of government as the supreme political end. In more general terms, C. J. Friedrich has said, "Reason of state is merely a particular form of the general proposition that means must be appropriate to the end, must, in other words, be rational in regard to the end, and that these means are the best which are most rational in the sense of being most likely to succeed.[37]

There is undeniably a close parallel between these European doctrines of "reasons of state" and Liang's political thought during these years. In 1903 and the few years thereafter, Liang gradually found that *kuo-chia* (the state), the new form of political order which he so fondly admired as a key element in modern Western civilization, once accepted by him as a "terminal community" and hence as a supreme political value, had a grim logic of its own. Placed in an age of rampant imperialism, China as a state was confronted with the overriding problem of survival and security. Driven by the inexorable logic of the organizational requirements of the state, Liang then found himself drifting away from his previous collectivistic advocacy of democracy toward the acceptance of an authoritarian state as a necessity.

Seen in this perspective, Liang's interest in enlightened despotism was but a natural development of his concern with "reason of state." But it must be noted in this connection that he was not interested in enlightened absolutism per se; he evaluated it primarily as a rational and effective means to cope with the problem of the security and survival of China as a state in an age of imperialism. But as a rational institutional means, political absolutism had a serious built-in limitation which Liang could not

37. Ibid., p. 5.

fail to detect; that is, it was by its very nature unstable. Within the framework of political absolutism there seemed to be no way to guarantee the enlightened nature of despotism except through the arbitrary will of the despot. Could the life of the all-important state ultimately rest upon such a precarious foundation? It was perhaps for this reason that Liang's commitment to enlightened despotism could not be whole-hearted and he remained more or less attached to some form of constitutional monarchism in spite of his occasionally professed belief in political absolutism.

In fact, if one looks more closely at the form of monarchical constitutionalism in Bluntschli's statism, Liang's ambivalence toward constitutional monarchism versus enlightened despotism may be explainable. We must remember that the point of departure for the development of German statism in the nineteenth century was Frederick the Great's ideal of enlightened despotism. As Rupert Emerson has suggested, the limited constitutional monarchy advocated by Bluntschli and other German political theorists in the nineteenth century was no more than an effort to prevent, by means of an institutional device, the will of a monarch from being arbitrary and thereby to guarantee his devotion and best service to the state.[38] In this perspective, both enlightened despotism and Bluntschli's limited constitutional monarchy may be seen as variant forms of the same principle of upholding the state as the supreme political value. The implication is that, however shifting and ambivalent Liang's political stance, his political outlook in the years after 1903 still remained within the basic framework of the "reason of state." In-

38. Rupert Emerson, *State and Sovereignty in Modern Germany* (New Haven, 1928), pp. 1–4.

deed, one may further suggest that his changes of heart were no more than reflections of the uncertainties he felt in groping for a means of rationalizing the state.

While Liang's overriding concern with the rationalization of the state led him to an ambiguous attitude toward Bluntschli's ideal of limited constitutional monarchy, it also led him to a whole-hearted espousal of such central concepts in Bluntschli's statism as the state and sovereignty. In Liang's search for "reason of state" he was concerned not only with what Weber called *Zweckrational*, which led him to accept any means required for the security and survival of the state; he was also concerned with what Weber called *Wertrational*, which justifies values or ends involved in his commitment to statism. He accepted Bluntschli's view that state is inseparable from sovereignty. As Liang emphasized, Bluntschli's view of sovereignty was different from both Bodin's and Rousseau's. While Bodin identified the bearer of the sovereignty of a state with its ruler, Rousseau thought that the sovereignty of a state should reside in the general will of the citizenry. On Bluntschli's authority, Liang rejected both, and maintained that sovereignty was neither in the ruler nor in the general will of the people but in the state itself.[39]

In so doing Liang followed the general tendency in nineteenth-century Germany to reify the state; in other words, the state was a moral and organic entity which had its own individuality independent of and superior to all its constituent individuals. Liang was especially emphatic with regard to this organic concept of the state, which he regarded as an outstanding achievement of political thought in the nineteenth century and as a great improvement over the mechanistic view of the state prevailing in

39. "Cheng-chih-hsüeh ta-chia Po-lun-chih-li chih hsüeh-shuo," pp. 86–88.

the eighteenth century. In Bluntschli's analysis, according to Liang, sovereignty consisted in the majesty or supreme public dignity of the state, its independence of other states, the power of choosing and altering its form of government, its irresponsibility, and its originality in relation to all the other powers of the state which were derived from and responsible to it.[40] Borrowing Bluntschli's theory of statism, Liang accomplished his rationalization of the state as the primary political value.

Liang's advocacy of the state as the primary political value is nowhere more clearly reflected than in his expounding of Bluntschli's view of the goal of the state. According to Bluntschli, there have been two principal historical views of the state. One view, represented mainly by peoples in ancient Greece and Rome, was that the state was an ultimate and intrinsic end for which people existed as a tool; people were to sacrifice themselves for the benefit of the state in case of any clash of interest between the two. The other view, represented by modern Germanic nations, was that the state existed as no more than a tool to serve the interests of individual people. In Liang's interpretation, Bluntschli leaned toward the first view. Though the private interest of the individual citizen often coincided with the collective interest of the state, in some unusual situations they did not. In these cases, the state could claim even the lives of its people. Thus on Bluntschli's scale the state was the primary value whereas the individual citizen was secondary.[41]

Liang's attitude toward nationalism had also undergone significant change, which might also be explained by his overriding concern with the rationalization of the state. Previously nation (*min-tsu*) and state (*kuo-chia*) had meant

40. Ibid., pp. 70–71, 86–88.
41. Ibid., pp. 88–89.

almost the same thing for Liang and in his writings he seemed to use them interchangeably. Now, following Bluntschli, he made a critical distinction between nation and citizenry (*kuo-min*), which Liang often identified with state in meaning. By nation he meant a group of people who lived in the same territory and were descended from the same ancestry, people who not only looked alike but shared the same language, the same religion, the same customs, and the same means of livelihood. By citizenry he meant a group of people who were not only a legal body but had also an organic and corporate personality capable of expressing its own will and formulating its own rights. A nation could transform itself into a citizenry and thus lead to the formation of a state, but it was not identical with a state.[42]

What is more important, Liang was very intrigued by Bluntschli's historical observation that a state need not necessarily be made up of a single nation. While it was true that in modern times the nation-state was the predominant type, previously, there were other types of states such as the city-state, the oligarchy, and despotism. Furthermore, even if the relationship between nation and state was often very close, it in fact varied considerably in different situations. When a nation was dispersed in several states, these states were often found to combine themselves into a single state. On the other hand, when a state contained several nations, the state might eventually split itself into several states along national lines, or some of these nations might join together and form a separate state.[43]

All these observations added up to one important lesson for Liang: nationalism, while important, was not the only

42. Ibid., pp. 71–77.
43. Ibid.

way to achieve statehood; the citizenry, the essential condition for the formation of a state, could be built up in several ways. The Chinese people, Liang felt, must be aware of this lesson, for they were polyethnic and the new state they wanted to build was necessarily a multinational state. Seen in this light, an appeal to nationalism for the purpose of constructing a new state might not be an unmixed blessing. An indiscriminate use of nationalism might very likely turn out to be a barrier to rather than a catalyst for the unification of a multiethnic China.[44]

At the time, Liang's emphasis on the distinction between state and nation was by no means academic. In the years around 1903 a debate arose among the Chinese intelligentsia and divided them on the question of the nature of Chinese nationalism. Until the early years of the twentieth century, the central stream of nascent Chinese nationalism represented by Liang Ch'i-ch'ao was mainly oriented toward anti-imperialism. But in the two or three years prior to 1905 the trend started to change and an increasing number of Chinese intelligentsia drifted away from the anti-imperialist orientation of nationalism and turned toward anti-Manchuism as the central tenet of Chinese nationalism. Before 1903 Liang's attitudes had been ambiguous until he accepted Bluntschli's statism and his increasing concern with the rationalization of the state had clarified the problem. In Liang's view, in committing themselves to nationalism, the Chinese people must make the choice: did they aim to build up China as a modern state or did they prefer to be carried away by a narrow revengeful spirit against the Manchus? The people must face squarely the multiethnic character of China and orient themselves accordingly. Thus he now proposed a new kind of nationalism which he called "broad na-

44. Ibid., pp. 74–77.

tionalism" (*ta min-tsu chu-i*) as opposed to the anti-Manchuism, which he contemptuously termed "narrow nationalism" (*hsiao min-tsu chu-i*). Under the platform of "broad nationalism" he meant to unite Han people and all the other ethnic minorities such as Mongol, Tibetan, Manchu, Muslim, and Miao for the common goal of building up a new state of China in defiance of imperialist aggression. "Broad nationalism" was, of course, no more than a rhetorical device; the underlying concern remained the political rationalization of the state.[45]

Liang's advocacy of statism was also illustrated in his refutation of socialism, which he undertook mainly in 1906. By this time socialism was nothing novel to Liang; much of the early Chinese literature on socialism was published either in his *Hsin-min ts'ung-pao* or by the Kuang-chih shu-chü (Extension of Knowledge Book Company), which he founded along with some other reformists in Shanghai in 1902.[46] In his own writing prior to 1905 he had occasionally discussed it briefly. In these discussions he expressed vague sympathy with socialism either on the ground that a socialist solution was necessary for Western society in view of the latter's "social problems" or because of his identification of socialism with the Confucian concepts of great harmony (*ta-t'ung*) and the equal distribution of land embodied in the utopian well-field system of land tenure (*ching-t'ien*).[47] However, in spite of his professed sympathy, he refused to be affiliated with the Western socialist movement when he was approached during his travels in America by a socialist who tried to convert him

45. Ibid.

46. Martin Bernal, "The Triumph of Anarchism over Marxism, 1906–1907," in Mary C. Wright, ed., *China in Revolution* (New Haven, 1968), pp. 99–100.

47. Liang, "Nan-hai K'ang-hsien-sheng chuan," p. 73; "Wai-tzu shu-ju wen-t'i" (The problem of the importation of foreign capital), in *YPSHC-WC*, ts'e 6, 16:1.

to his cause.[48] Liang did not state the reasons for his refusal until 1906.

Liang's exposition of his stance on socialism was primarily a response to the revolutionists who, under the leadership of Sun Yat-sen, had made socialism a definite part of their party platform since 1905. The concept of socialism as used in the revolutionists' writing was generally vague and sometimes even confusing. Some emphasized the nationalization of land; others stressed the public ownership of industry. Some admired state socialism; others sympathized with Western social democracy.[49] Even Sun Yat-sen himself did not develop a consistent position on socialism. True, a crucial part of his socialist thinking derived from Henry George's theory of the single tax: the state should claim all rent on site values and abolish other forms of taxation. Sometimes, however, his ideas on socialism were closer to those of John Stuart Mill than to those of Henry George in maintaining that the government should only tax the increase of land values brought about by the advance of civilization. Meanwhile he also allowed himself to be represented as an advocate of land nationalization.[50] It is little wonder that Liang's rebuttals of the revolutionists' arguments were correspondingly ambiguous, but in the last analysis his attitude toward socialism, as toward democracy and nationalism, was determined by his central concern with the

48. *YPSTC*, XII, 65–67.

49. Martin Bernal, pp. 104–106, 108–112.

50. Wang Te-chao, "T'ung-meng-hui shih-ch'i Sun Chung-shan hsien-sheng ko-ming ssu-hsiang ti fen-hsi yen-chiu," in Wu Hsiang-hsiang, ed., *Chung-kuo hsien-tai shih ts'ung-k'an* (Taipei, 1960), I, 161–166; see also Harold Schiffrin, "Sun Yat-sen's Early Land Policy: The Origin and Meaning of 'Equalization of Land Rights,'" *Journal of Asian Studies*, 16.4:549–564 (1956–57); Robert A. Scalapino and Harold Schiffrin, "Early Socialist Currents in the Chinese Revolutionary Movement: Sun Yat-sen versus Liang Ch'i-ch'ao," *Journal of Asian Studies*, 18.3:321–342 (1958–59).

security and survival of China as a state in an age of imperialism.

Liang's criticism of the revolutionists' espousal of the Georgian doctrine of the single tax was first of all on the ground that it ran counter to his concept of the rationalized public finance of a modern state. For Liang a rationalized state finance was an exceedingly important part of the rationalization of the state. Ever since he had taken statism as his central concern in 1903 and 1904, Liang's interest had been increasingly drawn to the problem of how to streamline public finance and to rationalize national economy.[51] One cardinal principle he found for streamlining state finance was that a modern state required a large budget to finance its varied and comprehensive activities. More important, in the modern world the general tendency was for the state to increase the size of the budget annually for the purpose of national growth. Thus, contrary to the traditional Chinese principle of state finance that government expenditure be determined by its income, the modern principle dictated the determination of government income by expenditure. This modern tendency of the state to increase the budget implied a dynamic and complex tax structure as its primary source of revenue. Seen from this viewpoint, Liang emphasized, the Georgian doctrine of the single tax was patently inadequate. For, according to this doctrine, the nationalization of land would provide the government with enough revenue from the sole source of land yields. A modern state in Liang's view must institute a variety of taxes to tap economic resources other than the land, not just to meet its increasing expenditures, but also to serve many other

51. Liang's interest was reflected in the fact that a large part of his writings during this period was concerned with the problems of public finance and national economy. See *YPSHC-WC*, ts'e 1, preface, p. 1.

important purposes of a modern state such as making the tax burden on the people equitable and fostering the development of domestic industries and businesses according to the needs of national interest.[52]

But Liang's attack on the revolutionists was not confined to their acceptance of the Georgian doctrine of the single tax. He also challenged their view of the Georgian doctrine of the nationalization of land as the core of a modern "ideology of social revolution," by which he meant Marxian socialism. Such a view, he emphasized, implied a woefully inadequate understanding of the "ideology of social revolution." In his view, the nationalization of land, while also a concern for the Western advocates of social revolution, was certainly not a central one.[53]

What came first, Liang stressed, was the nationalization of capital. The "ideology of social revolution" arose primarily as a reaction against capitalism; and the characteristic feature of capitalism was doubtless its tremendous capacity for creating and increasing industrial and commercial capital as a major factor of production. As a corollary, the "ideology of social revolution" inevitably considered the nationalization of industrial and commercial capital as its primary task. To be sure, socialism in the Marxian sense was also concerned with the problem of land. But land was never a problem in itself for socialism; it constituted a problem only insofar as the expansion of capitalism brought urbanization and thereby caused an increase in land values in the cities. Thus from the standpoint of modern Western socialism, the nationalization of land must be attempted as a part of the broader program of the nationalization of all major means of pro-

---

52. "Po mou-pao chih t'u-ti kuo-yu lun" (A refutation of a certain newspaper's proposal for the nationalization of land), in *YPSHC-WC*, ts'e 6, 18:1–20.

53. Liang, "Tsa-ta mou-pao," in *Hsin-min ts'ung-pao*, 86:21–24.

duction, preeminently industrial and commercial capital.[54]

For this reason the "ideology of social revolution" could not be applied in China in her present stage. Because its socialist program called for the nationalization of both capital and land, it was inevitably an undertaking of gigantic magnitude and tremendous complexity. Many of the problems involved had not yet been solved by Western scholars. In any case, given the educational level and political experience of the Chinese people, Marxian socialism was not an ideology which they could undertake to implement in the foreseeable future.[55]

The ability of the Chinese people aside, there was also the significant question of whether China needed a social revolution. In Liang's view such a need did not exist given the existing social and economic organization. One could see the truth of this observation as soon as the socio-economic background for the rise of socialism in the modern West was understood. The social and economic organization of modern Western societies, he noted, was laid on the foundation of the world-shaking Industrial Revolution, which began in the late eighteenth century. There is no question that the Industrial Revolution had tremendously augmented the productive capacity and the total wealth of the society. But this benefit of the Industrial Revolution was reaped at the price of the cruel exploitation of a large labor class. The result was that modern Western societies were polarized between the increasing impoverishment of the majority of the population on the one hand and the mounting concentration of wealth in the hands of a minority of capitalists on the other. This gross unequal distribution of wealth and its attendant social evils made the rise of socialism inevitable in the West.[56]

54. Ibid.
55. Ibid., pp. 23–24.
56. Ibid., pp. 6–11.

The deplorable effects of the Industrial Revolution might have been avoided had there been countervailing forces in the society to curb and regulate the development of capitalism. Surely the governments should be blamed, for they let themselves be misled by the prevailing laissez-faire policies. Some would argue that the oppressed working class was also to blame, for if they had formed co-operative factories among themselves, they could have prevented the dominance of the capitalists. But Liang challenged this sort of argument. In his view even if the working class had been conscious of all the dangerous tendencies inherent in the development of capitalism, they would not have been able to stem them.[57]

The reason was that the Industrial Revolution only intensified but did not initiate the tendency toward the polarization of the capitalists and the working class. In other words, the tendency toward polarization had long existed in European societies before the Industrial Revolution. In fact, Liang considered class opposition between the rich and the poor as an inveterate and endemic feature of Western societies. By the advent of the Industrial Revolution the tendency toward class polarization had developed so far that the poor were already powerless to resist the oppression of the rich. According to Liang the roots of the modern socialist movement must be traced to the socio-economic conditions of the West before the Industrial Revolution.[58]

In his view the fact that Western societies had already become polarized before the Industrial Revolution was important. For this was the difference between Chinese and Western societies and was the reason why China did not need a social revolution. Liang emphasized that Chinese

57. Ibid., pp. 10–11.
58. Ibid.

society, unlike Western society, was largely composed of middle-class families and hence was not an economically polarized one. The reasons must be sought in three important facts about Chinese society. The first was that, unlike traditional Western societies where the aristocracy had long held a monopoly of social wealth, Chinese society had been spared from the plague of domination by an aristocracy whose social role had been continuously shrinking in the past two thousand years. Furthermore, instead of primogeniture, which was practiced in the West, equal inheritance by offspring had long been the custom in China since the Han. Finally, Liang pointed to the fact that Chinese governments had traditionally imposed a lighter tax burden on their population than did European governments. All these facts, he claimed, accounted for a more equal distribution of wealth in Chinese society than in traditional Western societies. By the same token, when China underwent industrialization as she would be bound to in the future, the tendency toward the polarization of rich and poor and its attendant social evils could be at least much mitigated, if not completely avoided. If a society is not ridden with sharp class conflict between rich and poor, Liang observed, what is the need for a social revolution? [59]

If China had no need for social revolution, what, Liang asked, was her present need? The most acute problem facing China, he continued, was not the distribution of wealth but the problem of production.[60] China was caught in a life-and-death struggle with international imperialism which was primarily economic in nature. This economic imperialism, which arose inexorably out of the growth of

59. Ibid., pp. 10–16.
60. Ibid., p. 20.

capitalism, propelled a world-wide expansion which now converged upon China as its final prey. Thus, what China should be worried about was not internal class conflict between the rich and the poor, but international conflict between two classes of countries, the haves and the have-nots, which Liang elsewhere called the superior countries (*yu-kuo*) and inferior countries (*lieh-kuo*).[61] China, being a have-not country, and threatened with economic exploitation and subjugation by the imperialist powers, should naturally regard as her foremost concern maximum industrial production within her lands. In Liang's view, the best way to promote industrial production was undoubtedly the system which had already achieved such marvelous success in the West, namely, capitalism.[62]

Once again we see Liang's concern with external competition, which occupied the center of his attention and determined his attitude toward the problem of internal competition. Liang said: "The economic policy I advocate is primarily to encourage and protect capitalists so that they can do their best to engage in external competition. To this policy all other considerations are subordinate." This economic policy necessitated not only the borrowing of Western technology; it also required holding down rents and wages. Otherwise China would not be able to withstand the competition from foreign capitalists. From this standpoint the socialist concern for the welfare of labor was necessarily a barrier and hence must be sacrificed, at least for the time being, for the all-important purpose of encouraging and protecting domestic capital. Liang em-

61. Ibid., pp. 18–19; see also "Shih-chieh ta-shih chi Chung-kuo ch'ien-t'u" (The trends of the world and China's future), in *YPSHC-WC*, ts'e 7, 20:2–7.
62. Ibid., pp. 16–21.

phasized, "Encouragement of capital is the foremost consideration; protection of labor is the second consideration." [63]

But we must not be led to believe that Liang espoused capitalism in an unqualified sense. On closer examination, what he advocated was really a sort of regulated capitalism. In fact, almost from the very beginning of his contact with Western economic thought, he had balked at the doctrine of unrestricted capitalism. This was made clear in Liang's criticism of Adam Smith's version of economic liberalism, a criticism partly based on Liang's observation that the Chinese people were mostly uneducated and hence lacked the ability to be enlightened about their self-interest. Without this ability which underlay Smith's doctrine, how, Liang asked, could economic liberalism work? More important in Liang's mind was the fact that China was existing in an age of imperialism. Foreign business enterprises in general had the state power of their respective countries behind them in international competition. Thus no domestic private enterprises could withstand the competition from them. This fact was the principal reason why Chinese businessmen had always been on the losing side of their competition with foreigners. Thus Liang saw state intervention in business enterprises as an inevitable phenomenon in the age of imperialism. It was also for this reason that at the end of his study of Adam Smith's economic thought he rejected economic liberalism in favor of mercantilism as the most appropriate economic system for China.[64]

Seen against this background, Liang's championing of capitalism as opposed to socialism does not mean an unqualified acceptance of capitalism. At the end of the same

63. Ibid., pp. 28, 16–17.
64. "Sheng-chi-hsüeh hsüeh-shuo yen-ko hsiao-shih," pp. 21–22, 34.

long article in which Liang advocated capitalism as against socialism one finds a summation of his position, which bordered on social reformism. By capitalism he really meant a kind of mixed system where private enterprises were regulated by a strong dose of socialist policies established by the government, policies very similar to those instituted in Bismarck's Germany. In other words the kind of economic system Liang envisaged was one in which small private enterprises predominated but were effectively regulated by the socialist measures of the government not only to prevent the internal social conflict and oppression which usually attended a capitalist system but more important to facilitate the pooling of economic resources in the country so as to compete successfully on the international scene. Modern Western capitalism, according to Liang, had two foundation stones, symbolized by James Watt and Adam Smith. His idea was to preserve Watt's technology while replacing Adam Smith's doctrine of laissez-faire with German social reformism. This was the position he eventually adopted as opposed to both Marxian socialism and pure capitalism. The reason, he emphasized, was that his attitude toward socialism, just as toward nationalism, was ultimately governed by statism, which was also what lay behind his unstable and equivocal attitudes toward constitutional democracy.[65]

65. "Tsa-ta mou-pao," pp. 48–52.

9

The New Citizen
and Private Morality

The years following 1903 marked a significant development in Liang's thought not only with regard to political problems but also about traditional moral philosophy. This resurgent interest was first manifested in the appearance of a new section in his long serial, *New Citizen*, stressing the importance of traditional "private morality" (*ssu-te*). Liang had revived publication of the serial after suspending it during 1903 when he traveled in America.[1] This long article was followed in 1905 by the publication of two books which Liang edited for the purpose of elaborating his idea of promoting traditional private morality. One was *Te-yü chien* (Mirror for moral cultivation), a huge collection of Confucian moral precepts selected and arranged by Liang according to a number of categories of traditional moral philosophy. The other was an abridged edition of *Ming-ju hsüeh-an* (The intellectual history of Ming Confucian scholars), which Liang claimed resulted from his long and uninterrupted perusal of the book ever since he had studied with K'ang Yu-wei at Canton in the early 1890's.[2] Both books were interlaced with Liang's commentaries. All three publications, Liang claimed, were

1. *YPSTC*, I, 200–244.
2. *YPSTC*, II, 1–170; VI, 1–620.

designed to indicate the tremendous contemporary significance of Wang Yang-ming's moral philosophy.

Did these publications mean that Liang was returning to traditional Confucian morality and was revoking the commitment to civic virtues, which he had earlier tried to popularize in the first part of his *New Citizen?* This does not seem to be the case, for in his long article on private morality he stated clearly that the new civic morality could not stand alone but needed the indispensable support of private morality — the subject in which, Liang believed, Confucian moral thought excelled.[3] Since self-cultivation constitutes the focal point of Confucian moral thought, the question remains whether Liang's particular notion of private morality conformed with the Confucian pattern of self-cultivation, or whether its inspiration lay elsewhere.

Confucian self-cultivation referred to specific efforts undertaken for the purpose of realizing those moral values embodied in the Confucian personality ideal of sage-statesmanship. These moral values and efforts took on an imperative character in the framework of the distinctive metaphysical and psychological aspects of the Neo-Confucian world view. Thus the Confucian ideal of self-cultivation was first of all predicated on a set of metaphysical and psychological premises. Any concrete thing in the manifold world, according to the orthodox Neo-Confucian world view, was ultimately made up of a combination of *li* and *ch'i,* or principle and material. It followed that human life was basically constituted by such a combination. The *li* that subsisted in and governed individual human beings was called *hsing* (human nature). Moral degeneration began when *hsing* became obscured by the often turbid state of *ch'i.* In this framework, Confucian self-cultivation was

3. *YPSTC,* I, 201.

then seen essentially as an effort to "recover nature" (*fu-hsing*) or to "transform corporeal nature" (*pien-hua ch'i-chih*), that is, to cleanse and purify the sometimes turbid *ch'i* so that the *li* in the human body could shine forth and thus be the master of the human mind for a moral life.[4]

To Liang these metaphysical and psychological assumptions were no longer acceptable. This can be seen most clearly in the basic distinction he made between science and moral cultivation. Under the general category of science he made a further discrimination between material sciences and sciences of the mind. Liang believed that a fount of useful precepts and prescriptions could be found in the moral philosophy of Lu-Wang Neo-Confucianism from the standpoint of moral cultivation, but many Neo-Confucian metaphysical categories such as *li, ch'i, hsing,* and *t'ai-chi,* which served to explain human nature and the nature of the world, were no longer valid and must be replaced by those modern material sciences and sciences of the mind. Thus in collecting moral precepts for his *Mirror for Moral Cultivation* and in editing an abridged version of the *Intellectual History of Ming Confucian Scholars* for publication, Liang made a point of excising those parts which involved metaphysical and psychological assertions about human nature and the nature of the world.[5]

The second motif of Confucian self-cultivation was the realization of the specific personality ideal of sage-statesmanship, which had its definite content in a complex of moral values centered around the ideal of *jen*. In the course of the late nineteenth century this personality ideal had undergone a process of erosion so that by 1902 it was relegated to the periphery of Liang's moral outlook, if not

4. Mou Tsung-san, *Chung-kuo che-hsüeh ti t'e-chih* (Hong Kong, 1963), pp. 68–78; Fan Shou-k'ang, pp. 120–121.
5. *YPSTC*, VI, preface, p. 2.

completely replaced by his ideal of the new citizen. Liang's compilation of Neo-Confucian moral precepts in 1905 did not represent a resurgence of the Confucian personality ideal nor a renunciation of his new civic virtues; in fact, a scrutiny of Liang's writings on morality, especially the latter half of *New Citizen,* gives the impression that civic virtues not only held the center of his moral outlook but also tended to appear in a more intensified form.

This tendency to advocate an intensified form of civic virtue was evident in the great emphasis that the concept of obligation (*i-wu*) now received in Liang's *New Citizen.* We must recall that in the first part of *New Citizen* Liang had recommended the Western ideal of rights as an important civic virtue for Chinese people to cultivate. In that connection he had deplored the one-sided stress on an individual's obligation to others implied in the Confucian ideal of *jen.* Apparently frightened by the disruptive influence of the ideal of rights on many Chinese intellectuals who misunderstood it as a sanction for selfishness and licentiousness, Liang now reversed his emphasis and asserted the priority of obligations over rights. But in his discussion of obligation, he meant primarily the "public obligation," the obligation owed to one's group, particularly to one's country. It was this notion of "public obligation" that was particularly lacking in Chinese tradition, although the notion of personal obligation was at a premium. Apparently it was this civic obligation, not the traditional type of obligation, that Liang now wanted to foster in the Chinese mind. Without developing this sense of civic obligation, he said, there would be no citizenry, and hence no modern state.[6]

The group consciousness or the collectivistic sense which lay at the heart of Liang's ideal of public obligation was

6. *YPSTC,* I, 175–183.

developed to a religious intensity in Liang's new philosophy of death. According to this philosophy, all the major religious traditions and philosophical schools in the world shared one important belief, namely, that at the death of a human individual there was always something spiritual in his life which did not die with his physical existence and eventually constituted an element of collective spiritual heritage. He cited the doctrine of karma in Buddhism as an example. This doctrine taught that anything in the world, once its evanescent physical existence passed away, left behind a karma that would last forever. The karma of a human being was made up of the aggregate effects of all the actions and thought one had carried out in life. The total of all the karma of a group of human beings would constitute a collective spiritual heritage which was bound to condition the lives of later generations.[7]

Liang found a close parallel to this collectivistic view of karma in what he considered to be the Darwinian belief that improvements in human adaptability can be transmitted from one generation to another through hereditary transmission. By extension he believed in a sort of collective heredity by means of which the total character of a human group could be preserved and transmitted to posterity. This collective heredity Liang also called national psychology or social psychology, to the formation of which every individual, however little he might count as a member of the nation or society, had a share to contribute.[8]

Christianity and Confucianism, according to Liang, each in its own way, emphasized some collectivistic notions of spiritual heritage which subsisted over and above the individual physical existence. Thus, whatever differences

7. "Yü chih ssu-sheng kuan" (My view of life and death), in *YPSHC-WC*, ts'e 6, 17:1–12, 2–3.
8. Ibid., pp. 3–4.

there were between these major religions and philosophical traditions, they all shared some common beliefs: that human life was divided into two realms, material and spiritual; that the material body belonged to the individual while the spiritual life belonged to the collective whole of the community; and most important, that the individual's physical existence was bound to pass away but his spiritual life would last forever as a part of the collective whole.[9]

Liang's interpretation of these religions and philosophies may sometimes appear forced and awkward. The important fact, however, is that with these interpretations he took pains to urge upon his reader a new outlook on life and death. The physical existence of the human individual did not, he stated, have any intrinsic worth, for it was ephemeral and would pass into oblivion very soon. What really counted was the collective whole of the group, because it was this collective whole which embraced in itself all the spiritual values of individual members and would have an everlasting existence. The physical existence of the human individual Liang called "small self" (*hsiao-wo*); the collective whole of the group to which one belonged Liang called the "great self" (*ta-wo*). He compared their relationship to that between individual cells and the human body. Cells live and die through biological processes; yet it matters little as long as the body lives. Similarly, the life and death of the small self did not matter as long as the great self lived. Underlying this analogy was a life view which we might well characterize as radical collectivism.[10]

To this idea of radical collectivism Liang added a cult of martial prowess (*shang-wu*). According to him martial

9. Ibid., pp. 6–7.
10. Ibid., pp. 6–9.

prowess was made up of three components. The first was a kind of mysterious spiritual strength born of an unshakable and single-minded dedication to purpose which enabled people to defy danger and achieve amazing feats. The second was the raw courage involved in any heroic enterprise. Finally there was the component of physical strength. Liang was particularly struck by the physical weakness of Chinese people in comparison with the physical vigor of Western people, nurtured by the long Western tradition of physical education. Liang considered this physical strength an important factor in the Western quality of martial prowess. He did not hesitate to excoriate Chinese cultural tradition for this inadequacy. However, Liang did not see martial prowess as a prevailing quality even in the West. Only a few nations had cultivated it, for example, Sparta in antiquity and Bismarck's Germany in modern times.[11]

But martial prowess was not simply something he read about in history books. Liang, living in Japan at the turn of this century, could see it at first hand in the Japanese bushido which doubtless still constituted an important part of the national ethos of Meiji Japan. In fact in Liang's writing we find a virtual cult of Japanese bushidō. In 1904 he published a popular book titled *Chinese Bushidō*. The theme of this book was that although the Chinese had appeared historically as a physically effete and spiritually pacifistic people, originally they did not lack martial spirit. Liang's thesis was presented in the form of a historical argument, but his main purpose was patently didactic. He hoped to get the Chinese people to accept the value of martial prowess by showing its roots as being in the Chinese cultural tradition.[12]

11. *YPSTC*, I, 194–200, 186–195, 183–186, 198–199.
12. *YPSTC*, VII, 1–100.

The predominance of the combined ideals of radical collectivism and martial prowess in Liang's writings after 1903 meant that in terms of personality ideal there was no break with the civic virtues he had recommended prior to this time. They represented only a more extreme development, which tallied with Liang's increasing concern in the same period with the rationalization of the state in the realm of societal ideals. By implication the Confucian ideals of *jen* and sage-statesmanship which controlled traditional self-cultivation were weakened, for Liang's interest in Wang Yang-ming's moral teachings and his professed concern with the cultivation of personality was not directed to a moral life-goal, whereas Confucian self-cultivation was.

The foregoing examination demonstrates that Liang's interest in Neo-Confucian moral philosophy could only be mainly directed to the third aspect of Confucian self-cultivation, namely, precepts on the techniques of personality cultivation. This conclusion is borne out by a scrutiny of the meaning of the categories in which he tried to classify these moral precepts and under which he wrote commentaries.

These categories began with the concepts of *pien-shu* (discernment in motives) and *li-chih* (setting of the life goal). In the Confucian scheme of things, man was essentially committed to moral and political involvement in this world. This sense of involvement lay at the root of any school of thought in the Confucian tradition and also, naturally, of Neo-Confucianism. Thus it was imperative that the first and also the most basic thing in life for a Confucian gentleman was an act of existential decision — the decision on the direction of his life path, which meant, of course, a decision to commit himself to moral and political involvement in the world. This primacy of existential decision is as axiomatic for Liang as for Chu Hsi or for Wang Yang-ming, as is clear in his copious quotations from Confucian and Neo-Confucian literature to that effect. Liang seemed never to tire of emphasizing the primacy of an initial once-for-all decision which Mencius and Lu Hsiang-shan called the "head" of learning.[13]

But for Liang, decision was no simple act of will, but rather a deliberate process made up of two parts. An important part of this decision was what was generally known in Confucianism as *li-chih*. This task of goal setting was an all-important one in the framework of Confucianism, for the whole process of self-cultivation was designed to attain sage-statesmanship. But what now held Liang's interest in the plethora of Confucian dicta on this category was the general idea of goal setting rather than the specific life goal implied in the Confucian *li-chih*. Thus in his commentaries under this category he concentrated on elucidating the general importance of *li-chih* for patriotism and character discipline without specifying Confucian sage-statesmanship as the life goal.[14] In this action we witness the subtle process of transforming the content and yet preserving the form of a Confucian value.

What was distinctive in Liang's notion of goal setting was the fact that *li-chih* did not constitute the whole process of decision but was preceded by another category which also served to indicate the subtle ways in which the niceties of traditional moral thought might still influence Liang's mind. This other category involved in the process of decision was *pien-shu*, which almost defies English translation and can be rendered only roughly as "discernment in motives." [15] Liang's stress on this category as the be-

13. *YPSTC*, II, 23–35.
14. Ibid.
15. Ibid., pp. 1–23.

ginning of the process of moral cultivation doubtless reflected his intellectual affinity with the idealistic tradition of the Lu-Wang School. The Ch'eng-Chu School, Liang pointed out, featured a predominant interest in the search for written knowledge and an intellectual understanding of the principles underlying the external order of existence, which was apt to result in a distraction from Confucian moral concern. As a reaction against this overemphasis on intellectual goals, the Lu-Wang School stressed the priority of examining one's own inner motives before committing oneself to the pursuit of Confucian learning. The main purpose of examining motives was to discriminate between righteousness (*i*) and profit (*li*), or the public-minded (*kung*) and selfishness (*ssu*). In other words, at the beginning of a person's decision to set his life goal, he must ask the all-important question whether his motives for selecting the specific life goal involved any selfish considerations or whether he was completely motivated by altruism. According to Lu, Wang, and their followers, an answer to these questions required an unremitting and agonizing scrutiny of motives; for self-seeking motives were often very insidious.[16]

For Liang, this scrutiny of motives could be reduced to one single discrimination, that is, the discrimination between sincerity (*ch'eng*) and sanctimony (*wei*). The translation of *ch'eng* into sincerity, however, fails to convey the strongly religious overtones originally embodied in the Confucian concept of *ch'eng*. In its original sense this concept really meant a moral commitment unalloyed with any selfish motive, the intensity of which amounted to religious devotion. It was in this sense that Liang viewed it as the motivational root of any great achievement. But he also knew that *ch'eng* in the sense of unconditional

16. Ibid., pp. 1–8.

moral commitment was a rarity which required relentless scrutiny of motive for its inducement and constant vigilance for its preservation. The least slackening might result in sanctimonious piety (*hsiang-yüan*), which Confucius had deplored as the most insidious form of moral degeneration.[17]

Of course Liang knew that *ch'eng* in its original Confucian sense meant above all a *moral* commitment. But, he argued, did not devotion to a political goal like patriotism need the same kind and degree of motivational commitment? In fact, Liang found in these two Confucian concepts of *ch'eng* and *pien-shu* a timely antidote to a current cultural malaise. For, he observed, among new Chinese intelligentsia a misunderstanding of Western ideals of utilitarianism and individualism prevailed and often led them to an irresponsible assertion of selfish ends and a corresponding reluctance to commit themselves to a public cause. Too often a fervent espousal of patriotism turned out to be mere cant; too often a decision to serve the country was made casually and faded in the course of a few years. In view of these grievous tendencies Liang enjoined an unrelenting scrutiny of motives prior to the primary decision at the beginning of one's cultivation of character. In short, the existential decision which Liang envisaged was one which would set the life goal once and for all and command a motivational commitment as unconditional as that demanded by Confucian moral imperatives.[18]

After the initial primary decision was made, what followed was the actual process of character cultivation geared to fulfilling the life goal. Liang was confronted with the problem of how to commence. In the Confucian tradition

17. Ibid., pp. 15–23.
18. Ibid., pp. 4–7; 16–23.

the problem of the cultivation of personality was a center of controversy between the Ch'eng-Chu School and the Lu-Wang School. According to the Ch'eng-Chu School, in cultivating personality, emphasis was laid on seeking directions from the principles underlying the external order of existence, especially from traditional literature (*tu-shu*), which Chu Hsi considered as the royal road to the required exhaustive investigation of principles. Thus the intellectual study of traditional literature constituted an important part of the Ch'eng-Chu School's approach to the problem of self-cultivation. This study, however, was considered distracting and wasteful by the Neo-Confucianists of the Lu-Wang School who believed in the innate moral propensities of the mind. For the purpose of moral cultivation, one should turn to his own mind, or "inner light," so to speak, rather than to external sources for directions.[19]

Although the metaphysical assumptions of Confucian self-cultivation and the Confucian personality ideal and its related moral values, which self-cultivation was designed to fulfill, were either unacceptable to him or had only peripheral significance, those basic methodological principles of self-cultivation around which the intellectual controversy was centered seemed to Liang to remain valid for character discipline for modern purposes. What, then, was Liang's position on this traditional controversy over the priority of inner mind versus external direction in matters of personality cultivation? More important, what did his position on this controversy mean in his scheme of character discipline?

Liang's preference was doubtless for the Lu-Wang School, as is evident in his *Mirror for Moral Cultivation*,

19. Fan Shou-k'ang, pp. 147–153; see also Hsü Fu-kuan, "Hsiang-shan hsüeh-shu," pp. 29–46.

in which he urged people to recognize, after making the initial existential decision, the priority of inner mind over external direction with regard to personality cultivation. Taking cues from Mencius, Lu Hsiang-shan, and Wang Yang-ming, Liang called this recognition of the supremacy of the inner mind for personality cultivation *chih-pen* (awareness of the basic). His reason for preferring the approach of the Lu-Wang School to that of the Ch'eng-Chu, however, must be sought in the basic distinction he now made between two forms of education: intellectual study (*chih-yü*) and moral cultivation (*te-yü*).[20]

Liang did not doubt the validity of the approach of Chu Hsi as far as intellectual study was concerned — there appeared to be no other way to undertake intellectual study than to accumulate knowledge of the external world. But unfortunately, Liang noted, Chu Hsi tried to apply this approach to moral cultivation, which involved essentially a process of inner decision and inward scrutiny.[21] For this end, the accumulation of external knowledge, however great, would be irrelevant and might well be a distraction. For cultivating and disciplining character, Liang found no better approach than the Lu-Wang School's injunction to search for inner direction, especially as embodied in Wang Yang-ming's notions of the "extension of innate knowledge" (*chih liang-chih*) and "unity of knowledge and action" (*chih-hsing ho-i*).[22]

At the center of Wang Yang-ming's approach to personality cultivation, in Liang's view, was the concept of mind (*hsin*) and its substance, *liang-chih* (innate knowledge). By *liang-chih* Wang meant a kind of intuitive or pre-reflective knowledge of right and wrong or good and

20. *YPSTC*, II, 35–78, 37–41.
21. Ibid., pp. 38–39.
22. Ibid., pp. 41–65.

evil. Since this intuitive knowledge was innate in the human mind, the latter should naturally constitute the primary and ultimate source of moral directions. There was in the human mind, so to speak, a kind of inner gyroscope which, if set correctly, would provide unfailing guidance for personality cultivation.[23]

But unlike the quietistic mind in Buddhism and Taoism, Wang Yang-ming felt that the mind was essentially activist. It must be directed toward the outside world, which in Wang's framework meant primarily the world of everyday life. In other words, the substance of mind, *liang-chih,* must be applied and exercised in confrontation with the life-world. Thus the word *chih,* "extension," was critically important for Wang Yang-ming. In Liang's view the notion of the "extension of innate knowledge" indicated essential directionality, or if we are permitted to use a similar concept from existential phenomenology, "intentionality," of mind as understood by Wang Yang-ming.[24]

According to Liang, Wang Yang-ming's doctrine of "unity of knowledge and action" was but a complement to his notion of "extension of knowledge." [25] As we have noted, Wang Yang-ming's concept of mind was essentially activist. Thus, as the mind extended its innate knowledge to the outside life-world, knowledge and action could not be separated and could only form one unitary process. It was inconceivable for Liang that the moral imperative as ordained by the innate knowledge of the mind would not result in moral action. Action was inherent in the very moral character of the innate knowledge of the mind. To be sure, in this world one saw many cases where people's

23. *Chieh-pen Ming-ju hsüeh-an* (An abridged edition of the intellectual history of Ming Confucian scholars), in *YPSTC,* VI, 101–149.
24. Ibid.
25. *YPSTC,* II, 57–65.

words and deeds were not consistent. In these cases Wang could maintain that thoughts and words were motivated by knowledge already adulterated with selfish desires and hence were not based on genuine innate knowledge. If one were sincere (ch'eng) about innate knowledge, he would always unify thought and action.[26]

We can now understand why Liang had developed such a profound interest in these notions of "innate knowledge" and "unity of knowledge and action." In the first place, he thought that Wang Yang-ming's emphasis on innate knowledge was likely to produce a sort of inner-directed personality which would be less burdened by the traditional prescriptions of behavior and hence more dynamic in response to external situations and also more independent in its beliefs. Liang was well aware of the group of courageous and non-conformist personalities produced by the left wing of the Wang Yang-ming School in the late Ming. In spite of some reservations, Liang in general had a deep admiration for their great self-confidence and independent ways of thinking. His *Mirror for Moral Cultivation* was in fact sprinkled with quotations from Wang Lung-hsi and Wang Hsin-chai, the two leading scholars in the left wing of Wang Yang-ming School.[27]

More important than the images of dynamic and independent inner-directed personalities in holding Liang's interest was the primacy of action implied in Wang Yang-ming's doctrines of the "extension of knowledge" and the "unity of knowledge and action." In order to emphasize Wang Yang-ming's activism Liang had quoted copiously from the writings of Wang and his followers in the late Ming, especially from those of Liu Tsung-chou, the central figure in Wang Yang-ming's School toward the end

26. Ibid., pp. 61, 75–78.
27. Ibid., pp. 35–78.

of the Ming.[28] This heavy reliance on Liu Tsung-chou's moral thought was by no means accidental. It stemmed from Liang's effort to prevent any misunderstanding of Wang Yang-ming's thought, which might becloud moral activism as its central motif. For Liang knew very well that in the course of the development of the Wang Yang-ming School there was a prominent tendency to overemphasize Wang's concepts of mind and its substance, innate knowledge, to the neglect of Wang's injunction to act on inner light when confronted with the external life-world.

Liu Tsung-chou's moral philosophy seemed to Liang to be the right antidote for this distractive tendency, because Liang found in the central concept of Liu's thought the key to restore the primacy of action in Wang's system. If one could remain constantly on guard against even the faintest emergence of selfishness in the innermost recesses of his mind, he would be able to maintain the spiritual state of sincerity which would thereby further guarantee his action according to the dictates of innate knowledge. Liang quoted Liu Tsung-chou: "Constant self-surveillance (shen-tu) is the extension of innate knowledge." [29]

Liang knew, of course, that Wang Yang-ming's concepts of innate knowledge and its extension were all conceived within the framework of Confucian moral thought. But he had no doubt that these same principles could apply as well to the practice of civic virtues. Can we ignore the principles of sincerity and the extension of innate knowledge, Liang asked, in professing convictions about patriotism and group spirit? In his view, there was no other way than to use Wang Yang-ming's principles to prevent the degeneration of patriotism and group spirit into mere cant. This, he believed, was another illustration of the in-

28. Ibid., pp. 73–78.
29. Ibid.

dispensability of "private morality" to the working of "public morality." [30]

Thus Liang saw the images of an inner-directed and action-oriented personality reflected in Wang Yang-Ming's doctrine of the "extension of innate knowledge"; and Liang did not have the slightest doubt that this doctrine, if believed and put into practice, would have such effects on personality. For he did not deduce such effects solely from Wang's doctrines; he saw the actual effect of the latter on the formation of Japanese personalities in both the Tokugawa and Meiji period. For Liang the lives of outstanding personalities like Takae Toju, Kumazawa Banzan, Heihachirō Ōshio, Yoshida Shoin, and Saigō Takamori were perfect illustrations of such effects. Even in the military ethics of Meiji Japan which Liang had so much admired, he saw Wang's doctrines as a living force.[31]

Mind equipped with innate knowledge, for Liang as for Wang Yang-ming, was the inner source of direction for action. Since human life in Liang's view was a combination of mind and body, the mind naturally needed as much care as the body. According to his schedule for moral cultivation, after the inner mind was recognized as the primary source of guidance for action, there had to be deliberate efforts (*kung-fu*) to maintain the continuous functioning of this inner gyroscope and to check and rectify it. Liang found a mine of prescriptions in the moral philosophy of Confucianism and Neo-Confucianism which were valuable for these efforts. Drawing upon these prescriptions, Liang placed these efforts in three categories, namely, *ts'un-yang* (preservation and cultivation), *sheng-ch'a* (self-examination), and *k'o-chih* (self-rectification).[32]

30. Ibid., pp. 63–65, 70–71.
31. Ibid., p. 71.
32. Ibid., pp. 78–79.

While normally "preservation and cultivation" would constitute the major part of these efforts, self-examination and self-rectification were nevertheless almost equally important.

According to Liang, the mind needed "preservation and cultivation" for five reasons: first, this effort served to keep the mind free from all kinds of illusion and keep it constantly enlightened in order to see things as they were; second, it served to replenish mental energy and to maintain the mind in full vigor; third, it had the function of maintaining emotional stability and spiritual calm, even in the face of disturbing events and chaotic situations; fourth, it helped to keep the mind clear of preoccupations and thus receptive to new information and ideals from outside; finally, it served to keep the mind constantly firmly in command, in the sense that it would be invulnerable to either distractions from the external world or disturbances from the sensual desires of one's bodily organs.[33]

Liang spoke of these efforts with the utmost urgency, for in the back of his mind was an image of a spiritual self engaged in an unremitting war against a material world, which included not only the external world but also one's own bodily organs. The slightest slackening in vigilance and discipline would result in the subjugation, or in Liang's own terms, "enslavement" of the mind by the material world. The mere possession of innate knowledge was not enough to maintain the primacy of mind over the external world; the human mind needed constant and unrelenting effort to preserve and cultivate this innate knowledge.[34]

What were the methods for the preservation and culti-

33. Ibid., pp. 87–93.
34. Ibid., pp. 94–95.

vation of the mind? According to Liang Confucianism provided two principal methods for this purpose. One emphasized a kind of "single-minded seriousness" (*chu-ching*); the other stressed the inducement of a sort of "quiescent state of mind" (*chu-ching*).[35]

Although the notion of developing "single-minded seriousness" as a principal way to cultivate the mind was found in the moral thought of both the Ch'eng-Chu School and the Lu-Wang School, it was, however, the Ch'eng-Chu School that gave this notion greater stress. It was the literature of this school upon which Liang drew in developing this notion. In Liang's view "single-minded seriousness" meant no more than an imperative to cultivate the inner mind by way of controlling external attitudes. The human mind was constantly being impinged upon by all kinds of disturbances and distractions mediated through sense organs from the outside world. To prevent the mind from being led astray by the outside world, an unremitting and "single-minded seriousness" must be induced so that one's attitudes and behavior would be constantly on the alert.[36] In the context of Neo-Confucianism, this single-minded seriousness really bordered on religious awe generated in the presence of a transcendental deity. When one's mind was dominated by religious awe, no extraneous distractions could enter the mind.

In Confucianism, another equally important method of cultivating the mind was the inducement of a sort of mental quiescence. For Liang this ability to maintain a quiescent state of mind meant less vulnerability to emotional disturbances, which seemed constantly to beset one's daily life. The principal method of cultivating this ability

35. Ibid., pp. 95–96.
36. Ibid., pp. 96–101.

as recommended in Neo-Confucianism was, of course, quiet sitting. But in Liang's view, quiet sitting was only one such method. There were other methods, like the practice of calligraphy, walking alone in certain spacious areas, visiting a church, and even cutting wood, to follow Gladstone's example. The point was to ward off any disturbance of the mind so as to prepare oneself for strenuous actions and achievements in the world.[37]

Liang had no particular preference for either the cultivation of a single-minded seriousness or for the cultivation of a quiescent state of mind. As long as one sincerely practiced it, he held, either of them would be a great help. But beyond these two approaches commonly advocated by Neo-Confucian philosophers, Liang suggested another one which he claimed to have been developed mainly in Taoism and Buddhism. This was to cultivate the mind by enlarging spiritual vision as far as possible. The point was that one would not become egocentric and perturbed by worldly entanglements so long as one could often keep in mind the basic spiritual unity of the whole universe. For illustrations of such cosmic vision, Liang cited Chang Tsai's "Western Inscription" (*Hsi-ming*) and Ch'eng Hao's important essay "On the Realization of *Jen*" (*Shih-jen*). For Chang Tsai, and Ch'eng Hao, as well as other Neo-Confucian philosophers, however, such literature conveyed a world view which suggested a universal moral community. But for Liang such a world view became no more than a heuristic device to "cultivate the mind."[38]

Important as the category of "preserving and cultivating the mind" was in the scheme of Liang's moral cultivation, it had to be supplemented by two other closely related

37. Ibid., pp. 101–107.
38. Ibid., pp. 118–125.

categories, namely, "self-examination" and "self-rectification." [39] The reason must be sought in Liang's particular view of human nature. Certainly he still accepted the Mencian view that the human mind had innate moral propensities. From this view it was but natural to uphold the primacy of the mind and hence the central importance of preserving and cultivating the mind in the process of character cultivation. While the Mencian view was certainly true of the individual, it was only partially so for men who lived in a human group, a society, a nation, or a family. Original human nature might be good; but the habits which a man formed in association with other men would inevitably be colored by the social heritage, national character, and family upbringing, which might carry some evil influences to warp the original moral propensities of human nature. These acquired habits might add up to the formation of a sort of second nature almost as deeply rooted in human character as the original nature. Thus the fact that these habits are acquired and not innate must not be allowed to obscure their threat to human character as a potential source of weakness. For Liang this meant that the Mencian approach, which had its natural corollary in upholding the primacy of mind and in emphasizing the importance of cultivating the mind, must be supplemented by Hsün-tzu's approach, which recognized the inveterate tendencies in human character to evil doing and hence the urgent necessity for efforts to detect and then overcome these tendencies. Thus, the effort toward self-examination, self-reproach, and self-mastery could not be overemphasized. [40] Their absolute necessity in character discipline was evident in the lives of many Confucian statesmen and scholars whose unremitting and

39. Ibid., pp. 126–162.
40. Ibid., pp. 128–132.

painstaking effort in this direction Liang illustrated at length; it was also justified in the framework of Social Darwinism. Liang specifically referred to the concept of opposition between man and nature, between the ethical process and cosmic process in Thomas Henry Huxley's *Evolution and Ethics,* with which Liang had long become familiar in the translation by Yen Fu. In Liang's view, if social progress depended upon constant human effort to improve society in opposition to nature, improvement of human character naturally also required constant human effort to fight and overcome weakness in human nature.[41]

But self-examination and self-mastery are no easy tasks; they need constant alertness and unrelenting effort. They also need meticulous methods for daily practice. According to Liang, the methods of self-examination, as provided by Confucianism, could be divided generally into two kinds: the ordinary and the special. The former was designed for practice in everyday life when nothing unusual happened to disturb the mind. This could be broken down into two varieties: one variety was designed to make sure of the commanding place of the inner mind in our daily actions; the other was designed to check our actions, thinking, and words against the commands of our inner mind. The individual could practice this method either in a regular way, that is, whenever he did something, or thought something, or said something. Or he could practice it at certain specified intervals every day, as Tseng-tzu, Chu Hsi, and Tseng Kuo-fan did. All these methods were still meant for practice in everyday life. When something unusual happened that distressed the mind and emotions became perturbed, self-examination was to be practiced more frequently and more relentlessly than usual. Only by practicing these meticulous methods of self-examination

41. Ibid., pp. 131–132, 160–162.

could one overcome his weaknesses and cultivate his character.[42]

By now it should be clear that Liang's profound interest in Neo-Confucianism, especially Wang Yang-ming's moral philosophy as a source of ideas for personality cultivation, does not mean that his notion of personality cultivation can be simply identified with the Confucian notion of self-cultivation. To be sure, he derived important elements from Neo-Confucian tradition, namely, some methodological principles and precepts of Neo-Confucian character discipline. However, the two other important elements in the Confucian notion of self-cultivation, namely, the psycho-cosmological world view and those moral values organized around the Confucian personality ideal of sage-statesmanship, for the most part receded into the background.

A modern reader may dismiss Liang's works on Neo-Confucian moral philosophy as no more than an attempt to placate his emotional need to assert China's national heritage in the face of a massive cultural threat from outside. But as is clear from the foregoing analysis, Liang's writings were done on the genuine conviction that some methodological precepts of Neo-Confucianism for character discipline could be very helpful to the disciplining of personality required for his envisioned "new citizen." In his mind his interest in the Neo-Confucian techniques of character discipline designed to achieve an inner-directed and action-oriented personality involved nothing to contradict the new civic virtues and political values he advocated. Because Liang had lived in Meiji Japan, where tradition and Western impact often blended into successful synthesis, it was but natural for him to think that some traditional Chinese techniques could be made to serve

42. Ibid., pp. 139–142.

Western values just as Western techniques could sometimes be made to serve Chinese values.

Liang's persistent interest in Neo-Confucian moral philosophy as the source of ideas for character discipline is very instructive for it shows us some elements of the Confucian tradition which continued to exist in the ethos of modern Chinese culture. More significant, Liang was not the only person who retained this interest. Neo-Confucianism, especially the moral philosophy of Wang Yangming, had persistent intellectual appeal among modern Chinese and also among East Asians in general. Liang's thought, then, suggests some ways in which certain elements in Confucianism could blend with modern Western ethos. Confucianism was a complex system of thought; its varied and intricate interactions with the cultural impact of the modern West are yet to be explored.

10

Conclusion

In March 1907, the offices of the *New Citizen* were damaged by a fire and four months later the journal stopped publication. With the closing of this journal Liang passed the height of his intellectual influence. From then on he became increasingly involved in political activities. Although throughout his life his political involvements did not prevent his versatile mind from being active, he was nevertheless never able to recapture the kind of intellectual dominance he achieved in the first part of the 1900's. We may thus stop at this point and attempt to relate the intellectual role Liang had so far played to the larger context of the intellectual transition from traditional to modern China.

The point of departure of Liang's intellectual development is the reemergence of Confucian practical statesmanship as an operative ideal in the late Ch'ing. Since this ideal governed not only attitudes toward the world but also approaches to the problem of state and society, its cultural erosion was inevitable as Western impact set in during the nineteenth century. The undermining of Confucian practical statesmanship was most evident from the mid-1890's to the mid-1900's.

In that decade the radical erosion of that Confucian ideal left the polity of China in a state of cultural disorientation. In the minds of many Chinese, Chinese polity could no longer be effectively governed by Confucian cultural values. The emergence of an autonomous polity immediately created a series of critical problems: if those cultural values and norms embodied in the Confucian ideal of practical statesmanship were no longer applicable, where could their replacement be found to supply the polity with workable forms and organizing principles? And what new framework existed in terms of which the new forms and principles of polity could be made legitimate and meaningful in the cultural context of China?

In the search for answers to these problems Chinese intellectuals started to turn to Western ideologies in the decade after 1890. The West seemed to them to be a possible source of authoritative concepts, meaningful images, and suasive frameworks, which would provide them with guidelines as to the forms, goals, and organization of their newly differentiated polity.[1] In a sense it can be said that ever since that time Chinese intellectuals have never ceased in their frantic search for ideological reorientations of polity. Seen in this perspective this decade was an important cultural watershed in which the intellectual tradition of Confucian practical statesmanship drew to a close and the search for ideological reorientation which is still in process today was instituted.

The development of Liang's thought in this crucial transitional period may thus be regarded as an important intellectual link between the age-old tradition of Confucian practical statesmanship and the contemporary search for ideological reorientation. I have already traced the transformation of the ideal of Confucian practical statesmanship into new images of state and citizenship in

1. See Clifford Geertz, "Ideology as a Cultural System," in David S. Apter, ed., *Ideology and Discontent* (New York, 1964), pp. 60–65.

Liang's thought between 1890 and 1907. On the level of societal ideals two processes were involved. First, there was a turning away from the universal moral community (*t'ien-hsia*) and an acceptance of the state as the terminal community. Second, there was the transformation of the moral goal of the state into the political goal of collective achievement and dynamic growth. Integral to both processes is a clear differentiation of polity from morality, two concepts that were inseparably fused in the tradition of Confucian practical statesmanship. But the autonomy of polity also entailed a tendency to see the state as the highest locus of values.

To be sure, Liang had also accepted democratization as an integral part of the modern concept of state. But since he viewed democracy basically from a collectivistic and utilitarian point of view, his democratic convictions did not exert as much check on his inclination to statism as might be anticipated in the context of Western liberal tradition. Thus without the governance of traditional moral values and without the control of Western liberal values, concern only with the state and its rationalization always carried the possibility of political authoritarianism.

On the level of the personality ideal the metamorphosis of Liang's mind involved the change from the image of sage-statesmanship to the ideal of citizenship. The essence of Liang's citizen-ideal was collectivistic and activistic, very much akin to the Renaissance ideal of political *virtu*. Thus, unlike the Confucian ideal of sage-statesmanship, in which moral orientation was central, citizenship as conceived by Liang was not primarily a morally directed ideal. More specifically, his concept of citizenship was no longer, as was the personality ideal of sage-statesmanship, governed by the Confucian principle of self-

298

cultivation. This by no means implies that some elements of Confucian self-cultivation were not involved in Liang's ideal of citizenship. In fact, as is clear in Liang's formulation of "private morality" on the basis of Wang Yang-ming's moral philosophy, the technical precepts on character discipline which were part and parcel of the complex of Confucian self-cultivation still found an important place in Liang's ideal of the new citizen. In other words, he believed that instead of conflicting with those civic virtues embodied in his ideal of citizenship, many Confucian precepts on the techniques of character discipline could be used in forming the kind of personality he envisioned in his *New Citizen*. In this respect Liang was typical of many of his contemporaries who accepted the modern citizen-ideal and yet still found in Confucianism precious sources of precepts on character discipline.

Liang's formulations of new political values and civic virtues were significant not only because they broke radically with the Confucian ideal of practical statesmanship but also because they formed a cluster of values and images which seemed to be present in many of the ideological developments of twentieth-century China. Although Liang disagreed with his principal antagonists, the revolutionists, over a wide range of ideological issues, a closer look at the literature of both sides seems to indicate that they agreed far more than they disagreed on the level of basic values. Although the revolutionists disagreed with Liang's emphasis on the orientation of Chinese nationalism to foreign imperialism and stressed anti-Manchuism as the main theme of Chinese nationalism, one doubts very much whether they would ultimately dispute with the same seriousness Liang's vision of China as a modern state which would include the Manchus and other ethnic minority groups rather than exclude them.[2] They might differ with each other about the meaning of Western socialism and argue over the problem of the nationalization of land, but they both more or less ended up with some sort of state socialism.[3] It is true that the revolutionists advocated republicanism and Liang preferred constitutional monarchism. Yet we may question whether the revolutionist would oppose Liang's basic idea of democratization in the sense of political participation as a means to state building. For all their noisy controversy over the problem of reform versus revolution, their differences seemed to fall more on the approaches than on the ultimate societal goals. If in the last analysis they disagreed little in terms of basic societal goals, they differed even less on personality ideal. This conclusion is clear from the fact that the revolutionists concentrated their polemical fire on Liang's ideological formulations of the issues of society and state without challenging his depiction of the citizen ideal.[4]

Among the May Fourth generation of Chinese intellectuals the situation is more complex. Some new elements are so obvious that at first glance one would hesitate to postulate similarities between this generation and the preceding one. To be sure, in a very broad sense both generations shared a common cultural approach to China's problems, which meant a tendency to assume the decisive roles of values and ideas in shaping human action and thereby to give priority to the renovation of the mind as the basic

2. This is clearly evidenced in the fact that when the Republic was eventually set up in 1911 almost all the Revolutionists accepted the principle that all the ethnic groups, including Manchus, should be included in the new Republic on an equal footing.

3. Robert A. Scalapino and Harold Schiffrin, pp. 321–342.

4. A cursory look at the contents of *Min-pao* (The people), the official journal of the T'ung-meng hui, will indicate that practically all the subjects in that journal dealt with sociopolitical problems.

approach to the national rejuvenation of China. This shared cultural approach should not, however, blind us to the specific differences which distinguished the cultural approach of Liang in formulating his ideal of the new citizen from the approach used by the May Fourth generation in formulating the ideal of new youth. In the first place, while both stressed the primary importance of the cultural renovation of Chinese minds, there were important differences of degree between their specific attitudes toward Chinese cultural tradition. The iconoclasm of the May Fourth generation was whole-hearted and totalistic. Its attack on the Chinese cultural tradition was not confined to Confucianism and Taoism; Buddhism was also denounced without reservation. A total darkness thus began to come over the Chinese sense of the past, creating a tendency to see an irreconcilable contradiction between the future and the past. This Manichean outlook bred in Chinese intellectuals a disposition to seek holistic and all-embracing solutions for their problems.

In contrast, in his *New Citizen* Liang only partly rejected Chinese cultural tradition. He did sometimes call for a moral revolution and a complete destruction of the past. But this note of radicalism was more rhetorical than serious; basically Liang was a reformist at heart and discriminating in his attitude toward Chinese cultural tradition. He still saw considerable cultural value in Confucianism and Buddhism; only Taoism received his unrelenting excoriation. Even in his most radical years, he still retained a basic trust in certain Confucian moral values in the realm of personal conduct and family ethics. Moreover, he still looked to Confucianism and Buddhism as the primary sources of character discipline.

Another difference which divides the cultural approaches of the two generations lies in their divergent attitudes toward religion and science. The intellectuals of the May Fourth generation were known for their radical opposition to religion. Religion in their eyes was merely a complex of gross superstitions which were bound to be swept away by the march of civilization. Underlying this antireligious stance was a militant intellectualism, at the core of which lay the cult of science. For them science became the master key to solve any human problem.[5]

Liang's writings do not show such a cult of science, although Western secular knowledge held a prominent place. Science as a talisman, as a master key to the rejuvenation of China, had not yet appeared. Concomitant with the absence of a cult of science was a marked tendency toward a positive evaluation of religion. Instead of being regarded as merely a drag on intellectual enlightenment, religion was viewed as necessary for social solidarity and as a spring of motivation for human achievement.

As for the cluster of personality and societal ideals spelled out by Liang in his *New Citizen,* on the surface one would feel even more hesitant to draw a close parallel between the *New Youth (Hsin ch'ing-nien)* of the May Fourth generation and Liang's ideal of citizenship. It is true that in the *New Youth* one finds a cult of activism and dynamism and praise of wealth-producing activities. These themes, in fact, bulk especially large in Ch'en Tu-hsiu's strident glorification of what he thought to be the main features of modern Western civilization — the cult of youth and progress, the stress on economic activity, utilitarianism, and the worship of struggle, war, and "animalism" *(shou-hsing chu-i).*[6] All these qualities sound

5. See D. W. Y. Kwok, *Scientism in Chinese Thought 1900–1950* (New Haven, 1965), pp. 20–119.
6. See Ch'en Tu-hsiu, "Ching-kao ch'ing-nien" (My solemn plea to the youth), "Fa-lan-hsi-jen yü chin-shih wen-ming" (The French people and modern civilization), "Chin-jih chih chiao-yü fang-chen" (Directions for

like echoes of Liang's ideal of the *New Citizen,* except that the *New Youth* contained a note of individualism quite incongruous with the motif of collectivism in Liang's writings. One clear index of this new note was Hu Shih's espousal of what he called Ibsenism. As a consequence one saw in the *New Youth* an attack on an unprecedented scale upon Confucian family ethics, which were now seen as a deadening shackle on the development of the individual personality.[7] This attitude differed notably from that of the *New Citizen,* in which by and large Confucian family ethics were not yet felt as a serious hindrance to the development of citizenship.

On the level of the societal ideal, one finds in the *New Youth* a more pronounced cult of democracy: along with science, it was now accepted as the primary symbol of modern civilization. But unlike Liang's *New Citizen,* in which democracy was inseparably fused with a feverish cult of nationalism, the exaltation of democracy was concomitant with a toning down of nationalism. Pronounced as this de-emphasis on nationalism was in the *New Youth,* it should not, however, be construed as a total turning away from nationalism. At least it would be inconceivable that the May Fourth generation had gone so far as to become disillusioned with the idea of the nation-state. A more logical explanation is that the idea of the nation-state had by now become universally accepted and was indeed taken for granted by Chinese intelligentsia. Thus what made some of the intellectuals of the May Fourth

current education), "Ti-k'ang li" (The force of resistance), "K'ung-tzu chih tao yü hsien-tai sheng-ho" (The Confucian way and modern life), "Tung-hsi min-tsu ken-pen ssu-hsiang chih ch'a-i" (Basic differences of intellectual outlook between peoples of East and West), "Jen-sheng chen-i" (The true meaning of life), in *Tu-hsiu wen-ts'un* (Hong Kong, 1965), I, 1:1–40, 113–125, 181–187.

7. Hu Shih, "I-pu-sheng chu-i" (Ibsenism), in *Hu Shih wen-ts'un* (Taipei, 1953), I, 4:629–647.

generation suspicious of nationalism was not the idea of the nation-state but the overblown patriotic feelings usually built around it. These patriotic feelings might make for political extremism and for cultural exclusivism, which would run counter to the open-mindedness of the May Fourth generation toward modern Western civilization. This is perhaps what Ch'en Tu-hsiu had in mind when he urged the Chinese to cultivate a reflective rather than an instinctive patriotism.[8]

But nationalism was not something which the *New Youth* intelligentsia could hold in abeyance long. Very soon they were again carried away by the spirit of the May Fourth Movement. With the growing tide of nationalism and, later on, of socialism, collectivism again became increasingly dominant over individualism.

Thus, despite the note of individualism and the apparent toning down of nationalism which characterized the writing of some of the *New Youth* intelligentsia, the personality and societal ideals which eventually emerged from the May Fourth Movement were not much different from those Liang propounded in the *New Citizen*. Indeed, taking a broad look at the major ideological trends of the post-May Fourth China, one may even venture to maintain that Liang's ideal of citizenship has persisted through the May Fourth Movement to become an important and enduring part of the value system of twentieth-century China.

We may question whether the cluster of values Liang recommended in his formulation of the ideal of citizenship had any place in neo-traditionalism, a major intellectual trend of post-May Fourth Chinese thought. Strictly speaking neo-traditionalists referred only to those persons who were still basically committed to traditional values and

8. Ch'en Tu-hsiu, "Ai-kuo-hsin yü tzu-chüeh-hsin," *Chia-yin tsa-chih,* 1.4:1–6 (November 1914).

who accepted some elements of modern Western civilization primarily as a means of promoting or preserving the prized traditional values. But neo-traditionalism, as applied to the intellectual scene of contemporary China, was a very loose category. Of those who were counted in this category many might well have been reformists trying to introduce modern Western values in the guise of traditional thought. Some might have become interested in elements of traditional thought because they genuinely believed that these elements could be made complementary or instrumental to the Western values they upheld. Between 1903 and 1907, for instance, Liang might have had a profound interest in those aspects of Neo-Confucian literature dealing with the techniques of character discipline but might not necessarily have been committed to the specific underlying Confucian personality ideal. Thus it is likely that even for some so-called neo-traditionalists Liang's image of the new citizen struck a sympathetic chord.

In regard to another important current of twentieth-century Chinese thought — liberalism — one would presume that for those liberals who were admirers of modern Western civilization Liang's image of citizenship was highly congenial except for its collectivistic orientation. It is, however, important that, unlike modern Western liberalism, individualism was never deeply rooted in Chinese liberalism. Among Chinese liberals there seems to have been a widespread tendency to appreciate democracy more as an indispensable functioning part of a modern nation-state than as an institution to protect individual rights and liberties. This tendency was clearly illustrated by the fact that when the Nationalist regime gradually consolidated itself in the early 1930's a group of liberal intellectuals, including such notables as Ting Wen-chiang and T. F.

Tsiang, were critical of democracy from the standpoint of nationalism and became open advocates of dictatorship as a more effective institutional means to secure and strengthen the state in a time of international and domestic crisis.[9] This tendency was again reflected in the fact that the large majority of Chinese liberal intellectuals gave support to the Communists when they seized power on the mainland in the late 1940's. Doubtless for them nationalism and the rationalization of the state were more important concerns than liberal values. Seen in this perspective, the collectivistic orientation of Liang's ideal of citizenship was certainly more representative of Chinese liberalism than was the ambivalent note of individualism in Hu Shih's thought.

Similarly, in communism, which, in addition to neo-traditionalism and liberalism, constitutes a major ideological trend of contemporary China, Liang's ideal of citizenship could find a pronounced resonance. To begin with, in spite of the original internationalist claim of communism there is no question that nationalism has increasingly become a dominant theme in the Chinese Communist movement. Along with this prominent strain of nationalism is a growing tendency toward the cult of the state and a regard for the rationalization of the state as an overriding concern, again contrary to the Marxist prediction of the "withering away of the state." Were not these societal ideals already prominent in Liang's formulation of citizenship?

In terms of personality ideal the continuity between

9. For an understanding of this debate, which took place among liberals about democracy versus dictatorship in 1933 and 1934, see the essays published by Hu Shih, Wu Ching-ch'ao, T. F. Tsiang, Ting Wen-chiang, and others in *Tu-li p'ing-lun* (The independent tribune) from nos. 80 to 100. See also Hu Shih, *Ting Wen-chiang ti chuan-chi* (Taipei, 1956), pp. 35–39, 82–107.

Liang's *New Citizen* and Chinese Communist ideology is even more marked. The prominent strain of dynamism and activism shown in Mao Tse-tung's poems and other writings are strongly reminiscent of Liang's glorification of the enterprising and adventurous spirit. The continuity can be seen more clearly in the much publicized portrayals of model Communists — Lei Feng and Wang Chieh. The image which emerges from these portrayals and other related writings of Mao is that of a dynamic activist dedicated to public interest, oriented toward the future, rigorously disciplined in character, full of the spirit of adventure, and ready to sacrifice. One cannot help noticing the striking similarity between this image of the model Communist and Liang's image of the new citizen.[10]

In the final analysis it appears that Liang Ch'i-ch'ao's ideal of citizenship has had an enduring appeal for a great many of the Chinese intelligentsia of various ideological persuasions in the past half century, and even today it still constitutes an important component in the value system of Communist China. In this perspective the intellectual changes that took place in the decade from the mid 1890's to the early 1900's should be viewed as a more important watershed than the May Fourth generation in the cultural transition from traditional to modern China. In this transition period Liang Ch'i-ch'ao stands as a central figure, linked with the tradition of Confucian practical statesmanship in late Ch'ing thought and at the same time transforming the concerns inherent in that tradition into new personality and societal ideals, symbolized in his popular image of citizenship, which became a major and abiding part of the ideological ferment of twentieth-century China.

10. For a portrayal of the model communist youth see *Ts'ung Lei Feng tao Wang Chieh* (Hong Kong, 1966), pp. 1–65; *Wang Chieh* (Peking, 1966), pp. 1–170; *Wang Chieh ti ku-shih* (Peking, 1965), pp. 1–75.

Bibliography　Glossary　Index

BIBLIOGRAPHY

Berlin, Isaiah. *Two Concepts of Liberty*. London: Oxford University Press, 1958.

Bernal, Martin. "The Triumph of Anarchism over Marxism, 1906–1907," in Mary C. Wright, *China in Revolution: The First Phase 1900–1913*. New Haven: Yale University Press, 1968.

Chan, Wing-tsit. "The Evolution of the Confucian Concept of *Jen*," *Philosophy East and West*, 4.4:295–319 (1955).

——— "K'ang Yu-wei and Confucian Doctrine of Humanity," in Lo Jung-pang, ed., *K'ang Yu-wei: A Biography and a Symposium*. Tucson: The University of Arizona Press, 1967.

Chang Ching-lu 張靜廬. *Chung-kuo chin-tai ch'u-pan shih-liao* 中國近代出版史料 (Materials on the history of publications in modern China). 2 vols. Shanghai, 1957.

——— *Chung-kuo chin-tai ch'u-pan shih-liao pu-pien* 中國近代出版史料補編 (Additional compilation of historical materials on Chinese publishing enterprise). Shanghai, 1957.

Chang P'eng-yüan 張朋園. *Liang Ch'i-ch'ao yü Ch'ing-chi ko-ming* 梁啓超與清季革命 (Liang Ch'i-ch'ao and late Ch'ing revolution). Taipei, 1964.

Chang Shun-hui 張舜徽. *Ch'ing-tai Yang-chou hsüeh-chi* 清代揚州學記 (A study of the thought of some Yang-chou scholars in Ch'ing dynasty). Shanghai, 1962.

Chao Feng-t'ien 趙豊田. "K'ang Ch'ang-su hsien-sheng nien-p'u" 康長素先生年譜 (A chronological biography of K'ang Yu-wei), *Shih-hsüeh nien-pao* 史學年報 (Historical annual), 2.1:173–240 (Peking, September 1934).

Ch'en Ch'i-yün. "Liang Ch'i-ch'ao's 'Missionary Education': A Case Study of Missionary Influence on the Reformers," *Papers on China*, 16:111–113. Harvard University, East Asian Research Center, 1962.

Ch'en Chih 陳熾. *Yung-shu* 庸書, excerpted in *Wu-hsü pien-fa*, 1:231–248.

Ch'en, Kenneth. *Buddhism in China: A Historical Survey*. Princeton: Princeton University Press, 1964.

Ch'en Tu-hsiu 陳獨秀. "Ai-kuo-hsin yü tzu-chüeh-hsin" 愛國心與自覺心 (Patriotism and self-awareness), *Chia-yin tsa-chih* 甲寅雜誌 (Chia-yin journal), 1.4:1–6. Shanghai, 1914.

———— *Tu-hsiu wen-ts'un* 獨秀文存 (A collection of Ch'en Tu-hsiu's essays), 2 vols. Hong Kong, 1965.

Ch'i Ssu-ho 齊思和. "Wei Yüan yü wan-Ch'ing hsüeh-feng" 魏源與晚清學風 (Wei Yüan and the new trends in late Ch'ing scholarship), *Yen-ching hsüeh-pao* 燕京學報 (Yenching journal of Chinese studies), 39:177–226 (Peking, 1950).

Chiang Po-ch'ien 蔣伯潛 and Chiang Tsu-i 蔣祖怡. *Ching yü ching-hsüeh* 經與經學 (Confucian canons and canonical scholarship). Shanghai, 1948.

Chien Ch'ao-liang 簡朝亮. *Chu Chiu-chiang hsien-sheng nien-p'u* 朱九江先生年譜 (A chronological biography of Chu Tz'u-ch'i), in Chien Ch'ao-liang, ed., *Chu Chiu-chiang hsien-sheng chi* 朱九江先生集 (A collection of Chu Tz'u-ch'i's writings). 4 vols. Hong Kong, 1962.

Ch'ien Chung-lien 錢仲聯. *Huang Kung-tu hsien-sheng nien-p'u* 黃公度先生年譜 (A chronological biography of Huang Tsun-hsien), in Huang Tsun-hsien, *Jen-ching-lu shih-ts'ao chien-chu*.

Ch'ien Hsüan-t'ung 錢玄同. "Ch'ung-lun chin-ku-wen-hsüeh wen-t'i" 重論今古文學問題 (A further discussion on the problem of New Text and Ancient Text scholarship), appended to K'ang Yu-wei's *Hsin-hsüeh wei-ching k'ao*.

Ch'ien Mu 錢穆. *Chung-kuo chin san-pai-nien hsüeh-shu shih* 中國近三百年學術史 (An intellectual history of China during the past three hundred years). 2 vols. Shanghai, 1937.

———— "Chin pai-nien-lai chu-ju iun tu-shu" 近百年來諸儒論讀書 (Some scholars' discussions on study in the past one hundred years), in his *Hsüeh-yüeh* 學籥 (The key to scholarship). Hong Kong, 1958.

Chih-hsüeh ts'ung-shu ch'u-chi 質學叢書初集 (The first collection of the Chih-hsüeh series). Chih-hsüeh Hui, 1896.

Ch'in Han-ts'ai 秦翰才. *Tso Wen-hsiang-kung tsai hsi-pei* 左文襄公在西北 (Tso Tsung-t'ang in the Northwest). Chungking, 1945.

Chou Fu-ch'eng 周輔成. "Cheng Kuan-ying ti ssu-hsiang" 鄭觀應的思想 (Cheng Kuan-ying's thought), in *Chung-kuo chin-tai ssu-hsiang-shih lun-wen chi*.

Chou Yü-t'ung 周予同. *Ching chin-ku-wen-hsüeh* 經今古文學 (New Text and Ancient Text scholarship of Confucian canons). Shanghai, 1926.

Chu Fang-pu 朱芳圃, ed. *Sun I-jang nien-p'u* 孫貽讓年譜 (A chronological biography of Sun I-jang). Shanghai, 1934.

Chung-kuo chin-tai ssu-hsiang-shih lun-wen chi 中國近代思想史論文集 (A collection of essays on the history of modern Chinese thought). Shanghai, 1958.

Chung-yung hsin-chieh 中庸新解 (New interpretation of Doctrine of the Mean), in *Ssu-shu tu-pen* 四書讀本 (A reader of Four Books). 8 vols. Taipei, 1952.

Cohen, Paul A. "Wang T'ao and Incipient Chinese Nationalism," *Journal of Asian Studies*, 26.4:559–574 (August 1967).

———— "Wang T'ao's Perspective on a Changing World," in Albert Feuerwerker, ed. *Approaches to Modern Chinese History*. Berkeley: University of California Press, 1967.

de Bary, W. T. "Chinese Despotism and the Confucian Ideal: A Seventeenth-century View," in John K. Fairbank, ed., *Chinese Thought and Institutions*. Chicago: University of Chicago Press, 1957.

———— et al., eds. *Sources of Indian Tradition*. New York: Columbia University Press, 1958.

de Ruggiero, Guido. *The History of European Liberalism*, tr. R. G. Collingwood. Oxford: Oxford University Press, 1927.

Eastman, Lloyd E. "Political Reformism in China before the Sino-Japanese War," *Journal of Asian Studies*, 27.4:695–710 (August 1968).

Eisenstadt, S. N. *The Political Systems of Empires*. New York: The Free Press of Glencoe, 1963.

Emerson, Rupert. *State and Sovereignty in Modern Germany*. New Haven: Yale University Press, 1928.

———— *From Empire to Nation*. Boston: Beacon Press, 1960.

Fan Shou-k'ang 范壽康. *Chu-tzu chi ch'i che-hsüeh* 朱子及其哲學 (Chu Hsi and his philosophy). Taipei, 1964.

Feng Kuei-fen 馮桂芬. *Chiao-pin-lu k'ang-i* 校邠廬抗議 (Personal proposal from the Studio of Chiao-pin), excerpted in *Wu-hsü pien-fa*, I, 1–38.

Feng Tzu-yu 馮自由. *Ko-ming i-shih* 革命逸史 (Historical anecdotes of the Revolution of 1911). 5 vols. Chungking, 1943.

Feng Yu-lan 馮友蘭. *History of Chinese Philosophy*, tr. Derk Bodde. 2 vols. Princeton: Princeton University Press, 1953.

———— "K'ang Yu-wei ti ssu-hsiang" 康有為的思想 (K'ang Yu-wei's thought), in *Chung-kuo chin-tai ssu-hsiang-shih lun-wen chi.*

Friedrich, Carl J. *Constitutional Reason of State.* Providence: Brown University Press, 1957.

———— *Man and His Government: An Empirical Theory of Politics.* New York: McGraw-Hill, 1963.

Gasster, Michael. *Chinese Intellectuals and the Revolution of 1911.* Seattle: University of Washington Press, 1969.

Geertz, Clifford. "The Integrative Revolution," in Clifford Geertz, ed. *Old Societies and New States.* New York: The Free Press of Glencoe, 1963.

———— "Ideology as a Cultural System," in David S. Apter, ed. *Ideology and Discontent.* New York: The Free Press of Glencoe, 1964.

Halevy, Elie. *The Growth of Philosophical Radicalism.* London: Faber and Gwyer Limited, 1928.

Hao Yen-p'ing. "The Abortive Cooperation between Reformers and Revolutionaries," *Papers on China,* 15:91–114. Harvard University, East Asian Research Center, 1961.

Hayek, F. A. *The Constitution of Liberty.* Chicago: University of Chicago Press, 1960.

Ho Ch'ang-ling 賀長齡 ed. *Huang-ch'ao ching-shih wen-pien* 皇朝經世文編 (Compilation of essays on statecraft). Peking, 1826.

Hofstadter, Richard. *Social Darwinism in American Thought.* Boston: Beacon Press, 1955.

Howard, Richard C. "K'ang Yu-wei (1858–1927): His Intellectual Background and His Early Thought," in Arthur F. Wright and Denis Twitchett, eds. *Confucian Personalities.* Stanford: Stanford University Press, 1962.

———— "Japan's Role in the Reform Program of K'ang Yu-wei," in Jung-pang Lo, ed. *K'ang Yu-wei: A Biography and a Symposium.*

"Hsi-pao hsüan-i" 西報選譯 (Selective translations from English newspapers), *Shih-wu pao,* 15:12–13 (December 14, 1896), 19:14–15 (March 3, 1897).

Hsiao Kung-ch'üan 蕭公權. *Chung-kuo cheng-chih-ssu-hsiang shih* 中國政治思想史 (A history of Chinese political thought). 6 vols. Taipei, 1954.

———— "Weng T'ung-ho and the Reform Movement of 1898," *Ch'ing-hua hsüeh-pao* 清華學報 (Tsing Hua journal of Chinese studies). New Series, 1.2:111–245 (Taipei, April 1957).

———— "K'ang Yu-wei and Confucianism," *Monumenta Serica,* 18:88–212,

Nagoya, Japan, 1959.

Hsin-hai ko-ming wu-shih chou-nien chi-nien lun-wen chi 辛亥革命五十週年紀念論文集 (A collection of essays in commemoration of the fiftieth year of the Revolution of 1911). 2 vols. Peking, 1962.

Hsin-min ts'ung-pao 新民叢報 (New citizen journal). Yokohama. nos. 1–13 (February-August 1902); no. 79 (April 1906); nos. 85–86 (August-September 1906); nos. 90–92 (November 1906).

Hsiung Shih-li 熊十力. *Tu Ching shih-yao* 讀經示要 (The essentials for studying Confucian classics). Taipei, 1960.

Hsü Chih-ching 徐致靖. "Pao-chien jen-ts'ai che" 保薦人才摺 (A memorial for recommending of talents), in Yeh Te-hui, ed., *Chüeh-mi yao-lu*.

Hsü Fu-kuan 徐復觀. *Chung-kuo ssu-hsiang-shih lun-chi* 中國思想史論集 (A collection of essays on the history of Chinese thought). Taichung, 1959.

—— *Hsüeh-shu yü cheng-chih chih chien* 學術與政治之間 (Between scholarship and politics). 2 vols. Taichung, 1963.

Hu Shih 胡適. *Hu Shih wen-ts'un* 胡適文存 (Collected essays of Hu Shih). 4 vols. Taipei, 1953.

—— *Ting Wen-chiang ti chuan-chi* 丁文江的傳記 (Ting Wen-chiang's biography). Taipei, 1956.

Huang Tsun-hsien 黃遵憲. *Jen-ching-lu shih-ts'ao chien-chu* 人境廬詩草箋註 (Commentaries on Huang Tsun-hsien's poems). Shanghai, 1957.

Hunan li-shih tzu-liao 湖南歷史資料 (Historical materials on Hunan). 3:98–108, 4:65–126 (Hunan, 1958).

Huntington, D. T. "The Religious Writings of Liang Chi-tsao," *Chinese Recorder and Missionary Journal*, 38.9:470–474 (September 1907).

K'ang Yu-wei 康有為. *Ch'ang-hsing hsüeh-chi* 長興學記 (An account of study at Ch'ang-hsing Alley), in Su Yü, *I-chiao ts'ung-pien*, 4:35–63.

—— *K'ang Nan-hai tzu-pien nien-p'u* 康南海自編年譜 (A self-compiled chronological biography of K'ang Yu-wei), in *Wu-hsü pien-fa*, 4:107–169.

—— "Shang Ch'ing-ti ti-i-shu" 上清帝第一書 (The first memorial presented to the Ch'ing emperor), in *Wu-hsü pien-fa*, 2:123–131.

—— "Shang Ch'ing-ti ti-erh-shu" 上清帝第二書 (The second memorial presented to the Ch'ing emperor), in *Wu-hsü pien-fa*, 2:131–166.

—— "Shang Ch'ing-ti ti-ssu-shu" 上清帝第四書 (The fourth memorial presented to the Ch'ing emperor), in *Wu-hsü pien-fa*, 2:174–188.

—— *Hsin-hsüeh wei-ching k'ao* 新學偽經考 (An inquiry into the classics forged during the Hsin period). Shanghai, 1956.

—— *K'ung-tzu kai-chih k'ao* 孔子改制考 (A study of Confucius as reformer). Shanghai, 1958.

Klausner, S. Z., ed. *The Quest for Self-Control.* New York: The Free Press, 1965.

Ko Kung-chen 戈公振. *Chung-kuo pao-hsüeh shih* 中國報學史 (A history of Chinese journalism). Taipei, 1964.

Ku Chieh-kang 顧頡剛. *Han-tai hsüeh-shu-shih lüeh* 漢代學術史略 (A sketch of the intellectual history of Han dynasty). Shanghai, 1948.

Kwok, D. W. Y. *Scientism in Chinese Thought, 1900–1950.* New Haven: Yale University Press, 1965.

Levenson, Joseph R. *Liang Ch'i-ch'ao and the Mind of Modern China.* Cambridge: Harvard University Press, 1959.

—— "The Suggestiveness of Vestiges: Confucianism and Monarchy at the Last," in David S. Nivison and Arthur F. Wright, eds., *Confucianism in Action.* Stanford: Stanford University Press, 1959,

—— "Liao P'ing and the Confucian Departure from History," in Arthur F. Wright and Denis Twitchett, eds., *Confucian Personalities.* Stanford: Stanford University Press, 1962.

Lewis, Charlton M. "The Reform Movement in Hunan (1896–1898)," *Papers on China,* 15:62–90. Harvard University, East Asian Research Center, 1961.

Li Che-hou 李澤厚. *K'ang Yu-wei T'an Ssu-t'ung ssu-hsiang yen-chiu* 康有爲譚嗣同思想研究 (A study of the thought of K'ang Yu-wei and T'an Ssu-t'ung). Shanghai, 1958.

Liang Ch'i-ch'ao 梁啓超. *Hsi-hsüeh shu-mu piao* 西學書目表 (A bibliography of Western learning), in *Chih-hsüeh ts'ung-shu ch'u-chi,* appendix tables, ts'e 9–10.

—— *Tu hsi-hsüeh-shu fa* 讀西學書法 (Approaches to studying Western learning), in *Chih-hsüeh ts'ung-shu ch'u-chi,* ts'e 10.

—— "Shang Ch'en Chung-ch'en shu" 上陳中臣書 (A memorial to Governor Ch'en), in Su Yü, *I-chiao ts'ung-pien,* appendix, 1–3b.

—— *Yin-ping-shih ts'ung-chu* 飮冰室叢著 (A collection of works from the Ice-drinker's Studio). 4 vols. Shanghai, 1907.

—— *Yin-pin-shih ho-chi, chuan-chi* 飮冰室合集, 專集 (Collected works and essays from the Ice-drinker's Studio, collected works). 24 ts'e. Shanghai, 1936.

—— *Yin-ping-shih ho-chi, wen-chi* 飮冰室合集, 文集 (Collected works and essays from the Ice-drinker's Studio, collected essays). 16 ts'e. Shanghai, 1936.

———— "T'an Ssu-t'ung chuan" 譚嗣同傳 (A biography of T'an Ssu-t'ung), in T'an Ssu-t'ung, *T'an Ssu-t'ung ch'üan-chi*.

———— *Chung-kuo chin san-pai-nien hsüeh-shu shih* 中國近三百年學術史 (An intellectual history of China during the last three hundred years). Taipei, 1955.

———— *Intellectual Trends in the Ch'ing Period*, tr. Immanuel C. Y. Hsü. Cambridge: Harvard University Press, 1959.

———— *Ch'ing-tai hsüeh-shu kai-lun* 清代學術概論 (Intellectual trends in the Ch'ing dynasty). Hong Kong, 1963.

Lo Jung-pang, ed. *K'ang Yu-wei: A Biography and a Symposium*. Tucson: The University of Arizona Press, 1967.

Lo-sang P'eng-ts'o 羅桑彭錯. "K'ang Nan-hai chiang-hsüeh Wan-mu ts'ao-t'ang chih hsüeh-yüeh" 康南海講學萬木草堂之學約 (K'ang Yu-wei's syllabus at Wan-mu ts'ao-t'ang), *Cheng-feng tsa-chih* 正風雜誌, 4.5:407–413 (April 1937).

Lovejoy, Arthur O. *The Great Chain of Being: A Study of the History of an Idea*. Cambridge: Harvard University Press, 1950.

Lun-yü hsin-chieh 論語新解 (New interpretation of Analects). 2 vols.; in *Ssu-shu tu-pen*.

Ma Chien-chung 馬建忠. *Shih-k'o-chai chi-yen chi-hsing* 適可齋記言記行 (Notes from the Shih-k'o-chai [Studio]), excerpted in *Wu-hsü pien-fa*, 1:163–176.

Marshall, T. H. *Citizenship and Social Class and Other Essays*. Cambridge: Cambridge University Press, 1950.

Meinecke, Friedrich. *Machiavellism*, tr. Douglas Scott. New Haven: Yale University Press, 1957.

Mou Tsung-san 牟宗三. *Hsün-hsüeh ta-lüeh* 荀學大略 (A sketch of the gist of Hsün-tzu's philosophy). Taipei, 1953.

———— *Cheng-tao yü chih-tao* 政道與治道 (The political way and the administrative way). Taipei, 1960.

———— *Chung-kuo che-hsüeh ti t'e-chih* 中國哲學的特質 (The characteristics of Chinese philosophy). Hong Kong, 1963.

Nakamura Tadayuki 中村忠行. "Chūgoku bungei ni oyoboseru Nihon bungei no eikyō" 中國文藝に及ぼせる日本文藝の影響 (The influence of Japanese literature on Chinese literature), in *Taidai Bungaku* 臺大文學 (Taiwan University literature; Taihoku, Taiwan), vol. 8, nos. 2, 4, 5 (1942–1944).

Nelson, Benjamin. "Self-Images and Systems of Spiritual Direction in the History of European Civilization," in S. Z. Klausner, ed., *The Quest for Self-Control*.

Nivison, David S. "Protest against Conventions and Conventions of Protest," in Arthur F. Wright, ed., *Confucianism and Chinese Civilization.* New York: Atheneum, 1964.

North China Herald and Supreme Court and Consular Gazette. Shanghai, 1898.

Onogawa Hidemi 小野川秀美. *Shimmatsu seiji shisō kenkyū* 清末政治思想研究 (Studies in the political thought of the late Ch'ing). Kyoto, 1960.

P'i Lu-men 皮鹿門. *Shih-fu-t'ang wei-k'an jih-chi* 師復堂未刊日記 (P'i Lu-men's unpublished diary), in *Hunan li-shih tzu-liao,* 4:65–126.

Richard, Timothy. *Forty-five Years in China.* New York: F. A. Stokes Company, 1916.

Roelofs, H. Mark. *The Tension of Citizenship: Private Man and Public Duty.* New York: Holt, Rinehart and Winston, Inc., 1967.

Saneto Keishu 實藤惠秀. *Chūgokujin Nihon ryūgaku shi* 中國人日本留學史 (A history of Chinese students in Japan). Tokyo, 1960.

Sartori, Giovanni. "Constitutionalism: A Preliminary Discussion," *American Political Science Review,* 56.4:853–864 (December 1962).

——— *Democratic Theory.* Detroit: Wayne State University Press, 1962.

Schiffrin, Harold. "Sun Yat-sen's Early Land Policy: The Origin and Meaning of 'Equalization of Land Rights'," *Journal of Asian Studies,* 16.4:549–564 (1956–1957).

Schiffrin, Harold, and Robert Scalapino. "Early Socialist Currents in the Chinese Revolutionary Movement: Sun Yat-sen versus Liang Ch'i-ch'ao," *Journal of Asian Studies,* 18.3:321–342 (1958–1959).

Schiffrin, Harold. *Sun Yat-sen and the Origins of the Chinese Revolution.* Berkeley: University of California Press, 1968.

——— "The Enigma of Sun Yat-sen," in Mary C. Wright, ed., *China in Revolution: The First Phase, 1900–1913.* New Haven: Yale University Press, 1968.

Schrecker, John. "The Pao-kuo Hui: A Reform Society of 1898," *Papers on China,* 14:50–69. Harvard University, East Asian Research Center, December 1960.

Schwartz, Benjamin. "Some Polarities in Confucian Thought," in David S. Nivison and Arthur F. Wright, eds., *Confucianism in Action.* Stanford: Stanford University Press, 1959.

——— *In Search of Wealth and Power: Yen Fu and the West.* Cambridge: Harvard University Press, 1964.

Shih-wu pao 時務報 (Chinese Progress). 15:12–13 (December 14, 1896), 19:14–15 (March 3, 1897), 21:22–24 (March 23, 1899). Shanghai.

Smith, Wilfred C. *The Meaning and End of Religion.* New York: Macmillan, 1962.

318

—— *The Faith of Other Men*. Cleveland: World Publishing Co., 1963.

Smythe, E. Joan. "The Tzu-li Hui: Some Chinese and Their Rebellion," *Papers on China*, 12:51–68. Harvard University, East Asian Research Center, December, 1958.

Soedjatmoko. "Cultural Motivations to Progress: The 'Exterior' and 'Interior' Views," in Robert N. Bellah, ed. *Religion and Progress in Modern Asia*. New York: The Free Press, 1965.

Soothill, W. E. *Timothy Richard in China*. London: Seeley, Service & Co., 1924.

Ssu-shu tu-pen 四書讀本 (A reader of Four Books). 8 vols. Taipei, 1952.

Su Yü 蘇輿. *I-chiao ts'ung-pien* 翼教叢編 (The collection of writings for promoting sacred teachings). 3 ts'e. 1898.

Su Yüan-lei 蘇淵雷. *Sung P'ing-tzu p'ing-chuan* 宋平子評傳 (A critical biography of Sung Shu). Shanghai, 1947.

Talmon, J. L. *The Origins of Totalitarian Democracy*. London: Secker & Warburg, 1955.

T'an Ssu-t'ung 譚嗣同. *T'an Ssu-t'ung ch'üan-chi* 譚嗣同全集 (A complete collection of T'an Ssu-t'ung's works). Peking, 1954.

—— *T'an Liu-yang ch'üan-chi* 譚瀏陽全集 (The complete works of T'an Ssu-t'ung). Taipei, 1962.

T'ang Chih-chün 湯志鈞. *Wu-hsü pien-fa shih lun-ts'ung* 戊戌變法史論叢 (A collection of essays on the reform movement of 1898). Hankow, 1957.

T'ang Chün-i 唐君毅. *Chung-kuo che-hsüeh yüan-lun* 中國哲學原論 (On some fundamental problems of Chinese philosophy). 2 vols. Hong Kong, 1966.

T'ang Ts'ai-chih 唐才質. "T'ang Ts'ai-ch'ang ho Shih-wu hsüeh-t'ang" 唐才常和時務學堂 (T'ang Ts'ai-ch'ang and the School of Current Affairs), *Hunan li-shih tzu-liao*, 3:98–108.

T'ao Hsi-sheng 陶希聖. *Chung-kuo cheng-chih-ssu-hsiang shih* 中國政治思想史 (A history of Chinese political thought). 4 vols. Chungking, 1942.

Teng T'an-chou 鄧潭洲. "Shih-chiu shih-chi mo Hu-nan ti wei-hsin yün-tung" 十九世紀末湖南的維新運動 (The reform movement in Hunan at the end of nineteenth century), *Li-shih yen-chiu* 歷史研究 (Journal of historical study), 1:17–34 (1959).

Thompson, Laurence G., tr. *Ta T'ung Shu: The One-World Philosophy of K'ang Yu-wei*. London: Allen & Unwin, 1958.

Ting Wen-chiang 丁文江. *Liang Jen-kung hsien-sheng nien-p'u ch'ang-pien ch'u-kao* 梁任公先生年譜長編初稿 (First draft of a chronological biography of Liang Ch'i-ch'ao). 3 vols. Taipei, 1959.

Ts'ao Chü-jen 曹聚仁. *Wen-t'an wu-shih nien* 文壇五十年 (The Chinese literary world in the past fifty years). 2 vols. Hong Kong, 1955.

Tseng Hsü-pai 曾虛白. *Chung-kuo hsin-wen shih* 中國新聞史 (A history of Chinese journalism). Taipei, 1966.

Tseng Kuo-fan 曾國藩. "Yüan-ts'ai" 原才 (On talent), in *Tseng Wen-cheng-kung ch'üan-chi* 曾文正公全集 (The complete collection of Tseng Kuo-fan's writings). Shanghai, 1935. *Wen-chi* 文集 (Collected essays), pp. 4–5.

Ts'ung Lei Feng tao Wang Chieh 從雷鋒到王杰 (From Lei Feng to Wang Chieh). Hong Kong, 1966.

Tu Wei-ming. "The Creative Tension between Jen and Li," *Philosophy East and West*, 18.1 and 2:29–39 (January-April 1968).

"Tung-pao hsüan-i" 東報選譯 (Selective translation from Japanese newspapers), *Shih-wu pao*, 21:22–24 (March 23, 1899).

T'ung-ch'eng p'ai yen-chiu lun-wen chi 桐城派研究論文集 (A collection of papers on the T'ung-ch'eng School). Anhui, 1963.

Wang Chieh 王杰 (Wang Chieh). Peking, 1966.

Wang Chieh ti ku-shih 王杰的故事 (The story of Wang Chieh). Peking, 1965.

Wang Ch'ü-ch'ang 王蘧常. *Yen Chi-tao nien-p'u* 嚴幾道年譜 (A chronological biography of Yen Fu). Shanghai, 1936.

Wang, C. Y. *Chinese Intellectuals and the West, 1872–1949*. Chapel Hill: University of North Carolina Press, 1966.

Wang Hsien-ch'ien 王先謙. "Ch'ün-lun" 羣論 (On grouping), in *Hsü-shou-t'ang wen-chi* 虛受堂文集 (A collection of essays of Wang Hsien-ch'ien). 12 ts'e.

Wang Te-chao 王德昭. "T'ung-meng-hui shih-ch'i Sun Chung-shan hsien-sheng ko-ming ssu-hsiang ti fen-hsi yen-chiu" 同盟會時期孫中山先生革命思想的分析研究 (An analytical study of Sun Yat-sen's revolutionary thought during the United League period), in Wu Hsiang-hsiang 吳相湘 ed., *Chung-kuo hsien-tai shih ts'ung-k'an* 中國現代史叢刊 (Selected writings on modern Chinese history). Taipei, 1960, I, 161–166.

Weber, Max. *Sociology of Religion*. Boston: Beacon Press, 1963.

—— *The Theory of Social and Economic Organization*. New York: The Free Press, 1964.

Wilhelm, Hellmut. "Chinese Confucianism on the Eve of the Great

Encounter," in Marius B. Jansen, ed., *Changing Japanese Attitudes toward Modernization*. Princeton: Princeton University Press, 1965.

Wright, Mary C. *The Last Stand of Chinese Conservatism: The T'ung-chih Restoration, 1862–1874*. Stanford: Stanford University Press, 1957.

—— ed. *China in Revolution; The First Phase, 1900–1913*. New Haven: Yale University Press, 1968.

Wu-hsü pien-fa 戊戌變法 (The reform movement of 1898), in Chien Po-tsan 翦伯贊 et al., eds., *Chung-kuo chin-tai shih tzu-liao ts'ung-k'an* 中國近代史資料叢刊 (A collection of materials on history of modern China). 4 vols. Shanghai, 1953.

Yang T'ing-fu 楊廷福. *T'an Ssu-t'ung nien-p'u* 譚嗣同年譜 (A chronological biography of T'an Ssu-t'ung). Peking, 1957.

Yang Tu-sheng 楊篤生. "Hsin Hu-nan" 新湖南 (New Hunan), in *Hsin-hai ko-ming ch'ien shih-nien chien shih-lun hsüan-chi* 辛亥革命前十年間時論選集 (Selected essays on current affairs in the decade before the Revolution of 1911). 6 vols. Hong Kong, 1962.

Yeh Te-hui 葉德輝 ed. *Chüeh-mi yao-lu* 覺迷要錄 (Essential writings for awakening the misled). 4 chüan. Special series, 1905.

Yen Fu 嚴復. "Chiu-wang chüeh-lun" 救亡決論 (On the salvation of China), in *Wu-hsü pien-fa*, 3:60–71.

GLOSSARY

Arimura Shunsai 有村春齋

bushidō 武士道

Canton 廣州
Chang Chih-tung 張之洞
"Chang Po-wang Pan Ting-yüan ho-ch'uan" 張博望班定遠合傳
Chang Tsai 張載
Ch'ang-hsing hsüeh-she 長興學舍
Changsha 長沙
Ch'en Ch'iu 陳虬
Ch'en Li 陳澧
Ch'en Pai-sha 陳白沙
Ch'en Pao-chen 陳寶箴
Ch'en T'ien-hua 陳天華
Ch'en T'ung-fu 陳通甫
cheng 政
Cheng-ch'i hui 正氣會
"Cheng-chih-hsüeh ta-chia Po-lun chih-li chih hsüeh-shuo" 政治學大家伯倫知理之學說
cheng-chih hsüeh-yüan 政治學院
Cheng Hsüan 鄭玄
Cheng Kuan-ying 鄭觀應
cheng-shih 政事
ch'eng 誠
Ch'eng-Chu 程朱
Ch'eng Hao 程顥

ch'eng-i 誠意
"Chi Shang-hsien-t'ang" 記尙賢堂
"Chi tung-hsia" 記東俠
ch'i 氣
chia 家
Chia-jen ch'i-yü 佳人奇遇
Chia K'uei 賈逵
Chiang Piao 江標
ch'iang-ch'üan 强權
Ch'iang hsüeh-hui 强學會
chiao 教
chiao-hua 教化
Chieh-pen Ming-ju hsüeh-an 節本明儒學案
chien 儉
Chih-hsin pao 知新報
chih-hsing ho-i 知行合一
chih liang-chih 致良知
Chih-pao 直報
chih-pen 知本
ch'ih-shen 治身
ch'ih-shih 治事
chih-shih 志士
chih-yen 知言
chih-yü 智育
"Chin-hua-lun ko-ming che Chieh-te chih hsüeh-shuo" 進化論革命者頡德之學說

"Chin-jih chih chiao-yü fang-chen" 今日之教育方針

Chin-ku-hsüeh k'ao 今古學考

chin-shih 進士

Ch'in 秦

Ch'in Shih-huang-ti 秦始皇帝

ch'in-wang 勤王

"Ching-kao ch'ing-nien" 敬告青年

ching-shih 經世

ching-shih chih-hsüeh 經世之學

"Ching-shih-wen hsin-pien hsü" 經世文新編序

Ching-shih wen-pien 經世文編

"Ching-shih wen-pien hsin-hsü" 經世文編新序

Ch'ing 清

Ch'ing-i pao 清議報

chiu-shih 救世

ch'iung-li 窮理

Chou 周

Chou Chi 周濟

chu-ching 主敬

chu-ching 主靜

Chu Hsi 朱熹

Chu I-hsin 朱一新

Chu Tz'u-ch'i 朱次琦

ch'u-shih 出世

ch'uan-chiao 傳教

Chuang Ts'un-yü 莊存與

Ch'un-ch'iu 春秋

"Ch'un-ch'iu Chung-kuo i-ti-pien hsü" 春秋中國夷狄辨序

chung 忠

Chung-cheng 中正

Chung-kuo chih wu-shih-tao 中國之武士道

Chung-tung chi-shih pen-mo 中東紀事本末

Chung-wai kung-pao 中外公報

chü-jen 舉人

chü-luan shih 據亂世

ch'üan-li 權利

chün-hsien 郡縣

chün-tao 君道

chün-t'ung 君統

chün-tzu 君子

ch'ün 群

ch'ün-shu 羣術

"Erh-shih shih-chi chih chü-ling t'o-la-ssu" 二十世紀之巨靈托辣斯

"Fa-lan-hsi-jen yü chin-shih wen-ming" 法蘭西人與近世文明

fang-pi 防敝

Fang Tung-shu 方東樹

fei li-shih ti jen-chung 非歷史的人種

fei shih-chieh-shih ti 非世界史的

fen-li 分利

feng-chien 封建

fu-ch'iang 富强

fu-hsing 復性

fu-ku 復古

"Fu Liu Ku-yü shan-chang shu" 復劉古愚山長書

Fukuzawa Yukichi 福澤喻吉

Gamō Shigeakira 蒲生重章

Gesshō 月性

Han 漢

Hankow 漢口

hao-jan chih-ch'i 浩然之氣

"Ho-pu-shih hsüeh-an" 霍布士學案

hsi-cheng 西政

"Hsi-cheng ts'ung-shu hsü" 西政

叢書序

"Hsi-hsüeh shu-mu-piao hou-hsü"
西學書目表後序

"Hsi-hsüeh shu-mu-piao hsü-li"
西學書目表序例

hsi-i 西藝

hsi-lao 習勞

"Hsi-ming" 西銘

Hsia Tseng-yu 夏曾佑

"Hsiang-shan hsüeh-shu" 象山學術

hsiang-yüan 鄉愿

hsiao-k'ang 小康

hsiao min-tsu chu-i 小民族主義

hsiao-wo 小我

hsien-tsai chu-i 現在主義

hsin 新

hsin-cheng 新政

Hsin ch'ing-nien 新青年

Hsin Chung-kuo wei-lai chi 新中國未來記

Hsin hsiao-shuo 新小說

hsin-min 新民

Hsin-min shuo 新民說

"Hsin shih-hsüeh" 新史學

hsin-shu 心術

hsing 性

Hsing-chung hui 興中會

hsiu-shen 修身

hsiu-ts'ai 秀才

Hsü Ch'in 徐勤

Hsü Jen-tsu 徐仁鑄

Hsü Shen 許慎

hsüeh 學

Hsüeh-hai t'ang 學海堂

Hsün-tzu 荀子

Hu-Kwang 湖廣

"Hu-nan Shih-wu hsüeh-t'ang hsüeh-yüeh" 湖南時務學堂學約

Hua-yen 華嚴

Huang K'o-ch'iang 黃克強

Huang Tsung-hsi 黃宗羲

Hunan 湖南

i 藝

i 義

i ch'ün wei t'i, i pien wei yung 以羣爲體，以變爲用

i-li 毅力

i-li 義理

i-li chih-hsüeh 義理之學

"I-pu-sheng chu-i" 易卜生主義

I-shu chü 譯書局

i-wu 義務

i-yüan 議院

Ijinden 偉人傳

jen 仁

jen-cheng 仁政

jen-hsia 任俠

Jen-hsüeh 仁學

"Jen-hsüeh hsü" 仁學序

"Jen-sheng chen-i" 人生眞義

jen-tao 人道

jih-hsin 日新

Ju-chia che-hsüeh 儒家哲學

Juan Yüan 阮元

kai-chih 改制

k'ai-ming chuan-chih 開明專制

"K'ai-ming chuan-chih lun" 開明專制論

Kajin no kigū 佳人奇遇

Kao-teng ta-t'ung hsüeh-hsiao 高等大同學校

k'ao-cheng 考證

k'ao-chü chih-hsüeh 考據之學

Katō Hiroyuki 加藤弘之

Kiaochow 膠州

Ko-ming chün 革命軍

ko-wu 格物
k'o-chi 克己
k'o-chih 克治
Komai Saian 駒井躋庵
"Ku i-yüan k'ao" 古議院考
Ku Yen-wu 顧炎武
"Kua-fen wei-yen" 瓜分危言
Kuan-tzu 管子
Kuang-hsü 光緒
Kuei-hsüeh ta-wen 桂學答問
Kumazawa Banzan 熊澤蕃山
kung 公
Kung-chü 公車
kung-fu 工夫
kung-te 公德
Kung Tzu-chen 龔自珍
Kung-yang 公羊
"K'ung-tzu chih tao yü hsien-tai sheng-huo" 孔子之道與現代生活
kuo-chia 國家
kuo-chia ch'ün 國家羣
"Kuo-chia ssu-hsiang pien-ch'ien i-t'ung lun" 國家思想變遷異同論
"Kuo-chia yün-ming lun" 國家運命論
kuo-min 國民
kuo-min pien-ko 國民變革
kuo-tu shih-tai 過渡時代
"Kuo-tu shih-tai lun" 過渡時代論
Kwangtung 廣東

Lao-tzu 老子
li 理
li 禮
li 利
li 力
Li Che-hou 李澤厚
li-chiao 禮教

li-chih 立志
Li Ch'ü-ping 李去病
"Li hsien-fa i" 立憲法議
liang-chih 良知
Liao P'ing 廖平
lieh-kuo 劣國
Liu-chai pei-i 六齋卑議
Liu Feng-lu 劉逢祿
Liu Hsin 劉歆
Liu Tsung-chou 劉宗周
lo 樂
Lo-lan fu-jen chuan 羅蘭夫人傳
"Lo-li chu-i t'ai-tou Pien-hsin chih hsüeh-shuo" 樂利主義泰斗邊沁之學說
Lu Hsiang-shan 陸象山
"Lu-so hsüeh-an" 盧梭學案
Lu-Wang 陸王
"Lun cheng-fu yü jen-min chih ch'üan-hsien" 論政府與人民之權限
"Lun Chih-na tsung-chiao kai-ko" 論支那宗教改革
"Lun chin-shih kuo-min ching-cheng chih ta-shih chi Chung-kuo chih ch'ien-t'u" 論近世國民競爭之大勢及中國之前途
"Lun Chung-kuo chi-jo yu-yü fang-pi" 論中國積弱由於防敝
"Lun Chung-kuo i chiang-ch'iu fa-lü-chih-hsüeh" 論中國宜講求法律之學
"Lun Chung-kuo yü Ou-chou kuo-t'i i-t'ung" 論中國與歐洲國體異同
"Lun chün-cheng min-cheng hsiang-shan chih-li" 論君政民政相嬗之理
"Lun Fu-chiao yü ch'ün-chih chih kuan-hsi" 論佛教與羣治之關係

325

"Lun li-fa ch'üan 論立法權
"Lun min-tsu ching-cheng chih ta-shih" 論民族競爭之大勢
"Lun pao-kuan yu-i-yü kuo-shih" 論報館有益於國事
"Lun tsung-chiao-chia yü che-hsüeh-chia chih ch'ang-tuan te-shih" 論宗教家與哲學家之長短得失

Ma Jung 馬融
Mai Meng-hua 麥孟華
mao-hsien chin-ch'ü chih ching-shen 冒險進取之精神
"Meng-tzu chih-yen yang-ch'i chang shih-shih" 孟子知言養氣章試釋
min 民
min-chu 民主
min-ch'üan 民權
Min-pao 民報
min-tsu 民族
min-tsu ti-kuo chu-i 民族帝國主義
Ming 明
ming 命
Ming-i tai-fang lu 明夷待訪錄
Ming-ju hsüeh-an 明儒學案
ming-tao 明道
Mo-tzu 墨子

Nakae Tōju 中江藤樹
Nakamura Masanao 中村正直
Nakayama Tadamitsu 中山忠光
"Nan-hai K'ang-hsien-sheng chuan" 南海康先生傳
"Nan-hsüeh-hui hsü" 南學會序
Nanking 南京
nei-ching 內競
nei-hsüeh 內學
nei-sheng wai-wang 內聖外王

Oka Senjin 岡千仞
Ōshio Heihachirō 大塩平八郎

pa-tao 霸道
pao-chiao 保教
"Pao-chiao fei so-i tsun K'ung lun" 保教非所以尊孔論
Pao-huang hui 保皇會
Pao-kuo hui 保國會
Pao Shih-ch'en 包世臣
pei-chih shuang-hsiu 悲智雙修
pien-fa 變法
"Pien-fa t'ung-i" 變法通議
pien-hua ch'i-chih 變化氣質
pien-shu 辨術
p'ing-min chu-i 平民主義
"Po mou-pao chih t'u-ti kuo-yu lun" 駁某報之土地國有論
pu-min 部民
pu-tung-hsin 不動心

Saigō Takamori 西鄉隆盛
Sakamoto Ryōma 阪本龍馬
San-ho hui 三合會
"San hsien-sheng chuan" 三先生傳
san-kang 三綱
san-kang wu-ch'ang 三綱五常
san-shih 三世
san-t'ung 三統
"Shang Ch'en Pao-chen lun Hu-nan ying-pan-chih-shih" 上陳寶箴論湖南應辦之事
"Shang-hui i" 商會議
"Shang Nan-p'i Chang-shang-shu shu" 上南皮張尚書書
shang-wu 尚武
Shang Yang 商鞅
Shanghai 上海
Shao I-ch'en 邵懿辰

she 奢
shen-tu 慎獨
sheng-ch'a 省察
"Sheng-chi-hsüeh hsüeh-shuo yen-ko hsiao-shih" 生計學學說沿革小史
sheng-li 生利
sheng-p'ing shih 昇平世
sheng-wang 聖王
Shiba Shirō 柴東海
Shih-chi 史記
"Shih-chi huo-chih lieh-chuan chin-i" 史記貨志列傳今義
"Shih-chieh ta-shih chi Chung-kuo ch'ien-t'u" 世界大勢及中國前途
shih-hsing 實行
shih-hsüeh 實學
"Shih-jen" 識仁
"Shih-ko" 釋革
Shih-wu hsüeh-t'ang 時務學堂
Shih-wu pao 時務報
shishi 志士
shou-ching 守敬
shou-hsing chu-i 獸性主義
shou-tao chiu-shih 守道救世
shu 恕
Shun 舜
"Shuo-ch'ün hsü" 說羣序
"Shuo-ch'ün i: ch'ün-li i" 說羣一：羣理一
"Shuo-tung" 說動
Sonjō Kiji 尊壤紀事
ssu 私
Ssu-pa-ta hsiao-chih 斯巴達小志
ssu-te 私德
su-wang 素王
Sung-Ming 宋明
Sung Shu 宋恕

Ta-hsüeh 大學
ta min-tsu chu-i 大民族主義
ta-t'ung 大同
Ta-t'ung shu 大同書
ta-wo 大我
Tai Chen 戴震
Tai Wang 戴望
t'ai-chi 太極
t'ai-p'ing shih 太平世
T'ang 唐
T'ang Chen 湯震
T'ang Chien 唐鑑
T'ang Ts'ai-ch'ang 唐才常
tao 道
tao-te ko-ming 道德革命
tao-t'ung 道統
te-hsing 德行
te-yü 德育
Te-yü chien 德育鑑
"ti-k'ang li" 抵抗力
t'ien-hsia 天下
t'ien-hsia ch'ün 天下羣
Tientsin 天津
t'o-tu yao-ni 拓都么匿
Tokutomi Sohō 德富蘇峯
"Tsa-ta mou-pao" 雜答某報
ts'an-cheng 參政
Tseng-tzu 曾子
Tso Tsung-t'ang 左宗棠
Tsou Jung 鄒容
ts'un-lo ssu-hsiang 村落思想
ts'un-yang 存養
"Tu Ch'un-ch'iu chieh-shuo" 讀春秋界說
Tu-li p'ing-lun 獨立評論
"Tu Meng-tzu chieh-shuo" 讀孟子界說
tu-shu 讀書
tu-shu 獨術
Tu-shu fen-yüeh k'o-ch'eng 讀書分月

課程
tung 動
"Tung-chi yüeh-tan" 東藉月旦
Tung Chung-shu 董仲舒
"Tung-hsi min-tsu ken-pen ssu-hsiang chih ch'a-i" 東西民族根本思想之差異
tung-hsia 東俠
tung-li 動力
t'ung 通
T'ung-ch'eng 桐城
T'ung-meng hui 同盟會
tzu-chih 自治
Tzu-li hui 自立會
Tzu Mo-tzu hsüeh-shuo 子墨子學說
tzu-yu 自由
Tzu-yu shu 自由書
tz'u-chang 詞章
tz'u-chang chih-hsüeh 詞章之學

Urano Bōtō 浦野望東

wai-ching 外競
Wan-kuo kung-pao 萬國公報
Wan-mu ts'ao-t'ang 萬木草堂
"Wan-mu ts'ao-t'ang hsiao-hsüeh hsüeh-chi" 萬木草堂小學學記
wang-ch'ao ko-ming 王朝革命
Wang Fu-chih 王夫之
Wang Hsin-chai 王心齋
Wang Hsiu-ch'u 王秀楚
Wang K'ai-yün 王闓運
Wang K'ang-nien 王康年
Wang Lung-ch'i 王龍溪
Wang Mang 王莽
wang tao 王道
Wang T'ao 王韜
Wang Yang-ming 王陽明

wei 僞
"Wei-hsin" 唯心
wei-lai chu-i 未來主義
Wei Yüan 魏源
Weng T'ung-ho 翁同龢
Wu-hsü cheng-pien chi 戊戌政變記
"Wu-hsü pien-fa shih ti hsüeh-hui ho pao-k'an" 戊戌變法時的學會和報刊

Ya-tien hsiao-chih 雅典小志
yang-ch'i 養氣
Yang-chou shih-jih-chi 揚州十日記
yang-hsin 養心
Yang Shou-jen 楊守仁
Yang Wen-hui 楊文會
Yao 堯
yeh-man chuan-chih 野蠻專制
Yen Hui 顏回
Yokohama 橫濱
Yoshida Shōin 吉田松蔭
yu-heng 有恆
yu-kuo 優國
yu li-shih ti jen-chung 有歷史的人種
yu shih-chieh-shih ti 有世界史的
yung-ching-chih kuo 永靜止國
"Yü chih ssu-sheng kuan" 余之死生觀
"Yü Lin Ti-ch'en t'ai-shou shu" 與林廸臣太守書
"Yü Yen Yu-ling hsien-sheng shu" 與嚴又陵先生書
"Yü yu-jen lun pao-chiao shu" 與友人論保教書
Yü Yüeh 俞樾
Yüeh-hsüeh 粵學

INDEX

Absolutism, *see* Enlightened despotism

Account of Study at Ch'ang-hsing Alley, An (Ch'ang-hsing hsüeh-chi), 41, 46–47, 67, 120

Account of Ten Days at Yangchow, An (Yang-chou Shih-jih chi), 126

Activism: Liang's views of, 89, 177–178, 298; in Buddhism, 234–237; of Wang Yang-ming, 286–287; in Mao's writings, 307. *See also* Dynamism

Adventurous and enterprising spirit *(mao-hsien chin-ch'ü chih ching-shen)*, 182–188, 307

Allen, Younger J., 71–72

Analects, 8, 43

Ancient Text School, 21–22, 24–25, 48–50; Liang's views on, 74, 76

"Animalism" *(shou-hsing chu-i)*, 302

Arhat-Buddha, 233–234

Arimura Shunsai, 89n

Authoritarianism, in Liang's thought, 256, 298. *See also* Dictatorship; Enlightened despotism

"Barbarian": concept of, 110–111; "barbarian absolutism," 254–255

Benevolent paternalism *(jen-cheng)*, 196–197

Bentham, Jeremy, 206–208

Berlin, Isaiah, 205

Bibliography on Western Learning (Hsi-hsüeh shu-mu piao), 72

Bluntschli, Johann Kaspar, 248–249, 252–253, 257–260

Bodhisattva ideal, 232–234

Bodin, Jean, 255, 258

Book of Changes (I-ching), 88

Book of Great Unity (Ta-t'ung shu), 53n

Book on Liberty, The (Tzu-yu shu), 191

Book study *(tu-shu)*, 17, 92, 283

Bornhak, Gustav, 249–251, 253

Buddhism: and Confucianism, 10, 36–37; and K'ang Yu-wei, 36–39, 56–57; in Liang's thought, 64, 225, 232–233, 235–237, 301; in T'an Ssu-t'ung's thought, 67; concept of karma in, 178–179

Bushido, 145, 278

Canton: Confucian scholars at, 18–19, 75; K'ang Yu-wei's school at, 20, 40; Liang at, 59–60, 63, 70

Capitalism, Liang's view of, 265–271

Cavour, Camillo Benso, 222, 231

Chang Chih-tung, 123

Chang Tsai, 54, 66, 291

Ch'ang-hsing hsüeh-chi (An account of study at Ch'ang-hsing Alley), 41, 46–47, 67, 120

Ch'ang-hsing hsüeh-she (Wan-mu ts'ao-t'ang), 40–41, 59–60

Ch'en Chih, 32–33, 107

Ch'en Ch'iu, 32, 107

Ch'en Li, 4, 20, 24, 42

329

HARVARD EAST ASIAN SERIES